Technical Program Manager's Handbook

Second Edition

Unlock your TPM potential by leading technical projects successfully and elevating your career path

Joshua Alan Teter

BIRMINGHAM—MUMBAI

Technical Program Manager's Handbook

Second Edition

Copyright © 2024 Packt Publishing

All rights reserved. No part of this book may be reproduced, stored in a retrieval system, or transmitted in any form or by any means, without the prior written permission of the publisher, except in the case of brief quotations embedded in critical articles or reviews.

Every effort has been made in the preparation of this book to ensure the accuracy of the information presented. However, the information contained in this book is sold without warranty, either express or implied. Neither the author nor Packt Publishing or its dealers and distributors, will be held liable for any damages caused or alleged to have been caused directly or indirectly by this book.

Packt Publishing has endeavored to provide trademark information about all of the companies and products mentioned in this book by the appropriate use of capitals. However, Packt Publishing cannot guarantee the accuracy of this information.

Senior Publishing Product Manager: Denim Pinto

Acquisition Editor – Peer Reviews: Jane Dsouza

Project Editor: Parvathy Nair

Senior Development Editor: Elliot Dallow

Copy Editor: Safis Editing

Technical Editor: Aneri Patel

Proofreader: Safis Editing

Indexer: Tejal Soni

Presentation Designer: Ganesh Bhadwalkar

Developer Relations Marketing Executive: Vipanshu Parashar

First published: Dec 2022

Second edition: September 2024

Production reference: 2031024

Published by Packt Publishing Ltd.

Grosvenor House

11 St Paul's Square

Birmingham

B3 1RB, UK.

ISBN 9781836200475

www.packt.com

Contributors

About the author

As a Principal Technical Program Manager at Amazon, **Joshua Teter** has led complex and cross-functional projects that deliver innovative solutions for millions of customers. He has been with Amazon for over 11 years, starting as a Technical Program Manager and progressing to a Senior and then Principal role. He obtained his PMP® certification in 2018 and has a Bachelor of Science in Information Technology, and a Bachelor of Arts in Earth and Space Sciences.

Joshua's core competencies include agile methodologies, stakeholder management, risk mitigation, and communication. He is passionate about creating products that enhance customer satisfaction, efficiency, and quality. He values teamwork and innovation, and strives to bring diverse perspectives and experiences to any team he works with.

He enjoys sharing his knowledge and expertise with others, through writing as well as running a non-profit organization, TPM Events, to grow the TPM community through annual conferences, local chapter events, podcasts, and more.

Outside of the TPM community and work, Joshua has a partner, two children, and three cats. Above all else, he prioritizes as much time with his family as he can manage while juggling work, publications, and running a non-profit organization in his spare time.

I would like to dedicate this edition to the TPM community that I have become a part of since writing the first edition. So much has come out of this wonderful group of people and it will continue to grow, I am sure, for years to come.

This is also dedicated to my kids, whom I hope know of my contributions to the TPM community, such as this book, through hearsay and not because I am busy while they are growing. So far, this has been successful, and I will strive to keep it this way forever.

Most importantly, this work is dedicated to my life partner, Courtney. Writing is tough, especially when it must fit in around work and family. She has supported me and given me plenty of opportunities to sneak in writing time. Her compassion and understanding of the hard work I put into this are the only reason I am able to do this. She is my foundation in life.

About the reviewer

Prasad Gandham has over 18 years of experience in business transformation, helping enterprise customers achieve engineering goals and operational efficiency. He has delivered enterprise technology solutions from planning to implementation and maintenance. He has also led the development of numerous workflow and dashboard products and is skilled in coordinating dispersed teams for timely delivery and consistent productivity. Prasad's expertise includes multicloud environments including Azure and AWS, leading large-scale migrations, and driving cloud adoption strategies. He has published technical blogs, spoken at cloud events, and guided technical executives through organizational changes to maximize cloud value. He also holds a Bachelor's degree in Information Technology from Osmania University and is proficient in multiple languages.

I would like to thank my family, mother, wife, and kids for their support and for motivating me.

Zhanat Abylkassym is a highly accomplished TPM, bringing more than a decade of hands-on expertise from roles at Amazon, Uber, Robinhood, and now LinkedIn, where he leads TPM efforts within the AI Platform. As the organizer of the TPM Summit, an industry-wide conference for TPMs, Zhanat is dedicated to advancing the TPM profession and empowering others in the field. He is the author of *Evangelizing the TPM Craft*, which draws on a wealth of experience from the TPM community and offers practical strategies and insights that help TPMs unlock their full potential and make a meaningful impact within their organizations. He is also the founder of the TPM Tribe coaching program.

Join our book's Discord space

Join our Discord community to meet like-minded people and learn alongside more than 5000 members at:

https://packt.link/sKmQa

Table of Contents

Chapter 6: Plan Management   109

Section III: Technical Toolset 217

Chapter 11: The Technical Toolset 219

Chapter 12: Code Development Expectations 233

Chapter 13: System Design and Architecture Landscape   255

Chapter 14: Harnessing the Power of Artificial Intelligence in Technical Program Management · 281

Chapter 15: Enhancing Management Using Your Technical Toolset · 313

Preface

The role of a **Technical Program Manager (TPM)** has been around inside and outside of the tech industry for quite a while; yet somehow there is still quite a sense of mystery around what the role is and why it is beneficial, let alone how someone can succeed in being a TPM. This book looks to solve that mystery by diving into what it means to be a TPM, where the role came from, and where it is headed. You'll get a look into how the TPM works and develops their career in the "Big 5" – Amazon, Apple, Alphabet (Google), Meta (Facebook), and Microsoft. Though I focus on these companies, in my interviews and subsequent experience running the industry-wide TPM Summit, these concepts are common across an ever-growing group of companies.

I've been at Amazon for a little over 11 years now and I remember back to when I was first interviewed, I had a hard time remembering what the term TPM even stood for, let alone what the role entailed. In my onsite interviews, I asked what the job role was and what the day-to-day was like. Eleven years later and I'm asked those same questions by interviewees at least once a week. I attend conferences discussing what it means to be a TPM and have written papers on what it means to be a TPM within my own organization because, as you'll see in this book, it depends on where you are as to what the role entails.

No matter what, there are foundational principles that are followed across the industry that will set you on the right path and help you when you get stuck in a rut without a way forward.

A lot has happened between the first and second edition of this book. The first edition launched me into the world of TPM leadership in various LinkedIn communities and sparked the creation of a non-profit organization, TPM Events, to foster community, learning, networking, and ultimately a unified understanding of the TPM role across the tech industry. When I started the non-profit with my co-founders Zhanat Abylkassym and Josie Gillan in 2023, we set out to run a single conference. After the first TPM Summit in October of 2023, we kept going and expanded into local chapters to facilitate growth and learning in between the now-annual TPM Summit. We spun off a podcast, TPM Ridge, and have many other ideas in the works.

In the wider world, **generative artificial intelligence (GenAI)** has blossomed into a driving force of change. Our job descriptions are changing, new roles are forming, and everyone is looking to what the future will have in store for them. I believe that GenAI will necessarily change what we do by taking the easily repeatable and generative portions of our jobs and forcing TPMs to become prompt-engineering experts. To balance this out, I believe TPMs will need to lean hard on our emotional intelligence skills to remain relevant in the coming decade. GenAI won't replace our ability to form relationships with our stakeholders and use empathy to drive the change we need.

Hopefully the introduction of these two new topics will balance out your growth as we move into this new reality.

Let's get you ready to be a successful TPM!

Who this book is for

This book is meant for TPMs at every stage of their career, including those that are considering transitioning into the role. To get the most out of this book, there is an expectation that you will have some basic knowledge of project management. I tend to lean into the **Project Management Professional (PMP)** lingo and style but the book does not follow a specific methodology, as I don't believe a single methodology can be adequately applied to this role! While I will cover many topics that are familiar in certification courses like PMP, I will not cover those topics with sufficient depth to certify as that is not my goal. That means some topics that I feel are hyper-specific to the PMP-style of management, but not seen by an average TPM, I won't cover.

The book will cover some basic programming topics, although very little code is used except for illustrative purposes in *Chapter 12, Code Development Expectations*. Most concepts are explored using figures and text, as that fits the audience of the book the best.

To read the book, there's no expectation of a specific technical proficiency, although as you will discover in *Part 3* of the book, there is an expectation that you'll have that if you want to be a TPM. This book will guide you through the technical skills that are prerequisites for most TPMs.

What this book covers

Chapter 1, Fundamentals of a Technical Program Manager, is an introduction to what a TPM is and where the role originated.

Chapter 2, Pillars of a Technical Program Manager, sets out the three pillars of a TPM: project management, program management, and the technical toolset.

Chapter 3, Career Paths, examines the career paths available for a TPM using interviews and job data from across the 'Big 5' tech companies.

Chapter 4, An Introduction to Program Management Using a Case Study, covers the key management areas that will be covered throughout the book: plan management, risk management, and stakeholder management. It also introduces a case study that will be used for all examples throughout the book.

Chapter 5, Driving Toward Clarity, elaborates on the recurring trait that defines everything a TPM does: being clarity-driven.

Chapter 6, Plan Management, dives deeper into the plan management best practices and goes over scenarios that are common in the tech industry.

Chapter 7, Risk Management, explores the risk management best practices and goes over scenarios that are common in the tech industry.

Chapter 8, Stakeholder Management, discusses the stakeholder management best practices and goes over scenarios that are common in the tech industry.

Chapter 9, Managing a Program, explains the differences between managing a program and a project and how program management builds on top of project management.

Chapter 10, Emotional Intelligence in Technical Program Management, discusses the importance of **emotional intelligence (EQ)** in the TPM profession, along with how do determine your EQ and foster its growth.

Chapter 11, The Technical Toolset, is all about the three fundamental tools in a TPM's technical toolset: programming fundamentals, system design, and architectural design.

Chapter 12, Code Development Expectations, is an outline of the programming fundamentals that a TPM is expected to understand and draw upon.

Chapter 13, System Design and Architectural Landscape, clarifies the system and architectural design patterns and principles that are useful to a TPM.

Chapter 14, Harnessing the Power of Artificial Intelligence in Technical Program Management, dives into the technical foundations of generative artificial intelligence (GenAI) and how to utilize GenAI tools throughout your day-to-day role.

Chapter 15, Enhancing Management Using Your Technical Toolset, covers the technical toolset and dives deeper into how and where in a TPM's day-to-day work it can be used to enhance their career.

To get the most out of this book

This book assumes you have a basic understanding of project management concepts. Any word that is specific to management or a technical background is explained, so no specific methodology is required, such as Project Management Professional terminology, or phase cycles.

From a technical perspective, an introductory programming course is enough to get value from the technical explanations in the code, system design, and architecture chapters.

Project and program templates

This book comes with templates of the various project and program artifacts that are discussed in the book, they are available on GitHub. Each chapter that has related templates will mention this under the *Additional resources section*.

For each template, instructions or guidance for each will be added in a review comment attached to the title at the top of the document or in the first cell of a spreadsheet. Each project or program is unique so you are encouraged to use the templates as a starting point but to add, subtract, or simply move around the elements based on the needs of the project and your stakeholders.

Find them here: `https://github.com/PacktPublishing/Technical-Program-Manager-s-Handbook-2E`

Download the color images

We also provide a PDF file that has color images of the screenshots/diagrams used in this book. You can download it here: `https://packt.link/gbp/9781836200475`.

Conventions used

There are a number of text conventions used throughout this book.

`CodeInText`: Indicates code words in text, database table names, folder names, filenames, file extensions, pathnames, dummy URLs, user input, and Twitter handles. For example: "You are stating which data you need in the `SELECT` clause."

Bold: Indicates a new term, an important word, or words that you see on the screen. For instance, words in menus or dialog boxes appear in the text like this. For example: "In this chapter, we'll look into the paths you may take to become a **Technical Program Manager (TPM)**."

Warnings or important notes appear like this.

 Tips and tricks appear like this.

Get in touch

Feedback from our readers is always welcome.

General feedback: Email feedback@packtpub.com and mention the book's title in the subject of your message. If you have questions about any aspect of this book, please email us at questions@packtpub.com.

Errata: Although we have taken every care to ensure the accuracy of our content, mistakes do happen. If you have found a mistake in this book, we would be grateful if you reported this to us. Please visit http://www.packtpub.com/submit-errata, click **Submit Errata**, and fill in the form.

Piracy: If you come across any illegal copies of our works in any form on the internet, we would be grateful if you would provide us with the location address or website name. Please contact us at copyright@packtpub.com with a link to the material.

If you are interested in becoming an author: If there is a topic that you have expertise in and you are interested in either writing or contributing to a book, please visit http://authors.packtpub.com.

Share your thoughts

Once you've read *Technical Program Manager's Handbook, Second Edition,* we'd love to hear your thoughts! Scan the QR code below to go straight to the Amazon review page for this book and share your feedback.

https://packt.link/r/1836200471

Your review is important to us and the tech community and will help us make sure we're delivering excellent quality content.

Download a free PDF copy of this book

Thanks for purchasing this book!

Do you like to read on the go but are unable to carry your print books everywhere?

Is your eBook purchase not compatible with the device of your choice?

Don't worry, now with every Packt book you get a DRM-free PDF version of that book at no cost.

Read anywhere, any place, on any device. Search, copy, and paste code from your favorite technical books directly into your application.

The perks don't stop there, you can get exclusive access to discounts, newsletters, and great free content in your inbox daily.

Follow these simple steps to get the benefits:

1. Scan the QR code or visit the link below:

https://packt.link/free-ebook/9781836200475

2. Submit your proof of purchase.
3. That's it! We'll send your free PDF and other benefits to your email directly.

Section 1

What Is a Technical Program Manager?

The **Technical Program Manager (TPM)** role has been part of the technical industry since the beginning but is still shrouded in mystery. This section aims to set the foundation of where the TPM role came from, what it is, and why it is an important and in-demand position in the industry.

As I am discussing the role's history, I will also talk about available career paths that are open for the TPM role. Together, the chapters in this section will set the stage for the concepts discussed in greater details in *Sections 2* and *3*.

This section contains the following chapters:

- *Chapter 1, Fundamentals of a Technical Program Manager*
- *Chapter 2, Pillars of a Technical Program Manager*
- *Chapter 3, Career Paths*

1

Fundamentals of a Technical Program Manager

The **program manager** role has been around for as long as humans have organized to accomplish a goal together as a group. Although the name may not be as old, there were certainly program managers or project managers while building the ancient Egyptian pyramids. A program manager is a generalist in nature and can tackle any project with some proficiency, often running multiple projects concurrently within the same program or across many programs. The **Technical Program Manager (TPM)** role followed in the program manager's footsteps to fill a specialized niche with the rise of highly specialized projects and programs. The TPM plays a powerful role in any technical project or program and has carved its way into the tech industry culture as a mainstay position, right alongside software and hardware developers, development managers, and product managers. Even with its ubiquitous role in the industry, the question of what a TPM is and how we can be effective practitioners of this kind is still asked on a daily basis. This book aims to answer those questions.

In this chapter, we'll start by discussing how the TPM role became what it is today. We'll do this by exploring the roots of the TPM, the generalized program manager role, and the skills and traits that both share. We'll round this out by exploring the basic requirements that are specific to the TPM specialization – the systems development life cycle.

With the fundamentals under our belt, we'll explore the specific attributes that help a TPM thrive at their job. With a better understanding of the TPM, we can widen our perspective to look at the roles adjacent to the TPM, seeing how they complement one another and how we can fill in the gaps that our team needs us to fill.

Lastly, we'll look into the industry to get a grasp of how the TPM role is defined holistically by exploring job postings, as well as interviews that I conducted with fellow TPMs from various companies.

In this chapter, we will explore the fundamentals of what the TPM role is through the following topics:

- Understanding the modern TPM
- Learning the fundamentals
- Exploring what makes a TPM thrive
- Comparing adjacent job families
- Exploring functional competencies across the industry

Understanding the modern TPM

In the 1967 book *The Technical Program Manager's Guide to Survival*, by Melvin Silverman, the author defines a program as an organization created to accomplish a specific goal. This organization was a group within a company that existed for the sole purpose of achieving the program goals, and it was to be dissolved once the goal was realized. You can see where the computer definition of a program gets its origins – a bit of organized code that executes to accomplish a task or goal! Once the task is complete, the computer program will terminate. Computer programs have evolved in complexity since their early days, as has the TPM, but the origins have a clear connection in meaning and purpose.

I found Mr. Silverman's book while attempting to uncover the origins of the TPM role. What transpired during this research is that the usage of TPM had a similar evolution to the word *program*. The term went from a generic use to a more specific use over the course of roughly 40 years. Silverman's book was one of the first books that used the term *technical program manager*, although it only shows up on the title page, as the rest of the book uses the generic term *program manager*. Elsewhere, in the 1970s and 1980s, the term popped up in various United States government papers, listing someone as the TPM for a given project at NASA, the Department of Energy, and the Department of Defense, to name a few. One excerpt from a 1965 NASA authorization stated:

> *Staffed by a competent technical program manager with long experience in managing Air Force* **life science programs,** *this office has been assigned responsibility for maintaining and improving the day-to-day relationships of the two organizations.*

This had me perplexed, as I couldn't see any role or definition that was recognizable as those of today. Why was a program manager in the Air Force liaison's office a technical program manager? How would this relate to the modern TPM we see in the tech industry today where the program manager is expected to have a computer science or similar background and is, thus, seen as a TPM instead of a generalist program manager? Mr. Silverman did not divulge what he meant by *technical,* nor did any of the government references that I could find, although there were clues in the context, like the quote above. Since Mr. Silverman defined *program,* I looked to the definition of *technical* in the Oxford English Dictionary to gain insight:

 technical (adjective). 1. relating to a particular subject, art, or craft, or its techniques, and 2. of, involving, or concerned with applied and industrial sciences.

This first definition is where the term seems to have originated. When a program manager had specific knowledge in the domain they were managing, they were seen as technical program managers. There it was! This is why the program manager in the Air Force was technical, as they had prior expertise related to what they were managing. What we commonly refer to as a TPM—where technical denotes a background in computer science, electrical engineering, or another similarly technical-focused discipline—is actually just one of many instances in which the term technical denotes using a specialization. The pattern of specializing the program manager role has even penetrated the already-specialized TPM role where there are sub-specializations, like Privacy and Security TPM, that apply to program managers with a technical background that focuses on privacy and security concerns. This is just one of many different examples of specialized TPMs.

As far as the technology industry is concerned, I identified the use of the term TPM at least as far back as 1993, although I suspect it has been in use in the industry as long as the industry has existed, given its prevalence in other industries from the 1960s onward.

Old title, new meaning

While researching the origins of the term TPM, I utilized Google's **Ngram Viewer**, which indexes word usage in books and government publications by year between 1800 and 2019 (note that we stop at 2019, as there is currently no data available beyond that). Using the Ngram Viewer results as a starting point, I researched dictionary definitions, half-century-old books, and US government publications from NASA, and I found that the TPM title has been around for a while. However, as I'm sure many readers are thinking, it feels like it's a very recent addition to the workforce. I remember when I was first approached to interview at Amazon for a TPM role, I was confused as to what it was.

I asked, and sure enough, it was roughly what I was doing professionally, but the company I was at simply didn't use that term. In fact, very few companies seemed to be using the title in 2013 – let alone the 1990s!

It's worth noting at this point that Ngram Viewer's data is English-only with a heavy emphasis on the United States, although not exclusively. The conclusions I'm drawing here are based on this research and the tech industry's history from a US standpoint. Although there will be some differences from country to country where the events are not directly impacting, the shifts that occurred were industry-wide from a high level. With the annual TPM Summit that started in 2023, there are more chances to bridge together some of these TPM term differences across the world, and as I learn more, the story and history of the term will be updated.

Figure 1.1 shows the Google Books Ngram Viewer results for "Technical Program Manager" from 1955 through 2019 in the *English (2019)* dataset, with smoothing set to 3. This graph was generated via `http://books.google.com/ngrams` with these settings:

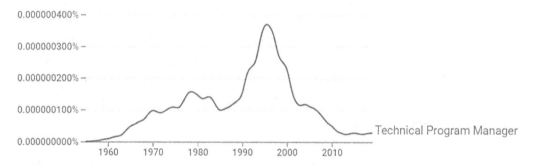

Figure 1.1: Google Ngram Viewer results of the occurrence of the term "Technical Program Manager" from 1955 to 2019 with a smoothing of 3

Figure 1.1 shows that there is a very large uptick to the highest vertex for the term TPM in the year 1995 —the early days of the World Wide Web and the mad dash of start-ups rushing toward the year 2000. With these technology companies sprouting up, the need for specialized program management arose—people with a background in and knowledge of the systems being developed so that they could be better facilitators and drivers of these new programs and websites. As is the case in the technology industry, trends that start at a few companies at the top slowly trickle down through the rest of the industry until they become commonplace. In some cases, this trend is still working its way down in the industry, as some companies are still not fully aware of the position and its benefits. I believe this explains the lag in the term being seen in publications and more commonly used in the industry.

Another likely reason for the downtick in the term being seen in publications in more recent years is the ubiquity of the internet that started to build in the early 2000s. As more articles were published on the internet, the term showed up less in printed media. This makes sense, given that the term is not a general term that you'd expect to continue seeing but is, instead, specific to the tech industry, which itself moved online. That's just to say that the downtick of the term is no reason for concern about the future of the TPM role!

Today, here we are with a title used to denote a specialized form of program management being wholly taken over by the tech industry, with its meaning changed to a program manager with a background in computer science or engineering—an old title with a new meaning.

We've explored briefly where the title of TPM originated, outside of the tech industry, and its transformation into a specific type of specialized program manager. Next, we'll review the fundamentals of being a TPM.

Learning the fundamentals

Throughout this book, we'll discuss many concepts that are core to any program manager, as well as some that are more specific to the TPM specialization. Let's briefly discuss some of these terms so that we have a shared foundation to build upon.

The first terms to discuss are project and program. There are some companies where the "P" in TPM actually refers to "Project" instead of "Program," and this can lead to some confusion. We'll cover it in greater detail in *Chapter 2, Pillars of a Technical Program Manager,* but suffice to say that a program comprises multiple related projects. A project manager may run more than one project at a time, but they may not have a common goal. A program manager runs multiple projects that share a common goal and possibly multiple programs too. With that, let's tackle some of the key management areas that are common between project and program managers and are shared across all program manager roles, including specialized roles such as the TPM.

Project planning is where we work through requirements, resourcing, and constraints and develop an action plan. This makes up the backbone of our work—all the other management areas build from this or feed into it, and it is paramount to a successful project. In *Chapter 5,* we will go into further detail on this.

Once you have a project plan, you analyze the plan and identify any *risks* that could arise. These can be related to tight scheduling, resourcing constraints, project dependencies, or scope concerns. Depending on the risk, you can amend your project plan to help mitigate it through mechanisms such as *swarming* (that is, increasing resources on a particular task to get it done quicker), in order to alleviate scheduling concerns.

Throughout these stages, you will be engaging with your stakeholders to provide insight. Requirements often come from one or more of the stakeholders, and they may identify risks or mitigation strategies to reduce risks. You'll also develop a strategy and cadence for regular communication with your stakeholders in a mechanism called a **communication plan**.

Figure 1.2 illustrates the key management areas we'll discuss and how they influence each other:

Figure 1.2: Key management areas

Project planning is at the top of this diagram because this is the foundation of the work we do in project management. Although no project goes exactly according to plan, it is important to see the planned path in order to make key decisions as they come up. Without a well-thought-out plan, a project is doomed to failure.

Just as project planning is centered at the top, **stakeholder management** is centered at the bottom. Just as all aspects of the project involve the plan, they also involve communication with your stakeholders. All areas we will talk about include some element of communication. As I have seen in many professional projects inside and outside the workplace, good communication is what separates average practitioners from exemplary practitioners. This cyclical nature can be seen throughout all areas of the project and program management.

Risk management includes both risk analysis and strategies to handle the risks that feed into the initial project plan and form a continuous feedback loop. As a risk arises, a schedule may need to be adjusted, and changes to the plan can introduce new risks to add to the risk register.

If a risk is realized and acted upon, or a new risk is introduced through a shift in the plan or other circumstances, this will be communicated to your stakeholders.

The same is true for **resource management**—if you lose or gain resources, your project plan will need to be adjusted. The available resources also play heavily into your initial timelines. Although some organizations' resources are based on an optimal plan, in that they will determine the quickest most efficient path to completion and the resources to meet this need, most tech companies provide resourcing based on prioritization of the project, and the schedule will adjust based on what is available. If a project is deemed to be a high priority, more resources may be given to hit a specific deadline, and conversely, fewer resources may be given if there are higher-priority projects elsewhere. Again, these types of changes must be communicated to your stakeholders.

An example from the real world

A few years ago, I was running a project with a tight timeline of 8 months, and to achieve that, I needed 10 developers on the project at all times. Though the top-down agreement was that this would happen, in the very first month, I had fewer resources than expected. I knew that a push-and-pull negotiation would be required every month throughout the project, and adding to the status report that resources were low would quickly lose any meaning. Nonetheless, the stakeholders needed to understand the implications of short-staffing the project, so I added a risk to the register about resourcing and included a simple graph with every report, which looked like *Figure 1.3*:

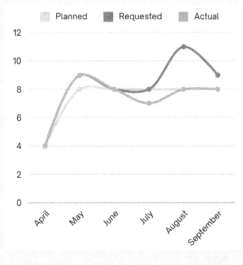

Figure 1.3: Communicating resourcing constraints

This contained a month-over-month view of the resources I asked for and the resources I actually received. This allowed me to sidestep most back-and-forth negotiations and easily show the impact of the resources I received. As soon as tasks started to slip because the buffers were used up, it was unmistakably apparent that the issue was due to resource constraints. I received a boost of resources to compensate for the dip without too much hassle, as the root cause was well-communicated and clear to all stakeholders. Although I never fully recovered from the resource dip, the project was delivered on time through long hours and an amazingly dedicated team.

The act of communicating with my stakeholders and updating the project plan, while handling risks and resources, ensured that I was able to stay on top of the project and keep things moving quickly and efficiently.

At this point, it's worth taking a moment to discuss the terminology I use to describe key management areas in this book and, in particular, how they relate to waterfall and agile methodologies. The terms I use in this book are most often associated with the waterfall methodology. However, the processes themselves are actually used in both waterfall and agile systems. Although waterfall is most often shown in diagrams as discrete steps, in practice, this is never actually the case. As I go into more depth later in the book, every step is a mini cycle where project planning informs risks, which when planned for can impact a plan and so on down the waterfall chain. For a TPM practitioner, no step should ever be seen as wholly separated from others.

Project planning is done in an agile system but not always to the same level of detail. For instance, the work breakdown may only go to a feature level. The features would then be added to the backlog and prioritized from sprint to sprint. This can either follow a high-level release plan or be highly iterative, with releases only being known about after sprint planning is complete and only for the items in that sprint. The issues that arise in project planning translate to the agile cycle as well.

In risk management, analysis happens at every step in an agile workflow, which I see as true of a waterfall approach as well. Although waterfall will have a heavier risk analysis phase in the beginning, this is only because the project plan is also largely planned early on. But any time planning is done, whether in a sprint plan or during project planning, risk analysis should always follow, and any comments on how to approach it remain true.

Lastly, stakeholder management is possibly more important in an agile system, as the number of interactions with stakeholders can be much higher due to the short iteration cycles. However, you still need to know your audience and decipher technical jargon for business stakeholders, among other advice this book will discuss.

All in all, the key management areas are transferable, and with little to no tweaking, all advice is applicable. Just think about how and when you plan, analyze risks, and work with stakeholders, and then the guidance in the book will apply.

Now that we've covered the program management fundamentals, we'll move on to concepts that are aligned more closely with the technical specialization aspect of the role.

The Systems Development Life Cycle

The **Systems Development Life Cycle (SDLC)**, sometimes written as Software Development Life Cycle instead, is fundamental for a TPM to understand, as it is central to both software and hardware development. As it is a cycle, it is, by nature, iterative. *Figure 1.4* illustrates the cycle, starting at the top with requirements analysis and following clockwise to come back around to this initial step:

Figure 1.4: The SDLC

The number of phases in the SDLC can vary, depending on the situation, as can the number of cycles. For instance, this entire cycle may repeat multiple times in a hardware setting, one per hardware iteration from the initial prototype (engineering validation and testing), the design validation and testing, and finally, the production validation and testing. For the purposes of his book, this configuration incorporates what I see as the main phases that need to be involved for the cycle to be successful. All of these steps should be part of the project plan and will also cross into the other key management areas. Starting at the top, the flow is as follows.

At the beginning of a project, the SDLC starts with the **requirements analysis** phase. The requirements may already be well defined and only need to be analyzed and broken down into a plan, or they may be newly discovered or added requirements to an existing project that need to be incorporated into the existing project plan. The analysis includes understanding prerequisite work, resource needs, and timing needs, as well as identifying known risks that need to be added to the project risk register.

While adding requirements to a project plan, the entire cycle should be considered in it. I have found the best way to do this is through adding buffers for each step that can later be addressed as each step is understood better (another cycle!). The buffers can be based on subject matter expert input (such as a developer's guess on implementation time), or a formula that takes complexity and scope as variables.

Once these requirements are better understood and incorporated into the project plan, the **design** phase is started, which takes the requirements and builds a design that meets the requirements. This may require more than one design, depending on the scope of the requirements. Requirements are often linear, dealing with a user story or task that needs to be completed. In highly distributed systems, a single requirement may impact several systems in order to get the correct user story outcome. You may also start with a high-level design that encompasses the entire requirement and then add in low-level designs for each system that is impacted. Either way, the design phase will give you better insight into the implementation time and the testing strategy. Both of the buffers that were added to the plan can now be refined to include the new information.

The design then drives the **implementation** of the actual requirement. As stated, this may end up being multiple implementations across services or components and involve several resources to be completed. The actual implementation may differ from what was planned, based on unforeseen issues that may impact the test plan, in which case, it can be updated during or after implementation is complete.

The implementation then leads to **testing**. This step will likely involve multiple types of testing – from integration testing, ensuring that the introduction of code functionally works, to regression testing, which focuses on ensuring no bugs were introduced that changed existing behavior, and possibly some form of production testing if the use case and project warrant this approach. This happens in cases where the code exists in a launched service that is readily available and active and tests live production traffic on the new code, testing for edge cases that may have been missed in regression testing. There are entire books, courses, and videos on this subject alone, and the actual testing steps you employ will depend on your needs and the architecture of your systems.

The final phase is **evaluation**, or iteration. This step involves examining a product and looking for improvements. These improvements can also come from feedback from stakeholders and customers. Once they are identified, you begin requirements analysis once more, and the cycle continues. This step tends to apply to products and might not exist in your cycle as a dedicated step at this level. In some cases, customer outreach may have its own cycle that is independent of the project.

Although this looks to be a waterfall approach, where all the steps of a phase are completed before moving on to the next phase, this cycle can happen as often as needed, and each step may spawn multiple next steps in the cycle. A single requirement can go through this entire cycle while another is still being clarified and will proceed to the design step much later. To that end, the cycle is utilized in waterfall, agile, and hybrid environments.

Many other pieces can contribute to the technical fundamentals, which we will cover in *Part 3*, where we discuss the technical skills needed to be a TPM in more detail. Those skills will vary from company to company, as well as from team to team within a company, as the needs of a team can vary. Keeping that in mind, the SDLC is a fundamental component across all variations of the TPM role.

Now that we've introduced the fundamental aspects of project management, let's take a look at what skills or traits make a TPM most successful in their role.

Exploring what makes a TPM thrive

This topic comes up in every interview I've conducted for the TPM position. I've put some thought into everything that a TPM does. The points that I'm going to discuss are not qualities specific to a company, team, or variation on the TPM role, but they are transferable from one position to the next.

Keeping forward momentum

For a TPM to thrive, their focus needs to be on moving the project forward and unblocking their team to get things done. This may sound like a cliché, as though you are reading it from a job description, but it is resoundingly true. Our innate drive to solve roadblocks, build a plan, mitigate risk, and drive toward deadlines are key to a project's success. It is important to keep momentum on a project because, without it, we risk losing progress and need to start over. Context switching is often to blame here because, during the time a project is blocked, the individuals working on it may move on to other priorities or lose context in the downtime. This necessitates more time to ramp back up once a project is ready to move forward. It is in our best interests to resolve issues quickly in order to keep engagement, focus, and motivation.

This driving motivation is a trait that isn't always present in roles that are adjacent to the TPM, such as the development manager and the product manager. This is because the primary function of those roles is not focused on project or program delivery like the TPM role is. A development manager's main focus is their people and their service or area of ownership, and a product manager's focus is their product. For the TPM, the focus is the project or program, which is where their drive and perspective are also focused. A blocker in a project blocks our main purpose, so it is extremely important to be aware of. This same blocker may be overshadowed by a performance review cycle for the development manager or by the product needs of the product manager.

Driving toward clarity

One of the most effective ways to keep forward momentum is to always drive toward clarity. The drive to clarify can come at any stage of a project or program. It's very common to see this during the requirements analysis and planning phases, as clarification is a key outcome of analysis and is needed to ensure a complete plan. We are always driving towards clarity through clarifying requirements, clarifying scope, clarifying the communication strategies and important stakeholders, and even unblocking development work.

Every roadblock we encounter requires us to drive toward clarity. We ask about the problem, the people or systems involved, any proposed solutions, and paths to escalation. Then, we take all of this data and define the problem to ensure that our solution is fixing the right thing. This then allows us to work toward the right solution. Think of it as asserting your acceptance criteria for a development task to ensure that it has the right outcome.

One way in which we drive toward clarity utilizes the last critical trait to make a TPM thrive—the communication bridge. We'll talk a lot about communication throughout this book, but this is a special form of communication that takes our technical background into account.

Communication bridges

Since we have a technical background, not only can we talk with our technical teams but also understand them! This is critical for our ability to understand the tasks it will take to complete a project and to push back on unrealistic estimates or provide feedback. This skill also allows us to explain the work that our developers are doing for other stakeholders. We can take highly technical information and transform it into language that a VP of marketing will easily understand.

This ability to translate from technical to non-technical works in reverse as well. In fact, we rely heavily on this early on in a project during requirement analysis. We take business requirements and translate them into functional specifications for our technical team.

We understand the business and their needs, and if required, we understand their knowledge domain. Knowing the domain isn't always required to land a job, but the ability to learn the domain on the job is key to being a successful TPM.

For many years, I've worked with the tax teams at Amazon. Our business partners are highly knowledgeable in worldwide tax laws and the implications of those laws, and they speak in a tax-skewed legalese that can be very daunting to someone outside of the tax domain. When I joined this team, I had heard terms like situs and jurisdiction, but I didn't know what they truly meant, or how important they were. Requirements documents were full of tax jargon, and every requirement was framed in the context of a tax-related concept. This made understanding what needed to happen very difficult, and to make matters worse, the people in the development team weren't trained tax experts either (nor should they have been). But this meant that it was my job to understand these requirements in a way that could be explained to the development team.

Not all communication bridging has to be in the moment, and this wasn't the case for that either. Instead, the team focused on creating courses to explain the tax domain for our developers – at least enough to understand the major concepts involved. We did the same for our business team to help them understand the data flow and major components of the software stack.

This allowed for easier communication between the technical and business teams, using a common understanding and lexicon. Any requirements that came up could more easily be talked through with a common understanding. By understanding our business and its needs, as well as our development team's needs, we can effectively bridge the communication gap between business and technology. *From a career growth perspective, this soft skill is by far the most important skill to perfect.* Due to this, it is also the skill that shows up most in the growth category for career progression. To improve this skill, ensure that you practice **active listening** by staying engaged with the speaker (put your phone away and stop checking email). Affirm your understanding through body language such as nodding — but don't interrupt. When they are finished, paraphrase what you heard and follow up with questions. This takes patience to do right, and that can be hard when you are trying to connect with someone quickly. I grew up in an environment where it was common to interrupt or talk over others during particularly engaging conversations. Although this can be fine among friends when talking about trivial matters, this is very disruptive in a work environment — especially given that, at work, we are often trying to solve a problem. When you interrupt, you aren't taking in what the other person is saying because you are looking for a space in the conversation to insert your own thoughts, instead of taking in what the other person is saying. Active listening will ensure that you truly understand the point of view of the other person. Often, this information can build on your understanding of their problem.

Follow-up questions can fill in the gaps in your understanding to paint a more complete picture of a situation. Over time, you'll understand your business teams and their domains, which will help you become a more effective communicator. The better you understand the pains of your business team, the better you can relay that to your development team in your functional specifications and conversations about scope. The more your development teams understand, the better the outcome of the software, and the more successful a project will be.

We now understand what makes a TPM thrive at their job, as well as the fundamentals to accomplish it. Next, let's compare the roles and responsibilities of a TPM to other roles that are often found adjacent to it.

Comparing adjacent job families

I love Venn diagrams because they show similarities and differences in a very concise and easy-to-follow way. Needless to say, you'll see a few in this book.

A common question in my profession as a TPM is, what is the value of a TPM? The question is understandable because there is a lot of overlap between our jobs and the jobs of the roles most often adjacent to us in a software or hardware team.

We'll start by exploring *Figure 1.5*, which shows the intersection of the roles most similar to the TPM: the **Program Manager (PM)**, and the **Product Manager – Technical (PM-T)**. Just as the TPM is a program manager who specializes in technology, the PM-T is a product manager who specializes in technology. The term PM-T may not be used at every company (just as TPM isn't used everywhere), but the particulars of the job as they relate to our discussion are the same:

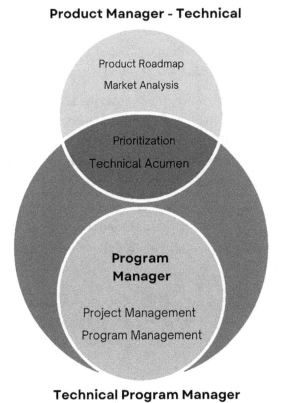

Product Manager - Technical

Product Roadmap

Market Analysis

Prioritization

Technical Acumen

Program Manager

Project Management

Program Management

Technical Program Manager

Figure 1.5: A Venn diagram comparing the TPM, PM, and PM-T role overlaps

The similarities between a PM, TPM, and PM-T are greater than their differences. The TPM, as a specialized version of the PM, shares the same skill sets with the PM. These are project management and program management aspects like project planning, risk management, stakeholder management, and resource management—all topics that the first half of this book covers. The TPM role adds the specialization on top of this foundation, which is a technical background for the purposes of this book but, as Mr. Silverman's book shows us, can really be any specialization.

The PM-T shares a similar technical depth with the TPM, as both roles work alongside or within a technical organization. The TPM and PM-T are often involved in prioritization exercises and where a product is concerned, a TPM can handle that if needed, but a PM-T will be more nuanced. The main focus of the PM-T is on the product roadmap and strategy, instead of projects or programs.

Next, we'll expand on the roles that are truly adjacent to the TPM role. Regardless of whether the TPM role reports to the technical team or they are in a parallel organization (such as a **Project Management Office**, or **PMO**), the TPM will work with these job roles in every aspect of a project or program. *Figure 1.6* compares the TPM, **Software Development Manager** (**SDM**) (sometimes called a **Software Engineering Manager** (**SEM**)), and PM-T roles:

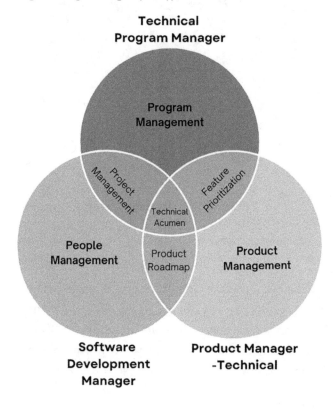

Figure 1.6: A Venn diagram comparing the TPM, SDM, and PM-T roles

Although this diagram is a simplification of the roles and does not list everything that each does, it does represent, and focus on, the typical alignments when they exist, as well as the main components that do not overlap. All three roles have a technical background, as they work within or alongside technical teams. Both the TPM and SDM can manage projects, although most SDMs will run projects that are related to their domain or services.

If a project goes beyond its domain boundary or is a cross-team program, a TPM is better equipped to handle that level of complexity. The SDM and PM-T can both create a product roadmap, and this is often a gap the SDM will fill when a PM-T is absent. Lastly, the PM-T specializes in product management and shares prioritization skills with the TPM. Simply put, in a pinch, these roles can often cover gaps in a team, but given that each role has unique skill sets, this would ideally only be short-term. The size of the team is also a factor in the relevancy of both the TPM and PM-T roles. A PM-T isn't necessarily needed for a small team with a single service, but as the team grows and a product becomes complex, or begins to serve many diverse types of clients, a PM-T should be brought on board. The same applies to a TPM—once the number of stakeholders becomes too large and complex, it begins to fall out of the expected comfort zone for an SDM, and a TPM should be hired.

Abbreviations and the overuse of PM

I use a lot of terms as written and used at the Big 5 tech companies (also known as **FAANG**, or **Facebook/Meta**, **Amazon**, **Apple**, **Netflix**, and **Google/Alphabet**). However, there is a tremendous overuse of "PM" as an abbreviation. Depending on which crowd you are in, it can stand for Project Manager (which is the original use of the abbreviation), Program Manager, or Product Manager. As such, each of these terms has alternate abbreviations of PjM, PgM, and PdM, respectively, among others.

I decided to use PM to mean Program Manager in this book, since the subject matter is Technical Program Management, and to have the PM in TPM be the same when it is also alone makes the most sense to me. Furthermore, it agrees with the common usage of the larger tech companies. For Product Manager, I use PM-T, or Product Manager – Technical, as both a common variant of the Product Manager role in tech and as a differentiator.

That being said, if there is possible confusion, I will opt to spell a term out.

Wearing many hats

At this point, you can see that the TPM role has many functions. The Venn diagrams show that we overlap with adjacent roles. This unique overlap allows our skill sets to merge and fill in any gaps, depending on the needs of our team. Over the course of my own career, I have found myself filling in the gaps of missing product managers, process managers, and even people managers by helping guide the developers in my projects. This is also the case for product managers working with small teams or products, which helps make sense of recent industry developments.

Some companies are shifting to product managers instead of TPMs, while others are doing the opposite and migrating toward TPMs. On a small scale, this swap is easy, and the gaps can be filled with minor inconvenience to a team. However, as the team scales, both roles become necessary.

This aspect of the job makes it extremely difficult to define the exact nature of what we do. The short answer is that we do it all. Our job is to ensure that our programs and projects are successful, and that may require different skills depending on the context of what is going on.

Even though this book talks about specific skills, they are not all required in equal measure and can even change from team to team within a company! The needs of the team are often unique to what it is trying to solve or how mature the team is. The reason I have filled in so many gaps over the years is that the team I have been on has grown 10 times in size while I've been here. This means that, at various times, the skill gaps or needs in the team at that moment have changed. In general, the more mature the team, the more defined your role in that team will be.

This is also a source of confusion and difficulty for the TPM role. Since there are gaps that TPMs fill in, it is harder to define a clear career guideline, as what defines success depends on what your team needs from you. It also means that any time you switch teams or companies, your ramp-up can be longer than other roles that enjoy a clearer industry-wide job definition. Even within a single team, if there are too many gaps to fill, this can lead to a large amount of context switching within a day. However, don't let this deter you. As with any skill, there are both good and bad aspects, but the adaptability by far outweighs the pain that it can cause.

Program management versus product management

The industry has seen a lot of change as COVID-19 has transitioned from a pandemic to an endemic phase. The shutdown from the pandemic created a surge in demand for online ecosystems, and the tech industry swelled in size. As we began to lift safety restrictions and return to the office, this demand fell away quickly. Since then, the industry has been going through waves of layoffs while it attempts to recover from falling demand and stock prices. It's these squeeze moments where we tend to see the most dramatic shifts in administration practices. One such shift has centered around the question of program management versus product management.

The question is valid in context, but outside of context, it has caused some anxiety in our profession as we all brace for what decision our leaders will take on the issue. Some companies have laid off their TPM force in favor of Product Managers and vice versa over the last year. But if you look closer, the answer is relatively simple in theory, although the results will vary by company.

As with most things, it depends, and in our case, it depends on the size and complexity of your organization.

To explain this, we need to understand what a product and program are. As a refresher, a program is a group of resources brought together to achieve a specific goal. Once that goal is met, the program is over, which means it is a temporary endeavor.

A product serves a specific purpose for a group of users. In this way, it is longer lasting, and although it may go through iterations, if it is successful, the intention is for it to be around for a long time. Microsoft Word as a product has endured over 40 years, having its first release in October 1983. Yes, some companies quickly iterate through products, and none last long, but the intention is that they do last, if they are successful.

For a small organization that has a single product, product management is likely more important to their success, as most of their work will revolve around a product development life cycle—very similar to the SDLC—as an iterative approach to releasing new versions of their product. So release management, roadmap prioritization based on customer feedback, and market analysis are of the highest value.

Let's say this organization grows and has multiple products that talk to one another (think G-Suite, or Microsoft 365). You still have a focus on product management for each product that you own, but a new complexity has been introduced, which is cross-product or cross-organization collaboration. Let's say a new feature that is common to the platform is introduced, like the ability to copy and paste information between products. Who would own this? One of the many product managers, on top of owning their release cycle? Instead, this is where a TPM becomes valuable for this type of organization.

In a similar scenario, say you are a small development team that owns a service internal to a larger ecosystem. You are small, but product releases may not be your focus, and instead, your concern is on integration with other services around you. Cross-team coordination can be handled by the development manager, but it may also require a TPM if the number of organizations involved becomes large. Here, the focus will likely be on a TPM rather than a PM-T.

Now, this small service team has grown in scope, and their service now has a user base. The complexities that require a TPM are still in play, but it's time to bring in a product manager to handle the larger scope and ensure that you are releasing what your user base needs.

Figure 1.7 illustrates the intersection of product and program management:

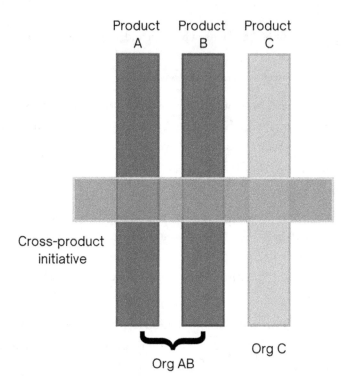

Figure 1.7: Product and program management comparison

As shown in *Figure 1.7*, a good visualization of this is to think of a product as a vertical construct in your company. There's a business team and a development team attached to that product. Anything that impacts that product alone can be done within the confines of a product manager.

Programs in this visualization are seen to work horizontally. They work across multiple products to achieve goals that impact the larger ecosystem. So, the more complex your ecosystem, the higher the likelihood that TPMs are needed to drive cross-organizational initiatives.

Now that we understand the functional aspects of the TPM role, and how that impacts how the job may manifest itself based on our team needs, let's see how consistent this holistic view is across the industry.

Exploring functional competencies across the industry

I've worked for most of my life as a TPM at the same company—as such, I was concerned about an unconscious bias of what a TPM is or should be. To combat this, I sought outside perspectives from as many high-profile companies as I could—Amazon, Google, Meta, Microsoft, and Apple. I interviewed TPMs from these organizations and combed through the job boards of these companies to see what each was looking for in a TPM.

I consolidated the interviews and job descriptions into a matrix in *Table 1.1* that we'll dive a bit deeper into. If something pops out to me as different in a particular interview or job post, I'll call out what it is and why it's interesting. Since the industry hasn't settled on a normalized level guideline, I created a three-tier leveling for the sake of brevity. The table covers positions that accept university graduates, which not every company supports. The industry level combines Senior and Staff positions, as these are middle positions that require some industry experience. Lastly, principal covers *principal and above* positions, although many companies stop at the principal level.

Normalized level	Company	Qualifications	Education
Entry	Apple	SDLC PM	CS or comparable
	Google	Alignment across multiple teams PM/SDLC	CS or comparable
	Microsoft	PM/SDLC Influence without authority Biz Intel	CS or comparable **Equivalent Work Experience (EWE)**

Industry	Amazon	PM/SDLC Remove ambiguity Thought leadership	CS or comparable EWE
	Apple	Leading a team Established PM/SDLC communication Strategy and program delivery	BS or MS EWE
	Google	E2E delivery System design Data analysis	CS or comparable
	Meta	PM/SDLC Works with other TPMs	CS or comparable EWE
	Microsoft	Experience writing code Defining program goals PM/SDLC	CS or comparable EWE
Principal	Amazon	PM/SDLC Remove ambiguity Thought leadership	CS or comparable EWE
	Meta	Proven PM/SDLC Cross-organization collaboration	CS or comparable EWE
	Microsoft	Proven PM Strong technical proficiency Excellent communication	BS/MS in CS or comparable

Table 1.1: A functional comparison of job roles across the tech industry

As you can see in the table, across the industry, there are more similarities than differences in the TPM role. This was a bit of a shock for me, to be honest. We've all heard of specific cultural stereotypes for Google, Meta, Microsoft, Amazon, and Apple—however, when it comes down to their expectations for the functional side of a TPM, they're close enough to call them equivalent.

The expected education, regardless of level, was pretty consistent, with some sort of technical degree or EWE being required. For qualifications, this varies somewhat based on the level, but the pattern is similar. At the entry level, the focus is on fundamentals such as the SDLC and basic project management. For industry hires, the focus is on program management and stellar communication, and then the principal level focuses on impact and proven results.

Insights into the TPM life from interviews

One thing that this matrix doesn't cover extensively is individual company style, which I was able to learn more about from the interviews I conducted. So, let's talk a little about the things that stood out here.

Of the companies I held interviews for, Meta (formerly called Facebook) was the youngest, having formed in the mid-2000s. Due to this, their standards for project management are, as the interviewer put it, based on a *"do what is needed"* mentality. This is by no means bad, as many companies use this strategy to great success. There wasn't much from the job boards that clued us in on this, but the focus on the SDLC does seem to agree with the *bottom-up* approach to management that the interviewee referenced, where the drive is from the engineering teams.

At the other end of the tenure spectrum is Microsoft. I think a lot of people think about Microsoft's own *Project* software and then lump it in as a highly regimented, **Project Management Professional** (**PMP**)-style organization. As it turns out, this isn't true! Although I am sure some people use Microsoft Project there, it isn't standardized. The interviewee I talked to said many of the individuals they've worked with use Excel! Also, due to their tenure in the industry, they pre-dated the **TPM** job role and, therefore, mainly used the program manager role title. Some organizations are starting to use the TPM role, both as seen on the job boards and also confirmed in the interview—the TPM title, and the matching compensation and requirements, are starting to be used in place of the PM title in areas that require technical expertise.

I've heard many people suggest that the TPM role originated at Amazon, and that does make some sense. Back in 2013, when I interviewed at Amazon, I had to ask what the TPM role involved, as I had never heard of it! A quick internet search didn't turn up any results either. But through some discussions, and simply looking at the timelines in *Figure 1.1* earlier in the chapter, you can see that the TPM role pre-dates Amazon.

I wouldn't be surprised if it was one of the first to widely use the job role based on conversations internally and externally, but it is hard to say for sure. Amazon is also a *"do what is needed"* organization, where the TPM role can vary quite a bit from team to team, based on the gaps and needs of a team.

An interesting takeaway in my discussions about Google is that they are heavily product-focused. A good portion—up to 30%—of the TPM's schedule is dedicated to working with product managers on the product roadmap and backlog grooming based on it. The job descriptions hint at this as well, which discuss that Google is product-focused and how cross-team communication with engineers and product managers is a must.

Lastly, we have Apple. As it turns out, Apple doesn't allow its current employees to be interviewed about Apple life, so for this iteration, we only have the job descriptions. However, one interesting takeaway is that they are the only company (of those that I researched) that lists having a PMP certification as a desirable (as in nice to have, but not required) skill to have. Personally, I believe the PMP certification is valuable to have, and as such, I currently hold the certification. It provides a common language and foundation in which to have discussions with fellow TPMs and even other project, program, product, and development managers. I have noticed that while companies like Amazon do not use the standard terminology that is used in the certification crowd, they do use the processes that are described. Once I realized this, it made a lot of my job easier, enabling me to relate a common foundation to what I do every day. That being said, just as Apple has taken a stance in favor of the PMP, some companies have taken a stance against it, so research well when looking at companies to ensure that they align with what you see as valuable.

A quick look into the main TPM career levels

Now that we've discussed different job families, let's dive a little closer into the TPM role itself across the life of your career. *Table 1.2* looks at the different levels of a TPM—entry, industry, and principal. Not every company has job postings for every level, and some, like Amazon, do not hire at the entry level anymore.

Normalized level	Company	Focus	Years of experience
Entry	Apple	Project delivery and fundamentals	None
	Google	Project delivery and fundamentals	0 to 1
	Microsoft	Project delivery and fundamentals Influence without authority	None
Industry	Amazon	Project delivery Cross-team collaboration Remove ambiguity	3 to 8
	Apple	Strategy and program delivery	5 to 10
	Google	E2E delivery System design	2 to 6
	Meta	Cross-team collaboration	4 to 7
	Microsoft	Program definition Cross-team collaboration	6 to 10

Principal	Amazon	Program delivery Identify ambiguous problems	8+
	Meta	Proven PM/SDLC Cross-organization initiatives	8+
	Microsoft	Program delivery Cross-organization initiatives	8+

Table 1.2: TPM levels and years or experience

These terms are not standardized, but they still line up well with the various levels that I've encountered in my research for the book. Entry level means being 0 to 3 years out of college, and the scope and expectations are focused more on the fundamentals of the job. The entry position is becoming less common, since the scope and impact are so small, the value-add of a TPM at this level is considered to be minimal. More often than not, the TPM type of duties that would warrant an entry-level TPM can also be done by either the development manager or the software developer/ engineer themselves. I'll cover what this means more in *Chapter 3, Career Paths*, but the general expectation is to start out your career tech-focused as a software developer or similar type of role.

The industry level means 3 or more years of experience in the industry with no hard upper cap. This is the most common row with the largest growth curve. You go from a relatively new TPM with a basic understanding of the role and expand into mastering your domain. This is often the highest level of your career as a TPM, as most either stay at this level or transition to other job families to continue upward growth. The last level that is common among these top companies is the principal level. Often, this is the highest level achievable as a TPM across the industry, which puts you at the same level as directors or senior managers. However, this means the expected scope and impact are also at the same level as those directors, making this level more difficult to achieve—although certainly not impossible!

Summary

In this chapter, we discussed the fundamentals of being a TPM. We started by explaining where the TPM overlaps with the generalized PM and program management and touched on the bare fundamentals for the technical aspect of our specialization.

Then, we examined the TPM role specifically to see what makes us thrive and found that drive, clarity, and being a communication bridge set us apart from our colleagues. Then, we expanded our view to look more closely into how our specialties overlap with the job families around us and across the industry.

We'll continue to build on these fundamentals as the book progresses and, as we dive deeper into these topics to get a solid understanding of our role, how to be the most successful at the job, and how to progress your career the way that fits your skills and desires best.

Next, in *Chapter 2*, we'll discuss the building blocks, or pillars, of the TPM role. We'll build on the fundamentals we tackled in this chapter and dive deeper into the program management and project management strategies that help make us successful. Lastly, we'll cover the technical nature of our role and how it feeds into the program management skills and techniques. Just as with the foundations found in this chapter, the pillars we will discuss in *Chapter 2* will be built upon and referenced throughout the book.

Join our book's Discord space

Join our Discord community to meet like-minded people and learn alongside more than 5000 members at:

https://packt.link/sKmQa

2

Pillars of a Technical Program Manager

For most of my professional career, I have been a **technical program manager (TPM)**—or a proxy to it. During this time, I have worked alongside other TPMs on large-scale projects, mentored junior TPMs on their journey, and interviewed a large number of TPMs from all corners of the industry. Over the years, I have gained a considerable perspective on what a TPM is and what makes them successful.

Without getting into complex sentence diagramming, let's take a look at the job title itself, *technical program manager*. The title is comprised of two parts, the noun *program manager* and the adjective *technical*. From this, it's easy to see that there are at least two foundational pillars to a TPM role: *program management* and the *technical toolset*. In my view, program management consists of two separate pillars since program management includes project management. You cannot have the skills to run a program without also having the skills to run a project. However, the reverse is not true—you can certainly have project management skills and not have the skills to run a program. So, that's our third, and final, foundational pillar. Every industry that has a TPM will make use of these three pillars, and the extent to which they are used most often varies greatly from company to company and even team to team. To that end, this book will treat all three as foundational and thus equally important, which I believe is the right approach for any TPM to take. Even if you work for a small company that doesn't have large programs, just projects, you should still understand program management to make it easier to transition to a different company should the need arise.

Why these pillars?

After the first edition came out, I was often asked about other skills that people saw as essential to being a TPM. Most of these can be categorized within these pillars but the one that stood out the most was **executive leadership skills**. To me, these skills are essential for all positions at the executive level or working alongside the executive leadership level. As such, I decided not to treat them as foundational. There are myriad books available for effective executive leadership and I would significantly derail the purpose of this book by diving into these aspects too deeply.

Another large shift has taken place since the first edition was released with the explosion of **generative artificial intelligence (GenAI)** across every aspect of life, including our profession. While this isn't a standalone pillar, it will be given its own chapter as it will help you elevate your effectiveness in all three pillars. I bring this up because GenAI has brought a very consequential discussion to the forefront of professional discourse: how will this impact my role? This has led me to include another new chapter—though not a pillar in and of itself—on emotional intelligence. While GenAI will steadily reduce many of the functional and administrative tasks like risk assessment, document generation, and even project planning, it will not replace our soft skills. This is our ability to interact with others, act on our intuition, and use empathy to help connect with stakeholders and make the right decisions for our programs.

Both of these additional topics exist within these pillars as added dimensions to consider in our day-to-day work as a TPM.

The foundational technical toolset is the key pillar that differentiates a TPM from a general practitioner program manager. But to fully understand why, we must first start with the pillars that the two roles share and build from there. So, in this chapter, we're going to dive a bit deeper into each of these foundational pillars by exploring them in the following order:

- Understanding project management
- Diving into program management
- Exploring the technical toolset

In this introductory chapter, I will introduce several topics at a high level to give you a sense of the scope of the three pillars. Each concept that is talked about here will be covered in greater detail throughout the rest of the book.

Understanding project management

Before diving into the first pillar, let's take a quick look at how the pillars support each other, as illustrated in *Figure 2.1*:

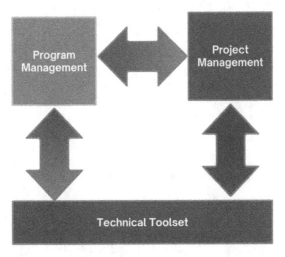

Figure 2.1: The pillars of a TPM role

Project management is the foundation of our functional toolbox. Certifications like **Project Management Professional (PMP)** from the **Project Management Institute (PMI)** exemplify the components of this space. Though the definitions have changed over time, I like the visualization of the 7th edition of the **Project Management Book of Knowledge (PMBoK)** guide, which uses management areas to describe and categorize the type of work that we do in project management. This is what I pull from when describing the key management areas that I cover in this book: project management, stakeholder management, and risk management. The skills learned at the project level are built upon as you manage multiple related projects in a program.

There is also a certification for program management from PMI called **Program Management Professional (PgMP)**. The PMP and more work experience are required to apply for the certification and it builds on top of the PMP principles and learnings. You can think of program management as an extension of project management in that you must have project management skills to build upon for program management. Program management phases and tactics build on top of the project management phases and tactics. Also, since a program involves multiple projects, they often share direct feedback, as risks at the program level can manifest at the project level and vice versa. The technical toolset supports both the program and project management pillars, as it provides the technical acumen to refine and more effectively utilize those skill sets.

To see how the three pillars relate to various managerial roles, we can look at *Figure 2.2*. The first two pillars are shared with other program and project manager roles. Nonetheless, they are an important part of a TPM's foundational skills:

Figure 2.2: The functional overlap between the role of program managers and TPMs

Though we call ourselves program managers, a lot of what we do day to day, especially earlier on in our careers, is related to project work. So, we'll start there.

Am I a project or program manager?

I've seen the "P" in TPM stand for both project and program depending largely on the company. I remember when I started at Amazon in 2013, I couldn't remember whether I was a project or program manager myself!

Since then, I've concluded that the "P" should stand for program. The difference between whether you are a program or project manager is more often about scope and impact, which comes with seniority. Though you may not own a program as an entry-level TPM, that is what the role's ultimate goal is, and what you are building on through the early years.

At the end of the day, a title is nothing more than what your HR team decided to use, and if you are listed as a project manager, this all still applies to you!

Most of what we do is measured through our ability to deliver results, either directly or indirectly. Did we reach the milestone on time? Did we effectively unblock the low-level design quandary from our developer? Was the stakeholder looped in to help drive a discussion to the right conclusion? These are all different ways that we move a project forward, drive toward clarity, and ultimately deliver our goals.

In the project management life cycle, there are many opportunities to deliver results—not just within the project itself. At every stage, we are tested on our ability to take what is ambiguous, add definition, and refine it. We analyze risks and mitigate them before they become problems.

In later chapters, we'll dive deeper into the major stages of a project to see how a TPM utilizes their technical toolset to effectively manage a project. For now, we'll go through the general steps we take as project managers to successfully deliver our projects.

Exploring the typical project management tactics

We'll go through a quick overview of the tactics used in a few of the high-impact areas of project management. These are the areas that utilize the TPM's skills the most. They will be explored throughout the book in various levels of detail and with various perspectives on the tools and work they involve:

- Project planning
- Resource management
- Stakeholder management
- Risk management
- Communication

Let's take a look at each of these in more detail.

Project planning

The steps to create a project plan are relatively straightforward. However, the work that goes into each of the steps can range from routine to highly complex. As a starting point for **project planning**, a project manager takes the given requirements and builds out a breakdown of the work structure and a work list, which then develops into a project timeline with dependencies, durations, and planned estimates. In many project management tools, all of these artifacts—work breakdown structure, activity lists, and dependency lists—are simply a single artifact along with the resultant Gantt chart.

A single spreadsheet will organize each task as part of the work breakdown and include durations, resource management, and task dependencies. From a textbook perspective, these are all separate steps. In this regard, this seems to be a lot of time and effort, but a seasoned and well-prepared practitioner can get through this quickly. The amount of time and effort also varies depending on the size and complexity of the project or program.

Starting out as a project manager, or in a new organization, each of these steps will take time. In the same way, many Western cultures learn math by starting out with writing down every logical step in solving a math problem before getting to the answer. These steps help the practitioner consider each artifact deliberately to ensure all information is present to make the project plan.

For instance, there may be cases where the requirements are not well understood. This is often the case the higher your career level as the problems you are solving are more ambiguous than entry-level positions. In a case where the requirements are not well understood or are simply too generalized, you have to strive for clarity to get a better idea of the scope of work before you can start to plan it out.

Requirements might also be vague depending on the problem space you are in. For many years, I have worked in the tax compliance domain, and the requirements that come in from government legislators are often vague. Sometimes this is on purpose and other times it is because they may not appreciate the nuance the legislation represents. In either case, requirements analysis is often one of the portions of a project that takes the longest and our plans actually start at the requirements phase to account for the time and resources it takes to simply get a clear understanding of what you are building.

Task dependency identification is often simple enough once the requirements are known, at least from a technical dependency perspective. It's always worth getting the dependencies in your plan checked by the technical team, but as a TPM, you should be able to take the first pass without help to identify task dependencies. An often-overlooked dependency comes from resource constraints where a key resource is required for multiple steps that don't share a task dependency. This means that given more resources, these tasks could be done in parallel as the work of one task does not rely on the output of the other task, but the realities of resource constraints limit your ability to optimize.

Add together all of these aspects that go into planning, and you end up with the high potential for a complex planning process. As with all steps in the project management process, they are revisited throughout the life cycle of the project in response to changing conditions.

During planning, as well as throughout the project, we manipulate the **project management triangle** to get the outcome we need. We often see it depicted as an equilateral triangle (as in, all sides and angles are equal) that represents the trade-offs between the project scope, timeline, and cost—this is done to illustrate that to remain equal, a change to one side of the triangle necessitates a change to one or both of the other sides. This concept extends to any system where three constraints are being considered for a given outcome and is often called the triple constraint triangle.

Figure 2.3 illustrates the project management triangle where scope, resources, and time are bound together:

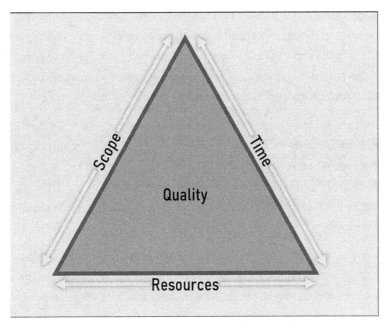

Figure 2.3: The project management triangle

As you can see, any change to a side length—which represents the number of resources, time, or scope of the project—will require an adjustment to one or both of the other sides to maintain equal (or balanced) sides. Without this balance, you cannot ensure the quality of the project or program goal. This isn't to say that time can't be reduced, or resourcing won't be tight, but this does mean that something must give and that is usually the quality. Many companies have a concept of a "beta product" that lives in a beta life cycle for years, or a "minimally viable product." These are instances where the requirements are reduced to the absolute bare minimum to get the product out the door. The expected quality of the new set of requirements can then be met with fewer resources or less time.

If someone is boasting that they can get a quality product with fewer resources or less time, then they are either having people work long hours and not reporting it or gambling with cutting corners on requirements, testing, or somewhere else in the life cycle to meet timelines. This certainly must happen from time to time, and as TPMs, we must be able and willing to make these challenging decisions, but that doesn't negate the fact that to do this, resourcing or time will be affected.

A common scenario that requires adjusting the triangle comes when people are moved off of the project. In this case, either the project timelines must move out to accommodate the reduction in resources, or the scope must shrink, or a little of both scenarios. Another frequent usage occurs when there is additional scope added to the project, either through a proper change request or simple scope creep, where features are added without going through a change process. In both cases, the outcome is the same: the constraints of the triangle have shifted to an unbalanced state and must be adjusted. In this example, a scope increase would necessitate increasing the time allowance for the project, adding additional resources, or a combination of both.

Of course, it isn't always this simple. Most projects are complex, and tasks have interdependencies that restrain your ability to simply add more people. If a task technically cannot be done in parallel with another task, additional people will not cause that to not be true, so the only course of action here is to increase the timeline for the project. As you can see, our day-to-day project negotiations are always tied back to the triangle and the trade-offs required to maintain the quality of the project.

The resulting project plan represents the vision of the project and is the basis for all the other stages that we'll cover. This is the metaphorical blueprint that TPMs follow. The ability to craft and maintain a project plan may not seem super significant, but I am often reminded of the fact that non-project managers have a hard time reading and interpreting a project plan. This is *our* language. Without a plan, the project is doomed to failure, leading to reactive actions instead of proactive delivery. It can reveal poor planning or estimations, a project trending yellow as time slips, or a risk rising in probability. It is a living document guiding our path and the decisions needed to reach our goals.

Resource management

Resource management, also referred to as cost in more traditional contexts, pulls directly from the plan, as it lays out the type of resourcing needed at each phase of the project as well as each task in the project plan. Resources can include software developers or engineers, **user experience (UX)** designers, software testers, vendors, contractors, and anyone else who is contributing to a task in the project plan. Additionally, this can also include hardware procurement, software installation, or other tangible needs of the project that are not people related but incur a cost.

Although this sounds straightforward, a project can very quickly stall if the right people and assets are not available when needed. How much of a problem this will be for you depends on how your company approaches resourcing and prioritization—it could be a constant struggle or a negligible one. In the critical chain methodology, resources are pooled or buffered at each step of the critical path of a project to reduce the chances of resourcing being a reason for delay. This was decided after extensive research showed that insufficient resources along the critical path caused the most delays. If a task is outside of the critical path, resourcing delays should not impact the overall timeline of the project. If it could, it would be part of the critical path by definition.

Stakeholder management

Stakeholder management, though separate from project planning, uses the plan to help inform the frequency and style of communication. In many companies, this style includes written status reports with varying levels of detail depending on the needs of the audience and meetings to convey the current status (which may or may not include a written report of the meeting).

A large number of teams may indicate a need for multiple types of stakeholder engagement—vendors likely require different status mechanisms to convey the needs or desires of the group than internal teams do. The reason is due to their unique perspective and what they need from the project. A vendor only cares about the components of the project that they are dependent upon, and giving them a status with overly detailed accounts unrelated to their deliverable introduces cognitive friction. It may also be that some information is sensitive and should not be shared with external teams. Conversely, internal teams have the context of the day-to-day changes and a more detailed recount since the last status update is more relevant. Within the internal setting, the seniority of the stakeholder may change the information shared. In the same way that day-to-day changes unrelated to the vendor's deliverable are unnecessary to share with them, the same may hold true for the vice president of your organization. Most executive summaries remain at a high level and touch upon only the most critical aspects of that status.

Each of these aspects plays into how the stakeholder communication plan comes together, from the number of communication formats to the frequency of the reports being sent out. Being consistent and reliable here instills confidence in your executive sponsors and leadership that the project is headed in the right direction.

The frequency can vary based on the number and type of stakeholders as well as the complexity of the project. For instance, a plan with tight timelines, or a lot of dependencies, may warrant a more frequent communication cycle to help ensure the project stays on track by surfacing problems more quickly to the relevant groups.

The frequency may also change during the life cycle of the project. I have found that it is useful to include a weekly status update when approaching the launch date and will often send out daily updates the week of launch. Not only does this help instill that you are on top of the project and in control, but it also gives quick feedback to everyone involved should issues arise during this time. Conversely, during the requirements and planning phase, the updates are published monthly as there is less movement to report. Of course, this varies from project to project and company to company, so be cognizant of the speed of change in your project and adjust communications accordingly.

Risk management

Risk management, or the identification of risks and the strategies that are planned to handle them once realized, is one of the most powerful cycles in managing a project. It interacts with and affects all other aspects of the project that we've talked about. This is because a risk—or opportunity—can occur anywhere! To that end, every management cycle also has risk identification and assessment as well as tracking embedded into the work being done. A good project manager never stops thinking about risks and opportunities. We see risks from a mile away and home in on them when they become relevant. We don't let them alter our course unexpectedly, as we have already planned a course correction.

It's important to remember that a risk to a project is anything that poses a change to the plan that is in place. In traditional project management, this means a risk may be a positive change in one aspect but can still cause an overall delay. For instance, a supplier you work with has been known to offer discounts for bulk orders in the past, but the discount often results in a delay in the product being supplied as the time to process the discount adds an extra week. This vendor is also known to offer this after the agreed terms as they wait for when it lines up with their promotion cycles. This means it isn't always known upfront during planning. Being a savvy project manager, you remember this pattern, log the risk—which is both an opportunity to save on costs and a potential time delay—along with possible strategies to handle the risk. The strategy could be to accept the opportunity for cost savings, as well as adding an additional time buffer to account for the possible delay. Or, it may be wiser to decline the savings if the time delay would end up costing you more than the savings. Maybe you tell them this ahead of time, greatly reducing the possibility of the risk coming up. You've identified a risk, added a plan to handle it should it arise, and are well prepared for this known risk.

Communication

The key to all of these aspects of project management is **communication**. Without it, none of these cycles carry weight or value. In general, it is better to over-communicate than under-communicate. Though some situations may warrant otherwise, this is the general rule. You must share your intended plan with stakeholders, work with your teams for resourcing, and discuss and analyze every risk you can think of. This is also true when working with your engineering team—you listen to them, understand their needs and concerns, and act upon them. Communication amplifies cohesion and is a vessel for transparency.

A well-written status report, whether it's a document, an email, a slide deck, or even verbal communication during a meeting, conveys urgency where needed and demands action. It calls attention to problem areas and aligns everyone to the next steps. It lays out all the risks so that when a risk is realized, it isn't a surprise. It instills confidence in all the right people in your ability to deliver the project.

Project planning, stakeholder management, risk management, and communication throughout are all core project management areas. Now that we've discussed the core project management areas and the typical tactics that we use while executing the project, we can take what we've learned and scale it up to program management. I say scale here because program management is an extension of project management that applies scale across multiple projects under the same program.

Diving into program management

As you progress in your career as a TPM, the scope and impact of the work you deliver will increase. One way in which your scope will increase is through running programs. Instead of just the day-to-day operation of one project or even multiple unrelated projects, you will manage or oversee multiple projects with a shared goal. The distinction here is the shared goal, which provides the opportunity for synchronization and mutually beneficial planning.

What is a program?

As discussed in *Chapter 1*, a program is a combination of multiple projects, often spanning multiple years, that achieves a common goal. Each project may have its own goal, but it will also contribute toward the goal of the program.

Though seemingly straightforward, let's take a look at it from the perspective of a large, multiple-month project, instead of a program. The first thing you would do is break the project up into smaller deliverables, or milestones. Each of these should deliver a feature or functionality that, when put together with all the other milestones, achieves the goal(s) of the project.

A program is very similar to this concept, but usually on a much larger scale. Instead of a single multi-month project, the end goal may take multiple years. Each of the *milestones* may be different enough to warrant different personnel or strategies. In that sense, each of these becomes a project in itself (with its own milestones) that spans the program timeline. They all come together to deliver the goal of the program.

An analogy for a project versus a program is the difference between planning a day trip an hour away from home (a single project) and planning a multi-week trip to another country (a program). With the day trip, all the plans are self-contained to that day and likely only concern things like when you are leaving, returning, and what food you may need to bring. The right clothes, a camera or phone, and similar are some likely considerations. The only people that need to be considered (your stakeholders) are your family taking the trip with you. Now, for the multi-week trip, you need to consider what you need to pack as you will be gone for more than one day. This includes clothes, toiletries, medicine, and, if you have young kids, toys, nighttime needs like a sound machine, and books to read. You also need to plan a trip from home to the airport, the plane trip itself, a hotel at your destination, and then the actual itinerary once you are at your destination. This might involve getting visas and passports, which adds dependencies to outside groups like your post office for the passport application. All of these segments together constitute the multi-week trip (the shared goal) but can also be managed separately. For instance, one person can manage how to get to the airport and get on the plane. Another can determine the itinerary and hotel stay once in the destination. A delay in the trip to the airport can impact the hotel and destination itinerary, but with enough buffer, delays should remain contained.

To better demonstrate this concept, let's take a look at a visual representation of a program and the projects that comprise its body of work:

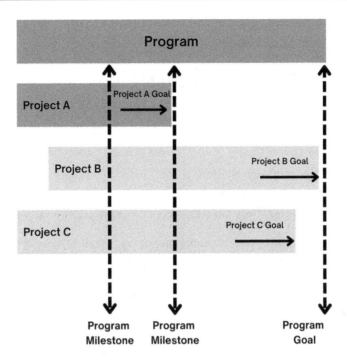

Figure 2.4: A program and its constituent projects

In *Figure 2.4*, a program has three planned projects, **A**, **B**, and **C**. All combined, the projects span the life of the program. Each project has its own end goal and its own internal milestones (which are not pictured). Notice that just as with tasks within a single project, not all the projects within a program start at the same time and can vary for the same reasons—whether resource constraints or internal and external dependencies. For this program, there are also program-wide milestones being tracked that align at different stages across the projects—project **A**'s end goal and the second program milestone are the same. A program-wide milestone can help provide cohesion and context across teams, driving better alignment for the program.

As referenced in *Chapter 1*, *Figure 1.7*, another common view of a program is to contrast it to a product. A product is a vertical organization in your company that often comprises the business, product team, and technology teams that support it—like a service offering to customers or even a standalone application. Many large companies have multiple products that often have some level of interoperability. In these companies, any feature that flows between two or more products would be introduced via a program initiative. In this scenario, the shared goal is the new feature and each project is what each product vertical needs to deliver in order for that feature to work.

Now that we know what a program is, let's explore how we use our skills to drive and manage a program through its various phases.

Typical program management tactics

As a program manager, technical or otherwise, the approach toward managing a program is similar. The stages are the same as they are for a project, just on a larger scale, which leads to changes in the skill sets and approaches at each stage.

Project planning goes from determining a single project plan for a single set of requirements to multiple sets of requirements and plans all contributing to the same end goal. The coordination and effort involved at this level increases as the number of projects increases.

Unlike a typical project where the planning stage happens once, the planning stage of a program iterates as projects open and close. Though a singular plan is created in the beginning, multi-year programs will revisit the planning stage often, as projects become clearer over time—similar to how planning the estimates for a task in the work breakdown structure is more refined once the breakdown of the task is understood better.

With multiple projects, there are often multiple leaders or drivers, each maintaining their own plan schedule that ties into the program plan schedule. This, again, is similar to a project plan but with a larger scope. A project's plan is overseen by the TPM with input from the people doing the work (developers, system developers, and so on) as far as estimates for the tasks are concerned. Further up, the program is overseen by a TPM with input from other TPMs, PMs, and SDMs with estimates and timelines for their respective projects.

Stakeholder management is similar to project planning in terms of the increase in scale from the project to the program level. While a project may move quickly and warrant a bi-weekly status update, a program may have a status update monthly or quarterly. The goal here is to let stakeholders know that the program is moving in the right direction. This could be that each project is delivering the right thing at the right time, or that a problem exists, and the right measures are being taken to correct it. In this scenario, the high-risk items from each project are showcased in a report, as opposed to listing all the risks when sending a status at the project level.

By now, you can follow the general pattern of project versus program—scope and communication complexities both increase at the program level. The same can be said for risk management as well. A program tracks the risks for each project within its scope as well as the risks present at the program level. These risks follow the same scope pattern; think of inter-project dependencies for a program instead of inter-task dependencies for a project.

Depending on the type of organization, funding may be of greater concern within a multi-year program compared to a multi-month project. **Projectized organizations**, or companies that fund and tie resources specifically to a project, may treat the program as a singularly funded entity for its life span. However, in the tech industry, funding tends to follow a yearly cycle. Within a given year, the funds are fixed to the project, and priorities are re-evaluated yearly where projects are re-prioritized or de-funded as other needs arise.

The communication of risks, as alluded to in the stakeholder discussion, will often focus on high-risk items that are a threat to the overall program and leave the project risks to the project level. A good analogy here—and true in general for all aspects of program versus project—is the satellite imagery of a city seen in the Google Earth application. From 17 kilometers above the ground, the city shape as a whole is well defined due to the density differences between it and the surrounding area, but spotting the city's medical district as compared to the core of the city's downtown is likely hard from this perspective as all buildings look the same. The only real differentiation here you can see is where a city park, wetland, or other green area is, as opposed to a commercial district with buildings stacked along the roads. Zooming in closer to the street level (around 4 kilometers), these distinct districts come into focus, yet the city-wide view is now gone. Next, zoom all the way down to the street level and you can discern one office building from the next, and one medical wing from another. Each of these views has its purpose, but to see the full city, you have to lose this specific focus on a singular building or district. You cannot see everything at once, but can only choose the level on which you focus.

Keeping in mind the varying levels of information, we can apply this analogy to a program's status update (the city-wide view) and compare that to a project-level update (at the city block or district level). First, let's see a program update:

Mercury Program Update

GREEN for Jul-1-24

Executive Summary

The program is green for a Jul-1-24 launch. We are tracking 3 program-level risks as their risk scores are high enough to warrant concern. Each risk has a strategy to handle it with only one that has the potential to delay the launch. We are working with the team in Project B on their resourcing concerns and escalating now to the director to align resources in order to avoid this

Top Program Risks

Risk Name	Description	Risk Score	Risk Strategy
Project A: Milestone 1	Production bug caused rollback and 1 week delay, 1 more week will cause program delay	90	Swarm
Project B Resourcing	Resource constraints are consuming program buffer on critical chain	75	Accept/Delay
Milestone 2 alignment	Misalignment of milestone 2 goal may cause scope creep	80	Swarm

Program Milestones

Milestone	Description	Date	Status
Milestone 2	Feature available in all services and products up to pre-production	Mar-30-24	Yellow
Milestone 3	Feature available in production under testing weblab	Apr-9-24	Green
Program Launch	Launch of feature in production	Jul-1-24	Green

Figure 2.5: A program status update

Early concepts seen in the status update

The status update here jumps ahead on a few topics that I'll cover in later chapters. Here's a quick description of the terms seen here.

Status is a summary concept that uses a word, sometimes combined with a color, to signify the high-level state of the project, program, or open issue. The most common system utilizes traffic light colors to signify the state, with red meaning a blocked state, yellow or amber meaning the path forward is uncertain, and green signifying that it is going as planned.

 Risk score is a rating rubric that is used to assess the level of a risk based on how likely it is to occur and how much of an impact the risk would have on the project. It's a way to remove bias from risk analysis and adds objectivity to risks. Most risk score ratings are on a 100-point scale where a 100 is essentially an inevitable risk that will cause a large disruption to the project plan. Any score above around 65 means the risk likely needs to be monitored closely. However, the exact numbering is subjective and depends on risk tolerance in your organization.

Risk strategy refers to the strategies the TPM will use to handle the risk should it occur. Common strategies are acceptance of the risk and the consequences, mitigating the impact of the risk, avoiding the risk, and transferring the risk to another party.

Figure 2.5 shows the type of details the audience of a program status update might want to see at a high level. The concerns are at the program level and only items that impact the program's **critical path**, or the sequence of dependent tasks that amounts to the longest time (and represents the minimum time in which a project can finish), are brought to light. As it relates to a program, the critical path is each critical path of the projects that comprise it put together. There may be additional work being done at the program level that will be part of the program's critical path as well, but the project's critical paths are a bare minimum.

The program status calls out a delay in Milestone 1 from Project A. The risk is surfaced, by the TPM, to the program status because Milestone 1 is part of Project A's critical path and therefore could cause a delay to the program.

Now let's look at the status of Project A to see how the details differ:

Project A Update

GREEN for Apr-9-24

Executive Summary

Project A is green for a Apr-9-24 launch. There is a high chance for a project delay, which would then result in an overall program delay. There was a production bug that required a code rollback that has eaten into the project buffer. Another week of delay will cause a day-by-day slip of the project and program launch. We are currently pulling in resources to swarm the remaining work to bring in Milestone 1.

Top Project Risks

Risk Name	Description	Risk Score	Risk Strategy
Milestone 1	Production bug caused rollback and 1 week delay, 1 more week will cause program delay	90	Swarm

Project Milestones

Milestone	Description	Date	Status
Milestone 1	Feature available in Service A up to pre-production	Feb-4-24	Yellow
Milestone 2	Feature available in service A under testing weblab	Mar-3-24	Not Started
Project Launch	Launch of feature in production	Apr-9-24	Green

Development Progress

Milestone	Description	Date	Status
Milestone 1: Story 1	Feature added to data model	Jan-15-24	Yellow
Milestone 1: Story 2	Weblab ready for feature in pre-production	Feb-4-24	Not Started
Milestone 2: Story 1	Weblab ready for feature in production	Mar-1-24	Green

Figure 2.6: A status update for Project A

Figure 2.6 shows a zoomed-in view of **Project A**'s status update. Just as in the program status, this calls out project risks and milestone progress. However, this goes deeper into the project deliverables down to the development tracks. This is because they have more meaning to the stakeholders reading the project status report. For instance, an engineering manager or SDM may want to see a delay in a story's progress even if it doesn't impact the current end date of the project because it may indicate another problem within the sprint team that they can address.

In both cases, we consider the audience of the report to tailor what is included to provide only the necessary information for that audience. Now that we've covered both program and project management and their tactics, which are shared across all program manager roles, let's discuss how your technical background provides you with the toolset to amplify your existing program and project management skills. This is the key to what sets a TPM apart from a generalized project manager.

Exploring the technical toolset

There's a reason why the *T* comes before the *PM*. The technical nature of the position is what differentiates a TPM from a generalist program manager. The area of focus is so deep within technology teams and technology products that specialized knowledge is needed to properly manage projects and programs. To be clear, not all companies actually use the term *TPM* and continue to use the generalized *PM* moniker instead. Make no mistake, though—positions that work with technical teams definitely require a technical background. This allows TPMs to dive deeper than just tracking milestones and deliverables, and also ensures that the right solution is being built for both the project and the organization.

As a TPM, you need to have some foundational knowledge in the technology space. We'll go over the particulars across the industry throughout *Part 3* of this book, but in general, that background should afford you some intermediary knowledge of software or hardware engineering. Although some jobs may cite a specific type of degree (for example, computer science), related degrees and experience suffice in many cases. At the end of the day, if your technical toolset allows you to navigate technical teams, technical requirements, system diagrams, and planning, then you will succeed.

Earlier in this chapter, we went over the general skills and tools that a generalist program manager utilizes. These tools are great for ensuring the proper delivery of a program or project across a wide range of disciplines. Now, we've learned that a technical background is key to the success of a TPM. Next, we'll learn why this technical toolset is so effective.

Discovering the effectiveness of your technical toolset

While studying for my **PMP** exam, the course instructor stated that the skills I would learn would allow me to walk into any job that requires a PM and perform the job. If that were true, why would there be a need for a specialized PM in technical situations? It comes down to the ability to eliminate *trial and error!*

The tech industry hasn't always had a TPM role—and as stated earlier, not all companies use the term, even today. However, over the last few decades, it's been shown that understanding the jargon, complexities, estimations, and designs of the software and hardware world leads to a more productive and successful program manager. The more successful the PM, the more successful the program, and thus emerges the TPM role!

This doesn't just apply to the tech industry. You certainly could take your PMP certification, walk into a construction site management office, apply for a program or project manager position, and get the job. You would have the skills, as you would understand the PM lingo and processes. You would be able to effectively handle change management, stakeholders, and multiple dependencies. However, you'd struggle because you don't understand construction at the level needed to be most effective. You might be able to manage a plan and reason out a good course of action, but it will take you longer to notice risks, mitigate issues, and estimate properly because you don't have the knowledge and experience for this. Over time, you'd learn patterns and standard behaviors that would accelerate your performance but every nuance with an unknown situation would slow you down.

Experience in the field you are managing is invaluable to your success.

If you have developed software in the past, you will have a good understanding of the software estimates that your developers give you and can challenge the estimates when needed. Your understanding of architectural landscapes and system designs can help you see how multiple projects fit with one another—how one project's design may cause risk through interference with another—or allow you to realize a positive risk, where two projects in a program share design elements and can thus shave development time off one or both projects.

An example from the real world: *Experience matters*

Here's a real-world example that might be closer to home for you from my professional software development days, where experience in your field matters. My first
job as a developer was at a geochemical laboratory writing software applications to
interface gas chromatographs and **Total Organic Carbon** (**TOC**) analyzers, among
others, into a central lab system for analysis and reporting. My first degree was in
geology, and I programmed as a hobby, so it was a natural fit to use my university
knowledge to help me in my software development. At the same time, I was fortu-
nate enough to have a desk right on the other side of the lab wall. I could see my
applications in action, run tests, and be called upon by lab technicians who had a
problem with the patch I had just pushed to their machines.

I had meaningful interactions with the lab technicians and actually understood their
problems because I understood their domain: oil. Sure, I had to learn the analysis
side and the nuances specific to the tests and situations in the lab, but my foundational knowledge set me up for success in that role. Near-instantaneous feedback
imprinted the concept of customer focus onto me. It also drove home the concept
 of customer obsession through near-instantaneous feedback.

Later in my career, when I switched to a TPM role, I started on a team that specialized
in updating services to be compliant with import and export laws. I knew nothing
about the compliance domain but spent two years with the team learning about the
services, as well as the intricacies of import and export legislation worldwide. When I
switched companies, I was able to pick up the business domain of my new team—tax
law—very quickly due to the legislative knowledge I had built up previously. Just as
in the geochemical lab, where I used my geology background to help my application
development, the legislation knowledge helped me contribute more quickly and
effectively to tax projects. Finding gaps in the requirements or requirements that
needed clarification was easier, as I understood the context of the requirements to
start with—I talked with developers about what changes were needed, and how
those changes would allow them to work faster and with more confidence that they
were building the right solution.

All of this is to say that a proper foundational knowledge, or toolset, can accelerate
your productivity and general efficiency at your job. Could I have written those applications without a geology degree? Yes. Was I faster, more focused, and able to provide
a better customer experience because of my background knowledge? Absolutely.

These tools enhance your existing PM skill set and allow you to apply situationally specific intentions to make all aspects of execution smoother and quicker.

Summary

In this chapter, we learned about the three pillars of a TPM role: project management, program management, and a solid technical foundation. We learned about project management as a common ground for all program and project managers and touched on the aspects of project management where the PM adds the most value.

We learned about program management being an expansion of the project management foundation and how the tools and phases involved are the same as at the project level but with a larger scope and more complex communication. We also discussed how communication is key to all of these exercises.

Lastly, we talked about what specialization can do and how a specific focus can amplify your existing program management skills to deliver with greater ease and proficiency.

In *Chapter 3*, we'll continue to explore program management in more depth. We'll talk about the specific methodologies that can be used in the various program and project phases. We'll also look more closely at the intersection of project and program management.

Additional resources

You can find templates regarding project and program status updates in the GitHub repo related to this book. Please check the Preface for the GitHub link.

Join our book's Discord space

Join our Discord community to meet like-minded people and learn alongside more than 5000 members at:

https://packt.link/sKmQa

3

Career Paths

In this chapter, we'll look into the paths you may take to become a **technical program manager** (**TPM**), followed by a closer view of the different career paths that are available to you once you are in the TPM job family. As the tech industry is large, the paths described here represent a generalized view of the career paths based on the interviews I have conducted and job descriptions that were present when researching this topic. I updated job descriptions for the second edition where appropriate but, from a career path perspective, not much has changed since this book was first published.

We'll also get a close look at two professional TPM journeys that showcase the different paths you can take, which will reinforce that no two journeys are the same, nor are they ever straight paths.

We'll explore the available career paths by doing the following:

- Examining the career paths of a TPM
- Exploring the **individual contributor** (**IC**) path
- Exploring the people manager path
- Wearing the hat of an adjacent role
- Moving up a level

Let's dive right in!

Examining the career paths of a TPM

The career paths of a TPM are as varied as the paths to becoming a TPM in the first place. Each person has their own story and path they follow, and the timing from step to step is also just as variable as the number of TPMs.

That being said, within the TPM job family, there are two main paths: the individual contributor path and the people manager path. I've combined job postings, interview notes, and personal stories of TPMs at different stages of their career to get to the perspectives in this book. What the data only hints at, however, is where we will start. *How do you become a TPM?*

The path to becoming a TPM

The TPM role is highly technical in most instances across the tech industry, as well as in industries needing technical expertise. A key component of a successful start as a TPM is having a strong technical foundation. This is traditionally in the form of a technical degree, such as **computer science (CS)**, **information technology (IT)**, or **informatics**, with CS being the most traditional. Regardless of the name of the degree, the knowledge you carry from the degree and your experiences is what matters both in the interview process as well as the job itself. We'll cover the technical competencies most often used on the job in *Chapter 12, Code Development Expectations*, and *Chapter 13, System Design and Architectural Landscape*.

I've seen TPMs start out their careers in various roles such as **Software Development Engineer (SDE or SE)**, **Development Operations Engineer (DevOps)**, and **Business Intelligence Engineer (BIE)**. On occasion, a TPM will start their career as a TPM out of college, though this is becoming a rare occurrence as many companies are removing entry-level roles for TPMs, as can be seen through job opening trends over the last two years, opting instead for people switching to TPM after obtaining *real-world* experience. This experience helps grow your depth of knowledge by working directly on solving real problems. Depending on how far you go down the pre-TPM path, you'll begin to work on your breadth of knowledge with system and architecture designs and possibly strategic product planning.

Some TPMs start out via a **Software Development Manager (SDM)** role or other people management role, which usually stems from a software development role or another IC role. In these cases, they may see a product, project, program, or situation that suits them as they switch back to an IC TPM role. In other cases, they find that they prefer honing their IC skills instead of people management skills.

We'll explore the journeys of some colleagues of mine in a bit, but I'll start with a bit about my personal journey to becoming a TPM. Hopefully, this will provide some insight into how the path to becoming a TPM truly can vary.

I grew up in the Puget Sound area of Washington State and, as such, Microsoft was in my backyard, so to speak. Likely in large part due to this proximity, I took an early interest in computers.

I really wanted to understand how they work, and when the opportunity came to install a dial-up modem, I took on the challenge. With no wizards or internet to guide me, I simply took the computer apart, read the paper instructions, and fumbled over the next several hours to get it installed. It was a lot of fun! From there, I took every opportunity to learn more about computers, which eventually led me to the Quick Basic language for early procedural-based programming. Writing programs quickly became a hobby for me.

Fast forward to college, I was still writing programs in my spare time as a way to learn. It may seem that a degree in computer science would have been a simple choice to make but I took some of the best advice I was given about college, which was to keep an open mind and spend the first year exploring different subjects. This is how I found geology, and I was hooked! It fulfilled the same need to understand how something works – in this case, the earth – that programming and hardware did for computers. Going into a supply store in the University District in Seattle to buy a rock hammer for class is still one of my favorite memories from college. This was my path, I was going to be a geologist, and so I graduated with a Bachelor's in Earth and Space Science.

According to a study by the US Federal Reserve in 2024, only 27.3% of college graduates work in a field that is closely related to their field of study. When I graduated, I was part of that 27%, but barely – my path had already begun to diverge. My first job out of college was working for a geochemical laboratory in Texas. However, I didn't become a project manager in the lab working with oil and rock samples, but instead I took a position writing the lab's applications. They largely used Visual Basic 6, a computer language that I used a lot as a hobby. This allowed me to use my knowledge to understand my users, their pain points, and to continue to explore my early fascination with computers.

I stayed with that company for many years and used it as a means to continue to learn new software development techniques. I eventually went back to college at night to earn an informatics degree – largely a computer science degree focusing on just the core major courses and not the higher science and math courses. This helped me build the rest of my foundational understanding of computers and how software gets them to do amazing things for us.

At this point, I wanted more and moved on to Hewlett Packard, where I became a software technical lead. This role was a little different from a typical software lead because I wasn't responsible for writing any code! Instead, I gathered and refined requirements, defined solution diagrams and data flow diagrams that met the requirements, and then guided a team of developers to write code and deliver the solution. This may sound a bit familiar – I was playing the role of a technical program manager.

My key takeaway from this journey is that every path is different, even if the path is shared by many people. One person might take detours along their road while someone else takes the shortest amount of time to reach their destination. This is okay and should be celebrated. The time or exact path does not define you as a TPM, but the knowledge you gain and apply to your work does.

I had major imposter syndrome issues in my first few years at Amazon due to my unorthodox path. I was surrounded by incredibly smart people with master's degrees in computer science and I felt I could not compare. However, my experiences in the lab and being close to my customer base gave me valuable insights and perspective on the implications of a software change that fostered my ability to think ahead to the customer's needs and think long term to the right solution.

Now that you've seen the journey I took to becoming a TPM, here are a few takeaways that are common regardless of the path you are on to become a TPM:

- **Technical background**: Whether this comes from a college education, on-the-job training, or a vocational program, a technical background is an absolute necessity.

- **Project management skills**: No matter which team you are a TPM with, a constant is that you will oversee projects, so some basic understanding is necessary. This doesn't need to be formal, like a PMP certificate, but understanding the key management areas will be needed.

- **Program management understanding:** Not every TPM will run a program as I am defining it here (which is consistent with the industry definition), but at least an academic understanding of running a program is helpful, though not as needed to begin with as the other two foundational pillars.

As you can see, there are many paths to becoming a TPM and it is easy to transition into this role given the right background, or willingness to expand on that background. A project manager can develop their technical acumen and then transition into the role. A software engineer can learn project management skills and become a TPM. Or, like me, you can grow both along your unique journey to become a TPM in your own time.

Now that we have seen what it takes to become a TPM, let's see what the path ahead will be for your career as a TPM.

The paths of a TPM

When I enrolled in the College of Earth and Space Sciences at the University of Washington, one of my professors, Dr. Stanley Chernicoff, told me that I was a geologist from that moment forth.

All of the courses and the degree serve to further my experience and knowledge. This was a profound statement to me and one that I come back to throughout my career when I am having doubts. I bring this up because I am often asked what it takes to be a TPM, and the bottom line is that once you land the role, you are a TPM. Everything else, including what we talk about in this book, is here to help you become a more experienced and knowledgeable TPM.

Once you are in the TPM role and on the path, you'll begin to strengthen your core competencies and expand both the depth and breadth of your knowledge. This serves to hone the foundational skills that are required, regardless of the path you take ahead. Each company defines its own career paths, which can vary depending on the size of the company or organization and the available opportunities. Within the tech industry, there is a general trend toward two distinct paths you can take to further your career and stay within the TPM job family – the IC path and the people manager path. Both are equally valid and have their own unique traits that may fit your style and aspirations. It's also worth noting that the path you take is not set for your entire career through a choice you make now. You may decide that IC is the right path for you now, and once that role has helped you grow how you want, you may decide to transition to people management, or the other way around.

Figure 3.1 explores some of the traits that are both shared and distinct between an IC and a people manager:

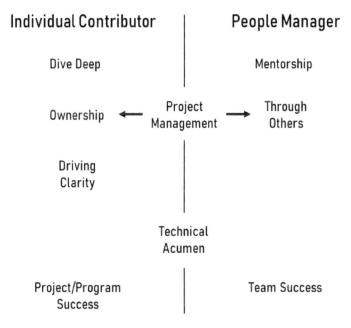

Figure 3.1: Traits of an IC versus a people manager

The IC role focuses heavily on the direct delivery of projects or programs with high value and impact. The skills that you have developed to manage a project and program, navigate stakeholders, and dive deeply into issues are the main skills in your toolset. In general, your focus is on delivering the project or program and that extends to ensuring your organization is on the right long-term path for project and program success.

The focus as a people manager is on the success of your team. You mentor your direct reports and grow their skill sets by sharing the knowledge you gained as an IC. They grow as an IC and your entire team benefits. In this way, you are focused on the success of your team and, by extension, the programs and projects that they deliver.

There are some focal points of your role that are shared between IC and people management; however, the emphasis on that focal point may be different. For instance, as a TPM, project and program management are a central focus to you. As an IC, this comes out via individual ownership of a project or program. You thrive in owning and executing programs and projects and dive deeply into every aspect of the projects. As a people manager, you work through others by guiding them so that they can be successful in delivering the program or project instead of delivering it by yourself.

Technical acumen is also shared across both of these different career paths, which makes sense given that they both share the same technical foundation. The depth and breadth of your technical knowledge, however, may differ based on your chosen path – for instance, people managers will focus on a deeper level of understanding of the systems their team owns and less breadth on the surrounding systems. As an IC, your technical acumen will depend on the needs of your projects and programs – you may dive deeply as an embedded TPM for a specific team and thus have good technical depth of that area, or you may have a broad understanding of the systems around you to better execute cross-functional programs. As your career develops and you go higher up, both the breadth and depth of your understanding will increase.

For people management, there are generally two paths available — a Software Development Manager and a manager of TPMs. Both paths are not always available, depending on the company philosophy, and it may be that a single manager role manages both TPMs and software developers.

Figure 3.2 shows the career paths available for a TPM who chooses people manager progression, and compares them to the IC path:

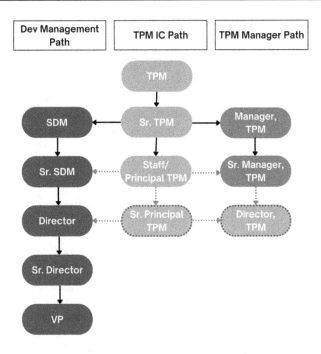

Figure 3.2: Possible TPM career paths within the TPM and adjacent job families

The center column represents the IC path, moving downward through higher levels. Not every role is available at every company and some role levels are omitted entirely, but the progression is the same. The graph starts with the entry-level TPM position, with no parallels in either column surrounding it. This is because the entry position for an IC does not exist in management roles as these are roles that an IC will pivot into within the same family. The Staff position is popular in small and medium-sized companies and sits as an intermediary step between the Senior and Principal roles. In large tech companies, Staff is omitted for the most part, but where both Staff and Principal exist, they are always in the same order from Staff to Principal. The Senior Principal TPM position is listed here as it does exist in some companies, and I expect this trend to continue, but it isn't mainstream as of now. In most cases, this is an executive-level IC position that converges with other IC paths and is a technical and strategic advisory role.

The columns on either side represent the two people manager paths mentioned: SDM and TPM manager. As you can see, the transition from IC to people management is lateral — meaning you stay at the same level, just in a different job family (for SDM) or classification (TPM manager). This happens most often at the Senior TPM level as this correlates to a first-level people manager in terms of corporate leveling. Though it is the most common transition, it can be done at higher levels as well but will vary greatly from company to company.

The SDM path is where the potential to move upward to senior VP is the most prevalent (though that doesn't mean it's easy, just that it's a path well taken!). Of course, this can go beyond senior VP, but this is a good stopping point for illustrative purposes. Each level increases your team and influence (thus, your impact).

The TPM manager path is often a shorter upward path as compared to the SDM route. Just like the Senior Principal TPM level, the director, the TPM position is available in some organizations though is not widespread. However, it is worth noting that once someone is a people manager, moving from a TPM manager to an SDM is a simpler move than from IC to people management.

Now that we've seen how IC and people management paths differ, let's look at each path in more detail.

Exploring the IC path

The IC role for the TPM job family is similar to that of other IC roles such as software developer or product manager. As the name suggests, an IC will contribute directly to the success of the company through deliverables, whether that's code for an SDE, a successful product release for a product manager, or delivering a project for a TPM. This role works as part of a team in the sense that they work with other ICs to deliver results. Unlike an SDE role though, a TPM will rarely work with other TPMs from their own team. Instead, when working with other TPMs, it's in a cross-organizational fashion.

Given that the IC role leans solely on the deliverables of the individual, the IC path tops off at the principal level in most companies. This is equivalent to a senior manager or director, depending on the company's verticality. The reason for this largely comes down to the ability of a single person to have a large enough impact to warrant the level. Though TPMs are force multipliers, the people we work with are still within different organizations and their successes are not directly our own. The deliverables are also measured at the scope of a single program, and though this is large, it is not as large as the deliverables under a director or VP since they are measured by the entire work of their respective organization. This makes influencing without authority much harder at higher levels.

That's not to say that a higher level isn't achievable in some cases. For instance, Amazon merged the career path of the TPM and the software developer starting at the L8 level, now called the Senior Principal in Tech. This allows a TPM to achieve up to L10 as an IC, which is a Distinguished Engineer in Tech (there is no L9 at Amazon).

These roles show that, at this level, your influence is geared toward the strategic goals of the company and the starting path is no longer relevant as you aren't writing code or delivering on projects directly. Of the TPMs I interviewed at the Big Five tech companies, this level for the IC path was only seen at Amazon; however, this will likely be a trend we see moving forward that more companies pick up.

Figure 3.3 denotes the career path and relative distribution of the IC TPM:

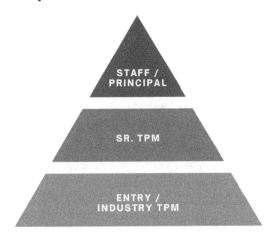

Figure 3.3: IC career path

The IC career path is shown as a pyramid to denote not only the upward path but also the relative distribution that each of these positions holds within a company. This helps illustrate the complications of moving upward, as well as the diverging paths that lead to a smaller number of positions the further up you go.

Like many places in this book, the figure uses normalized terms for the levels and represents them in three categories. The Entry and Industry TPM category consists of the entry level and first non-entry level of the path. The Senior TPM also includes the Staff and Senior Staff positions, depending on the company. The top category includes Principal, Senior Principal, and Distinguished where they exist.

The entry level TPM role only exists in a small number of companies now and is meant as a direct route from higher education into the TPM role and is essentially a stepping stone, meaning that upward movement is required. The industry TPM position is largely considered a career position, meaning that if you are happy at that level, you are not required to continue climbing. The senior position is also a career position, but it is also a crossroads for most TPMs as there is a split path at this point in your career.

In the words of *The Clash*, "Should I stay, or should I go?" You can choose the IC path and either stay a senior TPM, push upward to the principal, or you can pivot to the people manager path. As mentioned in *Chapter 1*, switching to people management is a popular shift at this level. This can be either through switching over to a software development management position or into a TPM manager role.

All of these paths are equally valid and which path is right for you depends on what you are looking for out of your career. Let's look at the path of a current Principal TPM to see why IC was ultimately the right choice for him.

An example from the real world: *An IC TPM path*

Oscar Jaimes is a Principal TPM at Amazon. His journey took him through both IC roles as well as people management roles. He received a degree in computer science and worked as a software developer for six years. Toward the end of that time, he went back and got a master's degree in business administration to help him move into project management, where he stayed for three years. From here, Oscar found an opportunity to lead both people and products, and then he became the chief technology officer for the Digital Business Unit at Latam Multinational. At each role switch, Oscar found positions that were strategic in nature, which allowed him to build businesses and ideas from the ground up. He expanded his leadership to thirty people as the director of innovation and business development – again, concentrating on strategically growing a product from idea to launch. Though his path changed often, the main driving focus was the product and seeing it through from ideation to launch. This is what led him to become a TPM at Amazon, where he was able to launch multiple global products on his way to Principal TPM in 2021.

Oscar's path led him back and forth between an IC path and a people manager path but there was always a focus on product delivery. In some cases, a people manager can also be responsible for concrete deliverables. This is particularly the case in smaller companies where every job function is expected to take on the needs of the company.

Now that we have a good understanding of the IC path, let's move on to the people manager career path and see what opportunities are available.

Exploring the people manager path

For TPMs, the people manager path goes in two directions for most companies in tech: SDM or TPM manager. Both of these paths switch focus from individual contributions to the company's success to team-based contributions. As such, it focuses on your ability to bring success through others. By growing the careers of the people who report to you, their contributions grow, and the collective contributions of your team grow. The difference between the two paths is the composition of your team as well as your mobility upward within that path. Each company is different, but this is true for the TPMs I interviewed from the Big Five companies. As you will see in an example later, companies outside of the Big Five, or really any of the other top tech companies, have their own progression route that may not differentiate between these two people manager paths. Beginning in 2023 or so, there has been a trend in some companies to remove the TPM Manager role and decentralize or embed the TPMs within the engineering teams. Though some have always done this or had a mix of both centralized and embedded roles, others are currently transitioning away from a centralized model. As with many changes in organizational structure and makeup, this is part of a larger pendulum swing that moves back and forth between the idea of project management offices. A pendulum tends to swing widely and always swings back in the opposite direction due to over-correction. Just like the IC role, the journey of a people manager can bounce between both SDM and TPM manager, as well as IC roles. Let's take a look at the journey of a people manager who held all of these roles.

An example from the real world: *A people manager path*

Faheem Khan is a senior TPM at Amazon. Throughout his career, he has been both an IC as well as a people manager in various forms. He started out ambitiously co-founding a start-up, Planetsoft, in India and found quick success with requests to build out enterprise solutions. He realized he needed to learn how enterprise software was created before committing to do so himself, so he got a job at a tech firm as a software tester.

When encountering a problem, Faheem was driven to get the right people together to find the solution. This tendency saw him get promoted to test lead, where he moved to Seattle to work for Microsoft. He first shifted into people management as a software test manager to build out the test framework used by Expedia. He enjoyed working with the users and stakeholders while building the framework. Faheem switched to the TPM job family to learn about business while still being close to technology at Expedia. He grew into a Principal TPM, then a director of TPMs, and then the director of technology and managed cross-functional teams. He bounced back and forth between people management and program management. This back and forth led him to think about what he was best at and what he enjoyed doing. He decided that he was a leader of people and enjoyed project management in the technology space. Knowing what he wanted, he found a TPM position at Amazon.

Faheem notes that whenever his career needed him to dive deep, he would take up an IC role so he could focus, learn, and hone new skills. Once those skills were present and he was ready to share and drive others, he would find a people manager role. This is an incredible insight and embodies both the breadth and depth of knowledge that is expected out of a TPM.

From both Oscar's and Faheem's journeys, we've seen the hallmarks of what makes a great TPM. They exhibit a drive to see a project through to completion, a willingness to learn and help those around them grow, and a desire to dig deep. Even with these common traits, different paths were taken for each, and both held IC and manager roles, and each ended up preferring one path over the other in the end. Faheem's insight that the type of role that was best suited for him depended on what he was looking to achieve rings true for all of us.

Until now, we've talked about the various roles within the TPM job family. However, there are other opportunities, and with the current volatility in the tech industry, they may be worth considering. So, we'll discuss switching to an adjacent role. At the end of the day, this will help your TPM career regardless. Let's take a look.

Wearing the hat of an adjacent role

One of the common mistakes people make is to make their career path too rigid. Coming from a non-traditional educational background, I know firsthand that there are many ways to move through your professional life. In *Chapter 1*, I talked about the adjacent roles to the TPM and how they all overlap with one another. This is intentional (or at least keeping it overlapped once it was noticed was intentional) because it gives the organization many ways to scale itself. A team can get by for a time when an adjacent role is not filled. The company can also try different ways to organize these roles into teams to maximize the output of their teams. Your ability as a TPM to assume these roles affords you flexibility in your role.

The tech industry is in another down cycle at the time of writing the second edition. Not only have there been massive layoffs across the industry, but the top companies also joined in, which some hadn't done in over a decade prior. As an example, Amazon had never performed a massive layoff prior to the 2023 layoffs. To make matters worse, the TPM role is undergoing some flux as the industry is trying to decide what is the right balance between program and product management.

2024 saw Snap eliminate 20 product manager roles in an attempt to speed up decision making. Their claim was that the product managers were spending too much time on strategic thinking and not enough on execution. Snap's bias was toward execution.

In 2023, Airbnb's CEO spoke about changes that the company had been working on since the 2020 pandemic in relation to the product manager role. The shift was to re-align the role to a product marketing style similar to Apple. In this role, the product manager is more focused on market trends, market research, and strategy. It was stated that the program management duties that the product managers used to do were given to actual program managers. In this case, Airbnb is solidifying the difference between and need for both product and program management. Lastly, Instagram, a subsidiary of Meta, removed the TPM role altogether. Though rumors said this would continue throughout all of the parent company, Meta, it has not. The truth is that Instagram was focusing more on product management as that matches the type of work that they do.

If you look back to the first chapter, I talked about the adjacent roles to the TPM, namely the SDM and product manager. We've talked about people management, which covers the SDM role, but we haven't discussed the product manager role. There are overlaps between program management and product management and many TPMs work on product-focused work. If you have ever worked on a service or product strategy document where you map out the next 3 to 5 years of direction a product should take, then you have worked squarely in the product manager area of focus. Depending on the company size and composition of roles, the amount of product work you would be expected to do within your role can vary wildly.

Taking a role as a dedicated product manager can broaden your understanding (and thus empathy) for those around you and strengthen your core product management strengths, which will make you a more versatile TPM. In some companies, like Microsoft, the product manager, program manager, and TPM are often fungible roles, and you can switch between them based on the needs of the team since the titles are all listed as program manager. The TPM role does exist at Microsoft, but only in certain organizations where the distinction is required or serves a purpose to denote the focus area of the work.

Remember that, as a TPM, you will be expected to handle product roadmaps, prioritization, and strategic vision as you get to higher levels, so having more formal experience in these aspects can only serve to advance your career.

Another adjacent role in some teams is a software or solutions architect. A software architect is a specialized role that focuses on the landscape architecture of a large system. This role is often played by a former software developer but can also be filled by a TPM. A solutions architect is similar but is focused on the cloud architecture of an ecosystem, specifically one that is moving from a local data store to the cloud. This is another good candidate for a TPM to fill this role, and in many small and medium-sized companies, this is exactly the case. In both roles, the architect is looking at the bigger picture of the landscape and how each system fits together and interacts with each other, and this is the type of impact and scope level that a higher-level TPM will have anyways, so this fit makes a lot of sense for when a specialized architect isn't available.

This chapter has focused on the paths and roles of the TPM and the different levels on the career ladder. However, we have not discussed how to move from one level to the next. Let's look a little closer at what this looks like.

Moving up a level

As is the case for any role, the particulars of how to move from one level to the next will vary from company to company. That being said, there are some general guidelines and tips that will help you make the leap. These are:

- Know your company's process.
- Talk with your manager.
- Document your body of work.
- Have a mentor.
- Write out a plan.

Know your company's process for moving up a level. Some companies are merit-based, meaning that once you have met certain criteria, your manager promotes you. This is not very common in the tech industry, which instead relies on proving oneself through their body of work and recommendations from colleagues. In either case, you need to understand what is expected of you as well as your manager. In cases where your manager is not a manager of TPMs explicitly, meaning that they manage a variety of roles and not just TPMs, they may not be fully versed with what is needed to get you to the next level. So, don't wait for them to start the conversation. Instead, know the path and the expectations ahead of time.

Talk with your manager now that you know your company's process. They either already know or need to know what the process is for the TPM as well as the particular level transition. Have an open conversation about your intention to move to the next level and discuss the gaps, if any, that need to be addressed to meet the requirements. In some cases, like Amazon, the criteria needed to progress in levels is laid out at each level guideline. This allows both the manager and TPM to be on the same page about the process and what to expect from each other during the preparation for the promotion. In some cases, the employee is expected to provide a body of work that details their current work that meets the definition of the next level. In other cases, your manager is responsible for this document, but your input will still be of benefit while they draft the document.

Document your body of work. This helps you demonstrate at any time what work you have done and how it maps to your career. It's especially important for concepts that don't lend themselves to typical artifacts such as persuading a stakeholder to do the right thing. The higher up in levels you go, the fewer concrete deliverables you will have that show your value to the organization. Emails, hallway conversations, and even meetings where you played a pivotal role in a decision being made are all areas where you will likely need to keep a record of your work.

For your consideration

Before you start to capture your work in a backlog, consider your company's data retention policies to ensure your body of work doesn't infringe on company policies.

Have a mentor to help you on your journey. Someone at the level you are looking to move to will have been through the same or a similar process as you are going through now. They will have valuable insight into gaps you may not have seen and can be a first line of review to ensure you have all the data you need to proceed. Aside from career growth, your mentor can also just help in general with any issues you are facing in your current role.

Write out a plan and share it with your manager and mentor. Reference it often to make sure you are on the right path and so your manager can help you find the right opportunities. This will be one of the most important plans you create so don't treat it any less than you would a project plan. It should have risks, a critical path, and key milestones (likely things like a specific project launch to showcase a needed skill).

When I was working on my promotion to Principal TPM, it took about 30% of my time for the last few months leading up to the submission while I worked on summarizing my work, checking in with peers on feedback, and getting artifacts ready for review. Though the process isn't as rigorous everywhere, treat it as seriously as any other deliverable you have. After all, it will have the largest personal return on investment compared to any other project you work on!

Summary

In this chapter, we examined the different paths that can lead to a TPM career, focusing on roles such as an SDE, DevOps, and even an SDM. We discussed the motivations for the switch to TPM as well as the paths that are often available once you are a TPM.

We saw that the IC role allows you to exercise your project and program skill sets and directly contribute to the success of your company. We followed the path of a principal TPM as he went from IC roles in product and program management to people roles as a director and development manager.

We then explored the people manager role and how you focus on the growth of others by imparting your IC experience to achieve success for your team.

We also followed two different TPM professionals through their career journeys to see how their choices led them to different paths. Most importantly, we got a glimpse of why they made the decisions they made to help us better understand what career path may be best for us.

In *Chapter 4*, we'll explore one of the most important characteristics of a successful TPM, *driving toward clarity*. This ability of a TPM to take an ambiguous situation and find or define clarity is what helps us solve problems, find opportunities to reduce risks, and deliver results.

Further reading

- *Solutions Architect's Handbook* by Saurabh Shrivastava and Neelanjali Srivastav: This book talks in great detail about what it means to be a solutions architect, so if you are interested in that adjacent role, this book is for you.

- *Software Architect's Handbook* by Joseph Ingeno: This book dives into software architecture concepts and the role in general so is another good resource to explore this adjacent role.

Additional resources

- **Levels.fyi** – This is a great resource to familiarize yourself with the human resource leveling guide across the tech industry. You can compare up to three different companies to see how their levels rank against each other. This is especially useful when looking at a new position as you can compare your current level and company to a position at a different company: https://www.levels.fyi

- **LinkedIn group: #TPMTribe Global** – This is a growing group of TPMs on LinkedIn that features great posts about the TPM craft as well as a good central place to find TPM job opportunities. Join here: https://www.linkedin.com/groups/13831478/

- **LinkedIn group: Technical Program Management** – This is the original TPM group on LinkedIn. It has occasional posts from the community but is focused more on job opportunities. Join here: https://www.linkedin.com/groups/13580146/

- **Slack server: Technical Program Management** – This is a community server where TPMs come together to share ideas, post jobs, and just generally talk about the craft. It's been growing a lot over the last year and is the place I most often post and lurk. Find it here: tech-pmo.slack.com

- **Discord server: TPMs unite** – This Discord server is very active in the community and is another great resource for connecting with other TPMs and discussing the TPM craft. I come here when I can, and I always see in-depth discussions going on. Find it here: https://discord.gg/VAtD9XW4hx

- **TPM events** – After I published the first edition last year, I joined up with two other TPMs to form a non-profit organization that aims to elevate the TPM craft to the highest standards. We do this through multiple efforts, including an annual TPM Summit, local TPM chapters holding monthly presentations, and most recently, a podcast! Find out more about the next TPM Summit and our other endeavors at `https://www.tpmevents.org`

Join our book's Discord space

Join our Discord community to meet like-minded people and learn alongside more than 5000 members at:

`https://packt.link/sKmQa`

Section 2

Fundamentals of Program Management

A large part of the TPM role is program and project management. However, the tech industry does not fit the mold for a standard **Project Management Professional (PMP)** style approach. It's dynamic, fast-paced, and views the project management triangle in a different light than is seen in other industries. This section will explore the approach I see used the most in the industry. We'll cap the section with a discussion on emotional intelligence, arguably the most important soft skill set for a TPM, especially given the recent rise in **Generative Artificial Intelligence (GenAI)**. As more of our role is delegated to GenAI, the more we will rely on our own emotional intelligence to drive change through empathy.

This section contains the following chapters:

- *Chapter 4, An Introduction to Program Management Using a Case Study*
- *Chapter 5, Driving toward Clarity*
- *Chapter 6, Plan Management*
- *Chapter 7, Risk Management*
- *Chapter 8, Stakeholder Management*
- *Chapter 9, Managing a Program*
- *Chapter 10, Emotional Intelligence in Technical Program Management*

4

An Introduction to Program Management Using a Case Study

In this chapter, we'll take the TPM pillars and key management areas introduced in *Chapter 1* and *Chapter 2* and explore them in more depth. As the book progresses, we'll go deeper into each of the pillars and the traits that define the pillars. To ensure we are not spending time on context building with new examples each time we dive a bit deeper, I'm going to set up the context in this chapter with the introduction of the Mercury program. I'll define the goals of the program along with the projects that comprise it as a good analog to starting a brand-new program and related projects. In each subsequent chapter, I'll use this program to examine each area or concept in detail as it makes sense in the book.

In this chapter, we'll introduce program management through the following topics:

- Introducing the Mercury program
- Examining the program-project intersection
- Exploring the key management areas

Introducing the Mercury program

Back in 2009, in my days as a software developer, I was working at a company that didn't utilize an internal messaging system. Phones weren't smart enough yet (the iPhone was introduced only in 2007, and Android came a year later in 2008), but messaging clients on desktop PCs were abundant.

However, they all required a central server to be configured in order to manage the messaging network. In the consumer world, this was achieved by the company that owns the messaging service maintaining the central servers; however, this would require logging in to these services at work with our personal credentials and friending everyone at work. The other option was to host the servers within the company and use open source or public messaging systems like Trillian. This wasn't something that I had access to do, nor was it something the company was willing to supply, so I thought about the idea of a distributed, or **peer-to-peer** (**P2P**), messaging system. This would allow messages to be sent without the need for a central server. So, I set out to write one myself, and some of us on the software team used the system for a year or so. It was a fun and distracting side project that we can build upon here as a thought experiment. Though the original premise was to not have a central server, for the purposes of this case study, we'll stick to the requirement to use a P2P network architecture. This distinction will become important later in the book as we explore various aspects of program management. I called the application *Mercury*, which is the Roman name for the messenger to the gods.

Let's take a look at a typical P2P network diagram in *Figure 4.1* and explore the benefits of a P2P network over a centralized network:

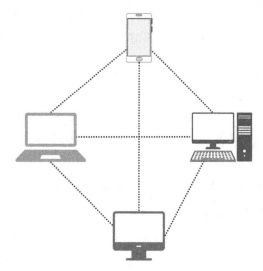

Figure 4.1: A simple P2P network diagram

In a P2P network, the devices on that network talk directly with one another, or through other connected clients when a direct connection is not feasible. The lines here do not mean that a physical connection necessarily exists between the devices, but that the communication is between the two clients.

This is opposed to communicating via a central server that relays messages between its users and maintains a map of the connected devices to the network. In this type of centralized setup, the central server can store the network and session data so only a single copy is needed. However, it means that without the central server, the network can't function. In a P2P network, each device on the network maintains its own list of connected devices and can relay information as needed. In this model, if one device goes offline, the network can still function, though there may be an increase in overall traffic for activities such as network discovery. Additionally, the P2P network has the added advantage of no central overhead of maintaining a server for the application.

Mercury program charter

A **program charter** is a document that defines the boundaries of the program. In companies that use a projectized organizational structure, where teams are formed specifically for a project or program, this document serves as a formal empowerment to the project team to proceed with the project. This usually comes with the ability to hire and enter into financial contracts. Outside of that setting, a charter is still a useful document as it serves as an overview of the program, who the key stakeholders are, who is on the program team, and the overall scope, timelines, and budget or resource constraints.

A program has at least one achievable goal and, usually, consists of more than one project to realize the goal(s). A program scope defines the goals in a way that bounds the program's area of impact. Just like a project scope, it is useful to reduce scope creep at the program level. The program scope is often included as part of the program charter as that document defines the start and end of the program.

Although I only built a simple application for Windows, that won't suffice for a good case study. So, for the purposes of this book, let's suppose that we wanted it to be available on devices other than just the Windows desktop.

Setting our goal

The *program goal* will be to create a P2P messaging application and have a 100% user base reach. As this is the goal of the program, the program will remain open until this goal has been fully achieved.

It may seem like an impossible goal to reach 100% of a user base, but the word "base" here is an important distinction. This implies that the program must make Mercury available to all of the potential users of the system, which is not the same as saying 100% of all people!

A formal way of looking at all of these components is to draft a program charter. *Figure 4.2* illustrates a formal program charter, including scope, for the Mercury program. Let's take a closer look:

Mercury Program Charter

Program Problem Statement

Centralized messaging systems have high operational costs, single points of failure, and privacy concerns due to data being stored and controlled by a central entity. This also makes the system's owner the gatekeeper to that information and network availability, increasing the risk of losing access. These issues can lead to inefficiencies, increased risk of data breaches, and a lack of control for the end users over their own communication data.

Business Case

A decentralized peer-to-peer network eliminates central ownership and reduces overhead by removing maintenance of large data centers dedicated for the program. It increases redundancy and availability while ensuring no single entity can remove access.

Program Goal

Develop a cross-platform peer-to-peer network that has the potential to reach 100% of our user base.

Program Core Team

Program Lead: Joshua Teter
Executive Sponsor: Vicky Preston

Decentralized Messaging System Corporation
404 Perdita Way
Los Alamos, MT 01001   Internal Use Only

Figure 4.2: Program charter for the Mercury program

A program charter can have many components to it as it originally serves as a sort of cover sheet for a program's paper trail of documentation. As such, it ties many aspects of the program together to offer a glimpse into the scope and impact of the program. These components include a problem statement, business case, program goal, program team, and key stakeholders, along with the budget and timelines for the program.

As many of these components are available elsewhere, like the key stakeholders and the timeline and budget, it may not be necessary to add them here.

In many cases, a formal document like this isn't used in the tech industry but the intent behind this document is captured in some form. At Amazon, it takes the form of a **PR/FAQ (Press Release/ Frequently Asked Questions)** document that is a fictional press release upon the launch of the program. It captures customer sentiment and describes the purpose of the program in newspaper-friendly terms. When done right, this will cover the problem statement and the goal, as well as the business case. It captures these because they are the most useful aspects of a charter. As the tech industry isn't a projectized organization, power isn't bestowed upon the program lead to build a team, and thus a formal document declaring as much isn't needed.

What is needed is a way to quickly bring new stakeholders or team members up to speed on the program, and these three statements provide the right framework to do that. It's important to understand why a program is trying to achieve something just as much as it is important to know what it is achieving. The why comes from both the problem statement as well as the business case. As an added bonus, both of these statements often provide good ideas for key metrics that the program can track.

Mercury project structure

The **program roadmap** is the end-to-end program plan that accomplishes the goals set forth in the program charter, including the number of projects, their boundaries, and their interdependencies. It is defined by the goals of the program. For the Mercury program, the goal was written in a way that has room for analysis and redirection. It states only that the application should have a 100% user reach, but not how to achieve that. This is where the project structure comes into play and how the projects can build upon each other to achieve the goal. For instance, 100% of the user base could, arguably, be achieved in a few different ways. You could target mobile-only **Operating Systems (OSes)** and focus on Android and iOS, as most people who have a computer also have a phone, and those **OSes** dominate the market. The user base is also not completely defined here, so shifting from a consumer user base to an enterprise user base could mean that only Windows and macOS are required to achieve that goal.

Lastly, you could go all out and utilize all major OSes: Windows, macOS, iOS, Android, and Linux. Unlike in 2009, when I wrote the Windows application, there are several cross-platform development environments that make sharing code easier. Work done for one platform can be reused in the others with less effort than having to rebuild from scratch. These ideas will be explored more in *Chapter 5, Driving Toward Clarity*, and *Chapter 6, Plan Management*.

A program goal can be more specific if the needs are already well researched, but this sort of goal can also help you start to move forward while working through some of the unknowns. In a real-world example, I was starting a program that impacted the customer experience as well as adding new data to our backend models. During the program initiation and early high-level designs, we realized that the customer-facing changes were ambiguous and would take a lot of iteration to get right. The goal was written in a way that didn't make it clear that the customer-facing interfaces would need drastic updates, which caused stakeholders to stop and focus on the goal wording. We were faced with either pausing the execution of the program to fully understand this impact or moving forward with this risk to the goal. To not lose the momentum we had, and with the active engagement of all stakeholder teams, we refined the program goal to state that it would include relevant customer experience updates and narrowed the project goal for the year to reference only the backend changes. This allowed us to move forward with diving deeper into the right changes we needed to make, while simultaneously working on the well-understood backend changes. Put succinctly, *the goal is a guiding principle to ensure the direction of each project is aligned with the purpose of the program.*

Given the high number of opportunities for shared code that reduces investment, we'll explore a project breakdown that delivers across all of the OSes. This has the added benefit of reaching the highest number of users as well. For now, we'll draw the boundaries for the projects at the OS boundary, as shown in *Table 4.1*:

Project/program name	Description	Goal	How does it help the program?
Mercury program	Program for P2P messaging app	Build and deploy a P2P messaging app to 100% of the user base.	N/A.
Android rollout project	Project for the P2P Android app	Deploy the app for the Android ecosystem.	Android represents 72% of the worldwide market share on mobile.

iOS rollout project	Project for the P2P iOS app	Deploy the app for the iOS ecosystem.	iOS represents 28% of the worldwide market share on mobile.
Linux rollout project	Project for the P2P Linux app	Deploy the app for the Linux ecosystem.	Linux represents 4.4% of the worldwide desk-top market share.
macOS rollout project	Project for the P2P macOS app	Deploy the app for the macOS ecosystem.	macOS rep-resents 15% of the worldwide desktop market share.
Windows rollout project	Project for the P2P Windows app	Deploy the app for the Windows ecosystem.	Windows rep-resents 72% of the worldwide desktop market share.

Table 4.1: The Mercury project structure

The preceding table lists the programs and program goals for easy reference when discussing the project goals. Each project has its own goal – to deploy the P2P app to a given ecosystem – while also contributing to the overall program goal of reaching 100% of the user base.

To ensure that the program is tackling the right OSes to reach 100% of the user base, I included market share statistics from *Statcounter Global Stats*, with a date range from August 2023 to July 2024, and used the percentages for July 2024. The numbers I use are rounded for readability and don't add up to 100% due to low-use OSes (unknown and ChromeOS) adding up to statistically relevant amounts. For more information, please visit `https://gs.statcounter.com/`.

Now that we have had an in-depth look at a use case program and the constituent projects, we'll continue with the introduction to program management by taking a look at the program-project intersection. We'll use this case study as we continue to explore the depths of being a TPM as a means to dive deeper into each area.

Examining the program-project intersection

In some companies, the TPM role is specifically listed as a project manager, not a program manager. For the majority of cases where it does refer to programs, the TPM still manages projects, too. This can lead to ambiguity as to the difference — if there even is a difference.

In *Chapter 2*, we briefly discussed the relationship between a program and a project. A program is made up of projects and works toward the goals of the program while still having its own goals.

Figure 4.3 illustrates the specific relationship between the Mercury program and the projects within it:

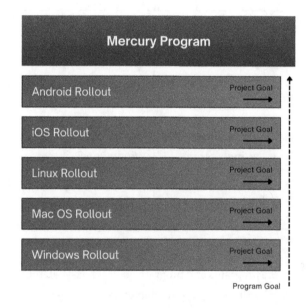

Figure 4.3: The Mercury program roadmap

The Mercury program's goal is related to user reach, and the projects are broken down by OS. This figure shows how the projects fit into the roadmap overall. Since we chose to break the program down by OS, there are currently no interdependencies. Because of this, the relationship is straightforward. As we learn about a key TPM trait in *Chapter 5*, *Driving Toward Clarity*, and project planning in *Chapter 6*, *Plan Management*, the program roadmap will change to take on more complexity and introduce some possible real-world scenarios that may necessitate a roadmap adjustment.

In the Mercury program example, each project's goal directly contributes to the program goal, as any increase in user reach by an ecosystem deployment will increase the overall user reach and get the program closer to the goal of 100% user base reach.

Program management for Mercury will start and end with these five projects, as they will achieve the stated goal of the program. As such, the program status will discuss the project goals in cases where they impact the delivery dates. It will also surface any major roadblocks that each project encounters. As the projects don't have any interdependencies, each project will only report on the work relevant to that project. They'll go into deeper details on development blockers, delays, and dependencies within the project.

With the way that the program and projects are currently laid out, a single status report might also suffice given how tightly related all projects are to the end goal of the program. At the end of the day, how you manage the program versus projects depends on many factors and can change from program to program. The number of organizations that are involved in a program can necessitate different status reports, for instance, as each organization cares about its specific contribution to the program. The individual complexity of a project may also warrant a separate status so that as much detail as is needed can come out. Many of the lower-level details can get lost or even omitted at a program level but may be vital information to disseminate.

I've introduced a case study and explored how the program and projects intersect with this example. We'll continue to build on this program plan and dive into how it is set up throughout the book. For now, we'll touch on the key management areas and use the Mercury program to explore those a bit deeper.

Exploring the key management areas

In *Chapter 1*, I introduced the key management areas: plan, risk, and stakeholder management. Using the Mercury program as an example, we'll examine each of the key management areas and continue to build on top of our use case study.

Program and project plans

Let's examine the Windows rollout project plan with a few assumptions so as not to overcomplicate the plan at this point in the book:

- We have as much resourcing as we need (so, every task that does not have a predecessor constraint at the beginning of the project will be scheduled to start).
- No resource timing constraints exist.
- Estimates are uniform across all platforms.
- All predecessors are considered **finish-to-start** (meaning the predecessor must be finished before the task can start).

- There are no cross-project dependencies.
- In other words, a *textbook* program example!

Given these assumptions, *Table 4.2* lists a simplified project plan for the *Windows project*:

ID	Milestone	Predecessor	Effort (weeks)
1	P2P Subsystem Ready		8
2	User Interface Ready	1	16
3	**End-to-End (E2E)** Testing	2	4

Table 4.2: A simplified view of the Windows project plan

In this example, there are a few simple dependencies shown: the user interface milestone requires that the subsystem is completed, and testing requires both preceding milestones to be complete. Now, this is extremely simplified, and many seasoned TPMs might be screaming right now at this optimistic project timeline. Don't worry! As we explore each management area in greater detail, the project and program roadmaps will be expanded to incorporate each of them. In the end, we'll have a more complete plan that demonstrates the strengths that the TPM brings to program management.

In *Table 4.3*, we'll show the Mercury program plan using a visual chart called a **Gantt chart**, showing the projects and project tasks with dependencies against a time plot. To get the program plan, we'll expand on the Windows project plan, apply the same milestones to each of the other OS rollout projects, and include some tasks for inter-OS testing:

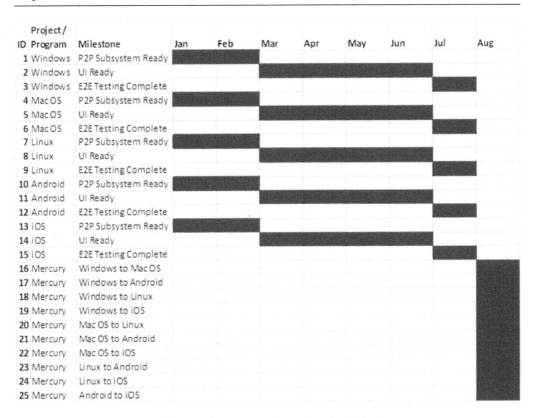

Table 4.3: The program plan with a Gantt chart

In the Gantt chart, a month is represented by a single cell, and we assume that 4 weeks is equal to 1 month. Given our initial assumptions of uniform task efforts and unlimited resourcing, we can see that all of the projects (Windows, macOS, Linux, Android, and iOS) start at the same time in January. The inter-OS tests are categorized under the Mercury program as inter-OS testing falls outside the bounds of the individual projects but is required for the Mercury program goals. This could also be a sub-project depending on the organizational structure of your company.

Program and project risks

At this point, we have a full, albeit simple, program plan including plans for all projects. We'll continue with our current assumptions for consistency while talking about risks. When we go through the exercise of risk analysis, we have a few different inputs to help us identify and categorize them:

- Plans
- Risk register
- Stakeholder input

Let's take a look at each of these in more detail.

Plans

Filling out the program and project plans can help us visualize constraint risks. Taking this program plan as an example, we can see that a few risks stand out, even with our infinite resourcing assumption. Let's look at a closeup of the risks in *Table 4.4*:

ID	Project / Program	Milestone	Jul	Aug
16	Mercury	Windows to Mac OS		
17	Mercury	Windows to Android		
18	Mercury	Windows to Linux		
19	Mercury	Windows to iOS		
20	Mercury	Mac OS to Linux		
21	Mercury	Mac OS to Android		
22	Mercury	Mac OS to iOS		
23	Mercury	Linux to Android		
24	Mercury	Linux to iOS		
25	Mercury	Android to iOS		

Table 4.4: A closeup of the Gantt chart, focusing on the integration testing

The first risk that stands out to me with our given assumptions is the 10 overlapping integration tests between the platforms. All 10 are running over the same two weeks. Our assumption is that we have the resources to do this, so that isn't the risk here. The risk is that this parallel schedule assumes that all testing is perfect and that nothing can go wrong. Every system is testing against every other system, and if even one of these integrations were to find a bug, let's say Windows to Linux, it means that every other Windows integration and Linux integration might potentially be blocked by the same issue.

This can lead to significant delays. In the planning stage, we can identify specific risks related to the actual tasks at hand; next, let's talk about a more generalized technique we can use to identify risks.

Risk register

The risk register is a central repository for all risks that have been identified in previous projects completed in a company or organization. Often, they are categorized in some fashion so that they are searchable based on similar project traits. This could include working with a specific system or team, dealing with the same clients, having the same level of complexity, and more. Honestly, I haven't found many instances where this risk register is a true database, but that is the perfect scenario.

Instead of a central repository, the risk register often relies on **tribal knowledge**. This refers to the implicit and explicit knowledge relevant to the organization that is not written down. **Explicit knowledge** is information that can be easily articulated and thus written down and learned by reading. **Implicit knowledge** is known but not easily conveyed information. In this case, you review a plan with your peers to seek out the known risks they can identify and also draw from your own experiences. However, if you do find yourself in a position to create an actual central repository, do it!

For the sake of demonstration, *Table 4.5* shows an example of a risk register. This company, which is running the Mercury program, deals with many other cross-platform business systems:

ID	Project/Program	Risk	Strategy
1	Windows To-Do App	Network testing failures	Acceptance – 3-week milestone slip
2	Linux To-Do App	Distribution regressions	Mitigation
3	Android Project Tracker	App approval delays	Acceptance – 2-week addition
4	iOS Project Tracker	App approval delays	Acceptance – 3-week addition

Table 4.5: A risk register for the Mercury program company, Decentralized Messaging System Corp

As you can see, there are a number of risks that can happen in one project and translate to the next. The network testing issue for Windows might be present and will need to be accounted for in the testing timeline. Based on the root cause, you might be able to mitigate the issue ahead of time, or just need to ensure you have extra time allotted for testing over the network. The app approvals in the Android and iOS stores are common and are likely to happen each time.

Again, knowing the root cause could help mitigate this, though the approval steps are constantly changing, so a more prudent approach might be to pad publishing timelines to account for the inevitable back and forth. Though the book *Critical Chain,* by Eliyahu M. Goldratt, talks about the perils of adding padding to every task, that concept is more geared toward linear tasks. By design, an effort estimate does not talk about calendar time, just effort in terms of hours or days. This also does not include overhead time like waiting for a code review for a code change or getting approval. These are either separate tasks or are accounted for using time buffers based on an average length of time for the administrative task to be completed.

Stakeholder input

Stakeholder input is similar to the tribal knowledge aspect of the risk register discussion. Stakeholders offer a different perspective on a problem or perceived risk. They might even have a risk register to share based on similar projects that they have been involved in. This also ties back to communication (which will be a recurring theme in this book) and just how important it is to communicate early and often. Talking with stakeholders about the plan and identified risks can lead to critical information that can prevent a risk from being realized and save you valuable time.

For instance, I was running a new program that involved teams and entire processes within the Amazon selling and order platform that I had never interacted with. The first few months involved learning about the systems and data flow across those platforms and determining the right places to change to get the program's data to the right systems for processing. We used the program requirements and the current system landscape diagrams to draft a new landscape diagram and high-level stories for each organization.

We took these stories, the new diagram, and rough timelines in front of all of our stakeholders and were quickly inundated with new teams to talk with and potential risks to explore and verify. One suggestion in this discussion was about a team that we may have overlooked that proved to be a key player in getting the data flow correct. Had we proceeded without this discussion, it would have been several months before we realized the gap and it would have cost us several more months to correct.

We've talked through the project plan and the risk plan, and we have even covered how they overlap, as demonstrated in this example of stakeholders contributing to the risk plan. Now we'll discuss the stakeholder plan itself in more detail.

Stakeholder plan

The stakeholder plan, which includes the communication plan, is another essential area of program management. It can make or break your project and your career. You can be excellent at delivering a project on time, but if your stakeholders are kept in the dark even where there aren't issues, it will come across poorly. People want to know what is going on.

Aside from just letting your stakeholders know about the status, knowing how to tell them is just as important. Your status report to a development team should read very differently than a status report to a senior leader. The stakeholders have different goals and perspectives regarding the project and their status report should reflect this difference.

For the Mercury program, there will be several different status reports and a layered stakeholder engagement and communication plan because of this. *Table 4.6* shows the different status reports across the Mercury program:

Id	Project / Program	Stakeholder	Development Report	Monthly Review	Quarterly Review
1	macOS	TPM Manager	Yes	Yes	Yes
2	Windows	Dev. Team Manager	Yes	Yes	No
3	Linux	Lead Engineer	Yes	No	No
4	Android	Android Division Lead	No	Yes	Yes
5	iOS	Director, Mobile Systems	No	Yes	Yes
6	Mercury	VP, Productivity	No	No	Yes

Table 4.6: The stakeholder plan for the Mercury program

This table describes three distinct types of reports: a development report, a monthly report, and a quarterly report. Not every company utilizes this many types of reports, and not all projects or programs will warrant sending this many out. This is to give you an idea of the types of reports you might encounter or wish to use yourself. Also, some companies don't do written reports at all but, instead, rely on review meetings. Whether the report is written in a Word doc, a Google Slide, or given verbally, the same principles apply.

The development report is a weekly or every two-week report that focuses on the development efforts. It discusses how the development cycle is going, including things such as a burndown or progress chart and velocity of a sprint cycle, along with any major blockers the team or teams are facing. Using the satellite analogy from *Chapter 2*, this would be the street view, as in seeing the buildings right in front of you.

The monthly review is directed toward stakeholders that are directly involved in the project or program (as in, they have resourcing involved), and upper management teams. The content is focused on the direction of the project or program including major milestones and their statuses. This will include any major issues or blockers that are directly impacting a major milestone but not the lower-level details such as standup and minor development blockers. Most importantly, the overall tone and narrative should focus on the aspects that have direct business value or impact. The business stakeholders are interested in understanding the value their involvement is bringing to the program. This is equivalent to the mid-level satellite views – you can see the neighborhoods of the city but can no longer make out exact details on the buildings.

Lastly, the quarterly review is directed toward senior leadership and executive sponsors for the project or program. Here, the content closely matches that of the monthly review but with a quarterly cycle. Some details may be taken out if deemed too granular, as the concern at this level is about the overall health and the end goal's trajectory. The executive sponsor wants to know if the end goal that they sponsored is on track, including any expected return on investment or incremental improvements or value added. The view here is at the city level, using our satellite analogy.

Chapter 8, Stakeholder Management, will cover how you can decide which of these communication cycles to utilize, as well as take a deeper look into each cycle.

Summary

In this chapter, we introduced a case study, the Mercury program, which will build a P2P messaging application across multiple ecosystems. We then used that case study to explore a simple program charter and the intersection between the Mercury program and its projects. We looked at how the audience level can change what a status report will contain and the tone that it carries. Lastly, we dug deeper into key management areas and refined the definition and roadmap of the Mercury program as a result.

In *Chapter 5, Driving Toward Clarity,* we'll explore one of the most important characteristics of a successful TPM. This ability of a TPM to take an ambiguous situation and find or define clarity is what helps us solve problems, find opportunities to reduce risks, and deliver results.

Additional resources

You can find templates regarding project and program charters in the GitHub repo related to this book. Please check the Preface for the GitHub link.

Join our book's Discord space

Join our Discord community to meet like-minded people and learn alongside more than 5000 members at:

https://packt.link/sKmQa

5

Driving Toward Clarity

In this chapter, I'll introduce the last foundational skill—driving toward clarity. It is not a single step in the management process but is instead a skill that is applied to every process we drive and every decision we make. It is the reason why you will hear the **Technical Program Manager (TPM)** in the room ask *why* and *how*. It's why you see TPMs run meeting after meeting, working session after working session, and attending every standup that they can fit into their schedule. They are constantly taking the information they have and clarifying it so that it has no ambiguity left and is easier to understand and follow. Driving towards clarity leads to consensus because, without clarity, you can't move past getting everyone onto the same page, and you can't continue on to driving consensus. It is truly the skill TPMs utilize the most and is even built into leveling guidelines as a clear expectation, as we will touch upon later in this chapter.

As this skill permeates everything we do as leaders, it is not a pillar but the mortar that transforms a pile of bricks into a wall. It is an integral part of who we are and the reason this topic gets its own chapter!

We'll learn how to drive toward clarity by exploring the following topics:

- Clarifying thoughts into plans
- Using clarity in key management areas
- Finding clarity in the technical landscape

Let's get started right away!

Clarifying thoughts into plans

Everyone drives toward clarity in some aspect of their life. It is the act of taking knowledge and applying it to a situation to make the path forward better understood, and to lead to the desired outcome.

As an example, a retail worker may look at a product layout diagram, along with the products they have on hand, and the shelving they have available, and do their best to match the diagram. All along, they'll make minor adjustments or judgment calls. They are driving toward the end goal of a properly stocked display. In the same situation, the worker may just be told to *make a display out of the seasonal summer products*. In this case, the level of ambiguity is much higher than the first—there is no diagram and no specific list of products, so the complexity and number of decisions are much greater. In this example, the worker first needs to decide what products to include in the display, possibly deciding on a theme in the process. As they build the display, they might make changes as it takes form based on new information, like whether they have enough of a specific product for the display as they designed it. At some point, they'll decide when the display is finished, it may not look like their original design, but it took on a new shape as they moved toward the end. In both cases, the worker drives toward clarity to end up with a properly stocked display.

This is also true for a TPM and the roles that surround them. What makes a TPM shine is that they drive toward clarity in every aspect of their job. We question *everything* and *everyone* to ensure that the objective is as clear as it can be. In this respect, a TPM must be willing to question requirements from upper management just as deftly as from a leader of a peer team.

The most common area where this comes into play is in the problem statement, as in, what is it that we are trying to solve? It is such a large part of our job that many role guidelines specifically mention the concept with varying degrees of complexity. *Figure 5.1* shows a common breakdown of the level of ambiguity a problem statement will have for a TPM based on their career level:

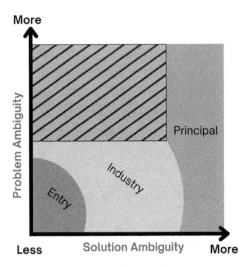

Figure 5.1: Ambiguity by career stage

In this figure, problem and solution ambiguity are plotted against each other. The ambiguity grows as you move outward (up and to the right). I used the normalized career stages here of entry, industry, and principal that I introduced earlier in the book.

The gray box with slanted lines represents an area where there is no intersection in ambiguity. If a problem is highly ambiguous, its solution cannot be well understood, as an example. To denote this, I chose the mid-way point of ambiguity to mark areas that don't plot. However, there is a point where the solution ambiguity is high enough that it can be plotted against the problem's level of ambiguity, hence the shaded-in area stops a little beyond the mid-point for the solution's ambiguity level.

As you can see, the entry-level position's problem statement and the solution are clearly defined, much like the first retail example. Both the problem and solution are laid out. There will be some minor ambiguities during execution that you'll need to resolve, but it will be fairly straightforward. At this level, you are focusing on executing a solution and expanding your project and program management skill set. Moving on to the industry TPM, there's a little less direction. You might be told the general solution but not how to accomplish it, so it is slightly more ambiguous than earlier. A senior TPM will simply be told what problem to solve but not how. In this scenario, the focus on driving toward clarity comes from the solution so your focus is on the right design and project plan to execute.

Up to this point in the TPM career, the problem statement is known but the amount of ambiguity in how to solve the problem is what increases the higher up in your career you go.

Beyond these levels, we get into high-impact positions where the ambiguity increases significantly. This can vary depending on your experience and the company but, generally, lands between being told that a problem may exist and to investigate and fix it, and to go *find* problems and fix them. In the first example, the problem statement is very ambiguous but, in the latter, the problem statement isn't ambiguous, it's non-existent!

An example from the real world: *Ambiguity in problems and solutions*

As I was moving towards a senior TPM position, I was presented with a unique and well-understood problem, the solution to which wasn't well known. I was working on the Tax Services team, which was responsible for calculating Sales and Value Added Tax. Amazon Chime was getting ready to launch at re:Invent, and as it is a video messaging client with the ability to call in to a meeting, it would incur tele-communications taxes in the US. These taxes are very different from standard sales tax, and our current architecture wasn't designed to handle the extra taxes and regulatory fees needed.

My team and I needed to find a way to get our system to handle these extra taxes. It was a complex problem, but the problem was well understood. However, there was no direction on how to solve it. I drove my team to find various solutions and pick the right one for long-term growth. We detailed the best solution and presented it to leadership for approval to move forward. It took about a year to get the solution to production. It's one of my favorite projects in my early career, and the solution has been expanded upon as the tax compliance landscape has grown more complicated since then.

Later in my career, with that same team, I was in a situation where the problem wasn't handed to me; instead, I uncovered it and drove an ambiguous solution to resolution over a 2-year span. The team had to get Amazon ready for Brexit—or the exit of the United Kingdom from the **European Union (EU)**. Legislation passed in the EU at the same time as the referendum in the UK in response to Brexit, which changed the way imports into the EU from anywhere in the world would be charged Value Added Tax. While the team was busy working on getting the UK ready to leave the EU, I realized there was a gap in the underlying architecture that needed to be addressed for transactions into the EU from outside of the EU data region to work properly.

In this case, there was no direct problem statement, nor a solution, as the problem wasn't known. My knowledge of the systems and recent work in that impacted services clued me in to the problem that we needed to solve. I took the problem and a solution that I worked with the development team to build to leadership to approve a program to get the architecture ready prior to launch. I assembled a team of developers and business domain experts and refactored the architecture to handle cross-region tax calculations. This example is on the other end of the spectrum on driving towards clarity and is the type of problem that a principal-level TPM would be expected to both find and solve.

We now understand the basics of clarifying thoughts into plans and the impact this skill has on our success in a project as well as in our career. Next, we'll see how this skill is utilized throughout the project.

Using clarity in key management areas

There are many ways in which driving toward clarity has an impact on project or program execution. We'll discuss the key management areas to demonstrate how seeking clarity is utilized in each of them.

Planning

Let's take the original problem statement for why I built the Mercury application as an example for driving thought into plans. This is my personal reason for building the application, not the fictional company's reasons. In the original iteration of the application on Windows, I had a problem I was trying to solve – I wanted to talk with my colleagues via a chat client but didn't have the resources or permission for a centralized server. I took the problem statement and looked for solutions that fit the need for no central server and landed on a P2P network. From this initial solution, I then dove into high-level designs, low-level designs, and then implementation. In every step, there was some level of ambiguity that needed to be clarified to proceed. I didn't have stakeholders to convince, nor a development team, but the need for clarity was still there as I knew the requirements I wanted to meet but not how to accomplish them.

The difference between my personal goal in building the application and the use case study's goals is in the scope and impact of ambiguity. In my personal example, the scope was limited to my colleagues on Windows machines, and there was no impact on the company or our work because it was simply a desired feature to have at the office.

Therefore, the ambiguity was limited to how to accomplish the requirements. In the **Mercury** program that I'm using in the book, the ambiguity stretches across both the requirements and solution, and there are stakeholders involved who are impacted by the work. The company also has a stake in the results because the application and its user base are a source of revenue.

Now, let's switch from the Mercury application I built to the Mercury program we're using as the use case for this book (essentially, expanding from a project to the program level). The problem statement is well understood, and the requirements are known at a high level. We need a low-overhead P2P system that can reach its target user base by making a client for each operating system (based on our assumptions from *Chapter 3*). However, there are many open questions that differ from platform to platform. For instance, mobile platforms need more clarity on the certification process for their respective app stores to form a project plan and a high-level design. Similarly, all platforms need details on how to initiate a broadcast call over **Transmission Control Protocol/ Internet Protocol (TCP/IP)** in order to finish high-level designs. This also helps determine the level of generalization the network communication layer component can be designed to work with across the platforms.

As the high-level designs for the broadcast call come into focus, further changes to the program plan, and each project plan, will be needed. To add to the complexity, each application will be developed by a team in the company that specializes in their respective operating system and may have additional requirements unique to their operating system, or the frameworks they use for development.

This iteration of the high-level design demonstrates how the planning cycles for the program and project can influence each other, and how driving clarity can feed right back into additional planning. Let's take a closer look at the cyclical nature between planning and seeking clarity in *Figure 5.2*:

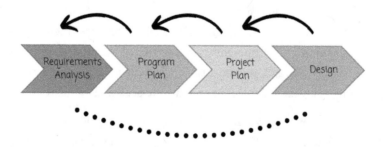

Figure 5.2: Driving clarity in plan management

The preceding figure shows the relationship between program and project planning, and how driving clarity plays a role in every step. As you work through the requirements for the program, you seek clarification on the specifics in order to understand the impact and scope better. These clarified requirements then feed into your program plan, which, in turn, sets up the basis for each project plan. The program requirements that are covered by a specific project will make their way to the project requirements with traceability back to the program. Then, during the execution of both the program and the project, as designs are finalized, updates to estimates and timelines are fed back into the respective plans. The designs are also checked against the requirements to ensure that the designs satisfy the requirements. Each of these cyclical paths is driving toward clarity.

> **An example from the real world:** *Driving toward clarity in planning*
>
> In the most recent program that I ran, the team needed to add new data entities that needed to be transmitted between 10 services, across 6 teams, and 2 **Vice President (VP)** organizations.
>
> However, starting out, we didn't know all of the teams, just the data that needed to get to a service several layers down from where it would be introduced. To get to this list of affected systems, I iterated together with another Principal TPM to build the data flow diagram and thus determine how it would alter the data flow landscape.
>
> We took the modified data flow diagram and reached out to the teams we believed would be impacted and iterated on the high-level design with each of these teams for a month. I took the resulting high-level design and built a program plan with projects for each service team to implement the changes needed within their domain. The teams involved took my plan and iterated internally to develop low-level designs and project plans so we could update the program plan based on their input.
>
> This process took about 6 months to get to a stable enough plan before we could start any real implementation work. Each iteration of the high-level design took some assumptions and drilled down until there was enough clarity to move to the next iteration.
>
> This was a complex distributed landscape of systems, so the number of iterations was very high and commanded cross-functional collaboration. Not all real-world problems are this complex, but I bet if you look closely at the projects and programs you are running right now, you will see this cyclical nature that requires you to drive toward clarity at every iteration.

What can happen when you don't clarify your plan enough?

We've talked a lot about the good things that can happen when your management practices are solid. However, it's worth talking about what can go wrong when clarity isn't sought out, or the level of clarity is insufficient.

The plan and the planning process are important for a successful project or program. Any lack of clarity in the requirements or elements of the plan can lead to long-lasting issues. The next three chapters will explore this concept in more depth, but let's walk through a few examples now.

Scope creep, or the increase in scope unexpectedly, can arise in a few different scenarios. We think of it mostly as additional requests that are added to the project after the scope is locked in, and this certainly does happen. However, it also occurs when requirements are not well understood. As requirements are fleshed out, they uncover complexities not seen at first, which will lead to additional tasks to meet the requirements. This is due to a lack of sufficient clarity in the requirements, resulting in poor estimations and understanding.

Conversely, scope creep can happen through **gold plating**, or the addition of features or enhancements not asked for in the requirements. This can happen during design, where the developer adds things to the design that they believe, or feel, are needed, and it can also happen at the request of the TPM.

Lastly, there are derived requirements, where the TPM gives the requirements or functional specifications to the development team, who then add additional requirements based on the needs of their service. This could be things such as scaling, latency, or code refactoring that are needed to make the required changes maintainable. As a TPM, the more you know about the roadmaps, architectural evolutions, and availability needs of the services you work with, the more you can anticipate these needs earlier on so they are not added during development but added into the scope at the beginning.

There is an important distinction to make here. This discussion on scope creep can make it sound as though iterative development is fraught with scope creep, but it isn't necessarily. The key differentiator here is that the unknown and exploratory nature of iterative development is planned for in those environments. The expected output of a sprint is one part finished work, and another part reflection on what is next. A sprint may deliver a proof-of-concept to inform which is the best feature design for the next sprint to pick up. This is a common approach in greenfield work, which is work that is new and not constrained by previous work. There is an element of exploration to determine the right path forward, and this is not the same concept as scope creep.

Scope creep would apply to an iterative development project if the end goal and end result do not match at the project or program level. This is either a symptom of a narrowly focused end goal that doesn't allow for a shift of requirements based on new data, or a true addition of requirements that were well beyond what was asked for or needed.

Change management, which is the process used to handle a change in scope, resourcing, or timelines, is negatively impacted by scope creep, as it causes constant churn on the project plan. This leads to delayed delivery of a milestone or the delay of the entire project. Though the nature of the project management triangle is that these elements are always tied to one another, a well-defined plan will reduce the friction between them.

In these examples, ambiguity in the requirements forces the late discovery of missed scoping during design and development. Ensuring that the project requirements are well understood and written in detail can mitigate these problems.

We've seen how driving toward clarity in project planning leads to a successful foundation for a project's execution, as well as some areas where a lack of clarity can increase the project scope or timeline. Next, let's see how the risk assessment process utilizes this same skill.

Risk assessment

For risk assessment, there are many ways to drive clarity. First and foremost is doing the exercise in the first place! I've seen plenty of projects that treat issues and risks synonymously — as in, an active issue is just a risk to the project, and risks are issues that cause timeline issues. However, a risk is something that might happen and impact the project timeline, scope, or resourcing, but hasn't happened yet. It's a known variability to your project plan. In a textbook example, meaning in theory, an issue is just a risk that has been realized—as in a risk that was already captured, and there is a strategy in place to deal with it. We also call this a *realized risk*. By knowing ahead of time when something might happen, you have a better chance of preventing it or at the very least being prepared to handle it.

We aren't in a textbook world, though, and in the real world, many unforeseen problems can crop up and need to be handled when they come up. These are unknown variables and should go into your risk register to reduce the chances of the same problem coming up again in future projects. The risk register for your project should be abundantly full to account for any issues that you can foresee. Though issues that arise may not match the risk perfectly, the stated risk and strategy are usually adaptable to the *real world* scenario that takes place.

As an example of a foreseeable risk that may or may not occur, I have worked with a team that has had trouble with consistent service deployments. There are multiple reasons for the inconsistency, from lengthy deployment timelines to consistent merge and regression issues. Owing to this, deployment delays are a standard risk for my projects when there is work on these services that have delays. Once I have my project plan and one of these services is identified in a task, I immediately add the risk to the project. The service could have a great month and not miss a single deployment, but that doesn't mean the risk is gone. This deployment risk isn't meant as a slight to the team that owns the service but is just a statement of fact, and if I ignore that fact, I put the project in jeopardy. (I'm happy to report that this team has made significant progress in their deployment issues, and I no longer include this risk in projects when I work with them!)

When driving clarity in analyzing risks, we see a cyclical relationship between risk assessment and planning. *Figure 5.3* shows this relationship:

Figure 5.3: Driving clarity in risk management

From our case study, we identified several risks in *Chapter 4*. The first pass at risk assessment is relatively surface-level; you find the risks that are obvious and capture them. These risks may help uncover more risks, which in turn find more, and so on. Every pass adds clarity to the project by adding more detail to the project plan and risk strategies.

What can happen when you don't clarify your risks?

Risk assessment follows many of the perils of the project plan. As seen in *Chapter 1*, it feeds into the plan itself and the plan, in turn, feeds into the risk assessment. A misunderstood risk can create a false sense of security by providing a risk strategy that may not fully address the problem.

For instance, a risk may be identified in the *Windows Rollout project* of the *Mercury program*, which states that there is a possibility of a network test failure that could add 3 weeks to the timeline (refer to *Table 4.5* in *Chapter 4*). However, if the type of network test failure isn't specified, the strategy of delaying by three weeks may not be accurate. It could also be the case that other risks, such as the **fast-tracking**—or running in parallel—of all end-to-end testing, could exacerbate the networking failures and thereby cause even more delays than expected. The deeper the analysis and cross-checking of risks and projects, the better the outcome will be.

Risk assessment benefits directly from seeking clarity but also influences your project plan in return. Without constant risk assessment, your carefully crafted project plan can quickly become useless as risk after risk causes constant shifts in the plan. This goes against the nature of a plan and negates the hard work of planning in the first place. Though a worst case, it is important to keep risk assessment in mind to reduce day-to-day churn on the project through poorly managed risks.

Risk assessment has a fairly straightforward relationship with driving clarity as a risk must be well understood. Now, let's examine the relationship between stakeholders and driving toward clarity, which is less direct in nature.

Stakeholders and communication

At first glance, working with stakeholders may not seem to have much need for driving clarity, but this is just as important as the more obvious methodologies we've already covered. We think of stakeholders as people or groups we need to communicate statuses to discuss timelines and blockers with, and so on, and while this is true, they are also great sources of information throughout the project, especially when the requirements or solution is ambiguous.

In order to get the most out of a stakeholder, you need to fully understand their role in the project or program. Are they merely an interested party, such as a VP of a department, or are they involved in the deliverables directly? If they are involved, what is their role in that involvement? A developer? A manager? A fellow TPM? These questions help determine who your subject matter experts are. A TPM is adept at seeing a problem at multiple levels and can connect a problem that one milestone is having with surrounding work or even other projects within their department.

Traditional program management treats stakeholder identification as a single step at the start of a program during the initiation phase. While this is true and an initial stakeholder analysis should be done early on, stakeholders can change through the life of a program and will constantly need to be reassessed.

New requirements may lead to new teams getting involved in a program and will bring along new stakeholders, or a stakeholder might leave the company, prompting a new stakeholder to represent the vacant space. For highly ambiguous problems or solutions, the adage of "building the plane while flying" often leads to discovering requirements and stakeholders as the program is being executed. Constant vigilance and driving toward clarity with who your stakeholders are will ensure your program runs as smoothly as possible.

Take the *Windows Rollout project* as an example. When getting ready for execution, the networking risk we discussed in *Chapter 4* may come up in the design. The list of stakeholders may reveal a subject matter expert in networking from within the *Windows Rollout project*, or even across the other projects within the *Mercury program*. If, for instance, the *Android Rollout project* has a dedicated networking team, they may be of some assistance given that three out of the four **TCP/IP** layers (the **Transport, Internet, and Network** layers) are going to be common across different application layers or, in our case, operating systems. This could be a chance to combine network specialists across the projects, forming a co-op group to help solve common network issues and ensure consistent network solutions for the program. Without knowing who your stakeholders are and what their roles are, this type of opportunity to clarify networking requirements and put in place mechanisms to ease the design and implementation may be missed or take a lot longer to piece together than is necessary.

Being a Windows developer myself, I know the TCP/IP implementation in Windows pretty well, at least as exposed through the .NET framework. I would highly optimize a solution towards the implementation found in Windows and may not be aware of constraints that exist in macOS or Android. The mere act of talking with others outside your sphere of knowledge or influence can garner valuable information and challenge assumptions you may not realize you had in the first place.

There are two avenues where you can drive clarity by communicating with your stakeholders. *Figure 5.4* shows the relationship between driving clarity and these avenues of communication:

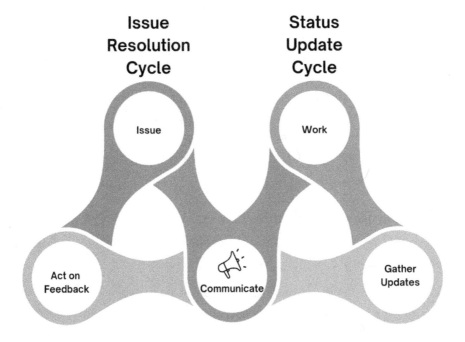

Figure 5.4: Driving clarity using stakeholder communication

Issue resolution and **status updates** are the main avenues of utilizing stakeholder communication to drive clarity. In issue resolution, you are communicating in order to get additional input to help solve the issue. This is important because each stakeholder will have a different perspective on the issue and may be able to provide useful information to drive a solution. Going back to the network discussion, a conversation between the Windows team and the macOS team may reveal that the TCP congestion control algorithms differ between the operating systems. Windows uses Compound TCP, whereas macOS uses Cubig congestion control—the same as Linux, on which it is based. This may not present an issue at closer inspection, but the difference is certainly a risk that needs to be accounted for, and a deep dive to determine if it amounts to an issue should be scheduled.

The status update mechanism is used when you are keeping your stakeholders up to date with current progress. Though this may seem like a passive exercise, it can help stakeholder teams prepare for milestone deliveries and reduce back-and-forth churn. It is also an indirect way to receive feedback from your stakeholders. For instance, you may include a path of resolution for a current issue and an expected resolution date. If there is concern with the path you chose, a stakeholder can call that out for you to address in your next status. If you think of your stakeholders as partners and resources of information instead of people to send reports to, you can create immensely powerful relationships to help propel your project forward, or at least keep it on track.

In the next section, we'll explore how omitting these cycles can cause problems.

Risks of excluding stakeholders in clarification strategies

Communication is key to our success. So is our ability to connect the problem with the right people to solve it, and to find out how problems may intersect.

I have found over the years that keeping all stakeholders up to date with all open issues is advantageous for a few reasons. Firstly, it provides the highest level of transparency to everyone involved, thereby building trust. The more the stakeholders know what issues are coming up and how they are being addressed, the more confidence they'll have in the project. Secondly, they'll have information to help resolve open issues. This leads to two main examples in which a lack of communication with stakeholders can cause even more problems.

When it comes to earning trust, it often comes down to the perception that stakeholders have of your ability to deliver on the goals. Your best avenue to control that perception is through status communications. Work with your stakeholders to draft the right message based on your audience and what they perceive to be important information to have in the report. Some of my best status reports were a result of several hour-long meetings with stakeholders discussing exactly how goals, risks, and issues needed to be formatted to be clear.

Aside from the content, it also needs to be consistent. If you promise that communication will come out weekly, and you miss a status or are a day late here and a few days there, this leads to the perception that you are disorganized and have a hard time following through. Even if you have a legitimate reason for missing or delaying—such as waiting on a resolution to an issue to report the most up-to-date status—there's a good chance it won't be seen that way. This is so fundamental to what we do as TPMs that consistent communication can come up in performance reviews and promotion documents. It's a measurable artifact that demonstrates our ability to be an effective communicator—you can literally see a gap in a status, or that dates don't line up to when they were promised. It can also lead to micromanaging from your stakeholders!

Note that this discussion is about perception, not your actual ability to deliver—this is an important distinction! It's easy to quickly get defensive in cases where your status report is being questioned. If your program is being run well, then there is a good chance the challenge is due to poorly worded or formatted information, which can leave too much room for interpretation. If left unresolved, it can negatively impact your trust. If stakeholders don't believe in your ability to manage the project, they may start to challenge your decisions. *Chapter 8* will go into more detail on the dos and don'ts of status reporting.

From a problem-solving perspective, not involving your stakeholders can lead to some negative impacts, all involving losing time. Let's examine two scenarios.

Avoiding wasted effort with clear communication

First up, I want to examine a use case of wasted effort. We'll use the *Mercury program* as the stage to discuss this. At a minimum, we have five projects going on in the program at once. Most of this work is contained within their respective operating system environments. However, there are examples of shared code from both the lower network layers, as well as a shared API library for the service itself. In these cases, each project team will be contributing to these shared libraries. As issues arise and problems are investigated, you may end up with multiple groups trying to solve the same problem, or simply working on the same code base at the same time. Without proper communication between teams, this can be missed. Worst-case scenario, you end up with code merges that remove, alter, or override behaviors in unexpected ways. Or, you simply end up with time wasted by having two teams working on the same problem. Proper communication can ensure the overlap is noticed, the plan is updated, and the situation is avoided or corrected as quickly as possible.

In my early developer days, I was working with one other developer on a shared code base. We had a check-in system for our code but if you didn't pull the latest version and apply your changes, you could still inadvertently overwrite code from each other. This happened almost every day as neither of us was in the habit of pulling a fresh copy of a package before making changes. And we even sat in the same room together and did this! The fix was, of course, rather simple. We let each other know when we were pulling and pushing changes and pushed every day before going home. It's a simple situation, but if you increase the number of developers, you can see how this can quickly get out of hand: even with the best diff analysis tools, code can be deleted or altered incorrectly.

A good analogy for this is *too many cooks in the kitchen*. If you've ever seen competitive cooking shows, you'll see multiple chefs in the same shared space and they're always yelling out something along the lines of *coming through, hot plate!* You've also seen what happens when they don't do that: plates collide and dishes are ruined. Communication can be the difference between winning and losing!

Reducing churn during issue resolution

The other consequence of poor communication when trying to find clarity is similar to the first example in that it results in wasting time. For instance, let's say there's a large, mature product that recently sent a new set of requirements to the development team via the technical writer. The technical writer's job is to write the end state of the requirements as documentation. The tester and developer then test the software to see whether it fits the requirements. However, it turns out that there are three requirements that logically cannot coexist—any two of them can, but not all three. The developer is doing integration testing and finds that one of the requirements breaks, so they fix it, which breaks the third requirement. Now the tester is running their tests, sees an issue, and reports a bug. This bug is fixed, but it breaks requirement two. This goes on and on, as the technical writer, developer, and tester are not communicating. A TPM gets involved due to the delay, gets everyone into a room, and within an hour the TPM sees that there is a problem with the requirements and works with the technical writer to decide which of the three to move forward with. Had the team members communicated about the issues they were facing, this may have come to light much quicker (or simply, had a TPM been involved from the start).

Often, in these cases, the missed opportunities are not intentional—you are simply in the weeds trying to unblock your team—but to be an effective practitioner, you need to always ensure stakeholders are in the know. It can save you a lot of time and unnecessary work.

As you can see, a lot can go wrong when stakeholders (including your project team) aren't involved in your quest to clarify. Conversely, a lot can go well when stakeholders, as well as the team, are handled correctly. As a TPM, your job is to be a force multiplier; you get the right people in the right place so that a problem can be solved quickly and efficiently. And when you don't know the right people, or the right place, communicate with your stakeholders to find answers quicker!

We've explored how to drive toward clarity in every step of a project and looked at examples of how seeking clarity benefits the project and what happens when you don't dive deeper into a requirement or problem to define it. All of these aspects are shared with a generalist program manager role as they will also drive toward clarity in all aspects that are directly related to project management.

Now, let's look at how driving toward clarity elevates our impact in a technical setting.

Finding clarity in the technical landscape

As a TPM, you are often aware of many programs and projects that impact your team or organization. You work with other TPMs, other teams, and leaders to deliver your goals. This gives you both a deep knowledge of where you directly run your projects, as well as breadth in the technical landscape surrounding you.

In a technical setting, we use this depth and breadth to our advantage as we have the ability to look at each problem from a different vantage point, all the way from the street level to the full cityscape. These varying vantage points allow us to connect the dots across projects and programs. Let's look at a few examples of seeking clarity and connecting the dots in a technical setting.

Let's explore a technical breadth example. As is often the case, people working on the implementation of a project are highly focused on the project goals. While this is desirable as it ensures a solid solution to the problem at hand, they might miss how these changes can impact other initiatives. As a TPM, you might be in a position to help drive the technical direction of your team. This involves knowing where your team and technology are headed, as well as the tenets that drive them. This knowledge will help drive your day-to-day direction and your design decisions by helping you connect problems and solutions across project and program boundaries.

In a recent example, my organization received a request from a client team to look into the behavior of a field we return in our service response. It was behaving incorrectly for an edge case, and they wanted us to fix it as they relied on that field to make a business decision. Our on-call developer was looking into the issue when I came across the ticket. Though it is always a good idea to fix edge case issues in your API responses, for this particular field, our team had decided that they wanted to remove this field from our response. The field was overloaded and not granular enough to convey the right information. I engaged with the client who submitted the ticket and asked them what they were trying to solve. I took this back to our team to help ensure that our long-term vision was not missing a use case, while also providing a different way for the client to achieve their desired behavior without relying on that field. Our on-call developer didn't know or wasn't thinking about the long term; they were in triage and trying to solve issues, so this connection was initially missed.

By recognizing that fixing this field went against our long-term goal of removing the field entirely, I was able to steer the client away from using it. We found a solution that aligned with the long-term architecture and removed the throw-away work the client would have done in the next year to move away from the deprecated field.

Inspecting broadly can help ensure you are influencing not just your project but your organization and driving everyone toward your shared goals. At the same time, we need to ensure we are diving deeply as well. Looking back at project planning, one key handoff is when a task is taken from the project backlog and given to the development team to design and implement. This handoff is a key point to ensure you drive as much clarity as possible. You do this by providing all of the context needed to do the task up front, and then by asking questions during design and estimation. Often, our project plan estimates are high-level at the beginning and as requirements go through design, we get a more confident estimate that we can then update our timelines with. If you don't ask clarifying questions, the design and estimates may not be as refined as they could be.

However, this isn't a static process as the capabilities and depth of understanding can vary from developer to developer. To mitigate this, I always clarify task estimations with the developer by asking how confident they are in the estimate. I follow up by asking what elements were included in the estimate (design, code review, testing, and/or deployment), as many new developers will just include the code writing itself. Lastly, I follow up by asking questions about the design to see what sort of responses I'm getting. This can help inform me of how big a buffer I might need to use for the developer's estimates. In these scenarios, it's good to remember that a developer's job is to estimate based on ideal conditions. It is your job as a TPM to look at how other factors may impact the developer's ability to deliver the task. Here are some questions to ask or think about when assessing a design and estimation:

- Are there deployment issues or blockers on the team release calendar?
- What is the experience level of the developer for the area the task impacts?
- Are there any unknowns or new technologies for this task that may take extra time?
- Are there other projects ongoing that may impact the changes being made?

You will need to go deep into the project and understand how these tasks are connected, the technologies behind them, and the people involved in order to bring the highest clarity to the project plan and ensure the success of the developer in their task. All of these questions reach out beyond the task itself to consider outside factors. Though some developers have the ability to look beyond the task when estimating, it is better to ask than to assume that these were taken into consideration.

You will need to balance how to get this information as you do not want to appear as though you are questioning their design or estimate. One easy way to remove tension is to add these questions to the sprint task template. Ensure the template has them fill out what the task is, what requirement it is meeting, and how they are going to do it.

From a soft skill or emotional intelligence angle, I will iterate what my role is during sprint planning. I tell the team that I am there to ensure the project runs smoothly and that tasks are delivered when they are agreed to be. In order to do that effectively, I must evaluate estimations and include appropriate buffers to account for outside influences. I have found that being direct in my intention smooths out any pushback as they understand I'm helping them succeed in the end. If you are open about why you are asking, they may start to supply that information ahead of time as I have had several teams integrate an estimation confidence score to help evaluate—as a team – the amount of buffer that may be needed for a given task.

Summary

In this chapter, we discussed in detail how a TPM is constantly driving toward clarity. From project initiation, all the way through to project closing, the TPM is clarifying requirements, assumptions, issues, plans, and estimates to continually steer the project in the right direction.

We looked at how everyone takes thoughts and clarifies them into plans, from building seasonal displays at a retail store to varying levels of ambiguity in the problem a TPM needs to solve. We also touched on how the level of ambiguity increases the further in your career you get.

We explored how driving clarity is used in all key management areas and tied it together with specific scenarios that you can encounter in a technology space.

In *Chapter 6*, we'll use the Mercury program and drive toward clarity to build out a more comprehensive project plan as we dive deeper into project and program planning.

Join our book's Discord space

Join our Discord community to meet like-minded people and learn alongside more than 5000 members at:

https://packt.link/sKmQa

6

Plan Management

In this chapter, we'll start delving deeper into the key management areas I discussed in *Chapter 1*, starting with plan management. We'll build on the *Mercury* program example, first introduced in *Chapter 4, An Introduction to Program Management Using a Case Study,* to inspect all stages of creating a plan both at the project and program levels.

We'll dive into plan management by exploring the following:

- Driving clarity from requirements to planned work
- Planning resources in a technology landscape
- Exploring the differences between a project and a program

Let's start planning!

Driving clarity from requirements to planned work

In *Chapter 5*, we discussed the importance of driving clarity in all aspects of a project or program. Out of all of the areas where driving clarity is needed, plan management is the most important.

When writing a project plan, we might find ourselves asking why we are doing it. "*Why are we doing this?*" I ask myself every time I'm writing one, even though it is one of the aspects of project management I enjoy the most. The answer to why we do it is simple: *it enables us to be a force multiplier.* We know the work that needs to be done and so does everyone else. The team spends less time on determining *what* and *when* and instead focuses on *how* to achieve the tasks and goals. Driving clarity in requirements early on takes less time than correcting the issue later in execution as this can lead to bad estimations due to poor understanding, which results in longer timelines.

The first step in driving clarity in your requirements and beginning your project plan is choosing the right tool or making full use of the tools you have available. Let's explore some of the most common project management tools on the market.

Project management tools

The project plan is one of the most crucial artifacts for your project. This includes many aspects, which we'll cover in this chapter, such as the task list, resourcing, and prerequisites that combine to produce a **Gantt chart** of the project timeline. This is a lot of work to do and there are several tools out there that can help you do it.

Through my interviews with industry leaders, I confirmed something I suspected was true all along—there is no standard tool in project management! It often comes down to personal preference combined with the constraints placed by your company, usually related to security concerns arising from your company data being stored on cloud servers, or budget concerns. In some cases, a company may have decided on a specific tool or ecosystem in which their work is done, and this might constrain you as well.

Nonetheless, I do have a list of tools and feature comparisons to help drive home the variability in the marketplace that exists today. I can say, though, that the one and only tool that was used at every company that I interviewed for this book was **Microsoft Excel**.

I must confess that I also use Excel from time to time—for instance, for the plans in this book! Sometimes, keeping it simple and in a well-known format is the best way to go. You lose a lot of the functionality that you will find in dedicated project management tooling, but you are also free from their preconceived notions of what project management must be. This last point is the main reason I've seen for there being multiple tools on the market—they all have a different feature set or a specific aspect of management that they concentrate on. Another benefit to a tool like Excel is the ability to add your own functionality through macros, scripts, or just simple cell-based formulas.

Taking a step up in functionality, **Microsoft Project** is ubiquitous in the industry—at least in name. It is certainly the standard in regard to features that other tools emulate and is a good introduction to purpose-built tools for project management. However, it doesn't span multiple projects easily, so for program or portfolio management, tools geared toward portfolio management will allow for better cross-project coordination.

Portfolio, program, or project?

Portfolios are a collection of related programs, just as programs are a collection of related projects; the tools are often called portfolio management tools since that is the highest level in which they organize. This means that they naturally manage programs and projects as well.

I use a portfolio management tool in my day-to-day program management so I can easily track multiple projects and build a program roadmap. I often start in Excel as the resource constraints on how project tasks are planned in most tools do not fit well with how my team handles resourcing. I'll get into this a bit more later in the chapter.

In *Table 6.1*, I've listed some tools, though certainly not all, that cover portfolio and program management and some high-level features for comparison. Again, it comes down to personal preference and company need, but this may help you in making decisions as well as knowing the tools that are out there and in use across the industry.

Tool	Project Management	Portfolio Management	Resource Management	Stakeholder Management
MS Project	✓		✓	✓
Smartsheet	✓	✓	✓	✓
Clarizen	✓	✓	✓	✓
Asana	✓	✓	✓	✓
ClickUp	✓	✓	✓	✓
Coda	✓	✓	✓	✓
Monday.com	✓	✓	✓	✓
MS Excel, Google Sheets				

Table 6.1: Comparing program management tools

The project and portfolio management industry has matured a lot in the last eight years and now includes quite a few options that are strictly online and require no local setup. From the areas that we are looking at, most of these tools will provide the basic needs to track a project down to the task level and tie it to resourcing. Stakeholder management for most tools is relegated to an entry list and dashboards to share information with stakeholders.

Some tools have recently explored report automation, but none that I have seen offer capabilities here that would truly set them apart. Generative artificial intelligence using large language models will make this job easier for sure, and we'll discuss that in *Chapter 14*.

The two outliers on this list, **MS Project** and **MS Excel/Google Sheets**, are added because of their ubiquity. MS Project handles project management well but doesn't offer portfolio management to the degree you see in other tools in the field. It does have good portability to other tools due to its maturity, so it can be a good starting point. MS Excel offers literally no specialized functionality for project management—it is a blank canvas. You can start working and add new fields (columns) and entries (rows) to the upper limit of the software itself. To this end, there is no barrier to entry or learning curve and most people know how to use it. A word of caution: to be effective, it takes a lot of work to add formulas, lookups, and straight-up manual manipulation.

Different types of tools

MS Excel and Google Sheets have no built-in functionality for project management but are widely used and thus included in the comparison table.

There are plenty of other tools that cater toward **task management** and, to an extent, **agile methodology** management like scrum boards and sprint planning, but these are not project or program management tools. They don't offer risk logs, milestone tracking, or resource management to a degree that allows them to be effective for higher-level management needs that TPMs require. For this reason, I would have left the spreadsheet entry off, but you can't ignore ubiquity!

Each of the proper management tools in this list will help you develop a good plan. But it's worth understanding the steps to create a plan without the use of a tool. We'll do that next.

Diving deep into the project plan

We're going to explore the step-by-step process of getting a project plan built. This is similar to learning math in the way that you start out writing down every step even when the step is obvious. As you get better, steps are done in your head, or multiple steps are performed at the same time. For now, we'll show all of the steps. In real life, I usually combine the first two and then the next two together. The steps we'll cover are the following:

- Requirements gathering and refinement
- Building use cases from the requirements
- Task breakdown with estimates
- Assembling the project plan

Let's look at each of these in detail.

Requirements gathering and refinement

This is a crucial step where a TPM drives clarity into the requirements. As this is the first step toward building a plan, everything builds from this foundation, so clarity is key.

Table 6.2 shows the high-level requirements for the *Mercury program's Windows Rollout Project.*

ID	Requirement
1	Create a **peer-to-peer (P2P)** messaging system
2	The system must allow sending text messages to other peers on the system
3	Standard UX elements from other messaging apps should be available
4	All messages sent and received by a user must be accessible to the user within the app until the user explicitly deletes a message

Table 6.2: Initial requirements for the Mercury program's Windows Rollout Project

The requirements are pretty straightforward here but are high-level. Reading through these, there are quite a few gaps and generalizations. Let's take a look at them one by one.

Requirement 1 doesn't mention the type of **P2P** system. Specifically, it doesn't mention that no central servers should exist. This is crucial as some P2P systems do have relay servers that are centrally managed and specific to the network. Though we don't explicitly say no centrally managed servers are allowed, our goal is to reduce the overhead of a centralized network.

Requirement 2 doesn't specify anything about the nature of the *text* of the message. The meaning of the text can vary depending on the situation and should be clarified. For instance, rich text supports formatting, whereas plain text does not.

Requirement 3 is vague in that each messaging application has its own look and feel and feature set. There is no common reference here, so assumptions will be made by whoever is doing the design, and their assumptions may not match those of the business team. The desired UX elements should be clearly called out.

Requirement 4 is a compound requirement; it is asking for multiple features in the same line. Though this can be okay, it makes traceability more difficult, so this should be broken up into multiple requirements.

Table 6.3 takes the feedback we just discussed and expands on the requirements:

ID	Requirements
1.0	**A P2P messaging system, with no central servers, should be created**
2.0	**The system must allow sending text messages to other users on the network/system**
2.1	The text message should support all Unicode characters, including emojis
2.2	The text should support rich text formatting (bold, italic, underline, font type, and size)
3.0	**Standard UX elements seen in other messaging apps should be available**
3.1	Address book of saved contacts
3.1.1	Add to the address book
3.1.2	Remove from the address book
3.1.3	Load the address book entirely or a single address
3.1.3	Export the address book entirely or a single address
3.2	User profile
3.2.1	User profile image
3.2.2	User alias should be changeable
3.2.3	Short bio section including description/bio, company, and title
3.3	Presence indicator
3.3.1	Configurable statuses
3.3.2	Configurable locations
3.4	Access control
3.4.1	The user should be able to accept contact requests
3.4.2	The user should be able to block contact requests
4.0	**All messages sent and received should be visible to the user**

4.1	Exception for when a message is deleted by the user
4.2	Messages should contain a status indicator of {sent, received, read}

Table 6.3: Clarified requirements

The new requirements utilized an outline numbering system, so the original four requirements keep their ordinals and additional requirements are listed below them. The bolded lines are the original requirements. A messaging system is bound to have a lot of requirements and this list is meant to just be illustrative of some of the expansions that could be made.

For *requirement 1*, I added the clarification that no central server should exist as a standard P2P network is decentralized. This is enough for the moment to ensure that the right type of P2P network is being developed.

For *requirement 2*, two additional requirements were added to provide context that the text should support all Unicode characters as well as rich text formatting. The specific formatting required is also listed to clear any doubt.

For *requirement 3*, we added the specific features we want to include: an editable user profile, an address book, presence indicators, and access control.

Lastly, *requirement 4* was broken down into components for traceability, and a status feature was added.

Every person reading this book has a different perspective while reading and thus may find requirements or features that they would add, and possibly some expansion on those I've included here as well. There might be a stakeholder who has worked on a P2P system at a past company or spent a lot of time using the various centralized messaging systems to offer UI comparisons. Conversely, you may have someone who has never used a messaging system at all (hard to believe these days, but at some point, this was absolutely the case). Each of these people will have a unique perspective on the requirements. This will always be the case, and I suggest that requirements analysis is not done in a closed room and that multiple stakeholders are involved, at least at some point, as they may see a gap that you do not.

Building use cases from the requirements

To provide context to the requirements and make it easier to test and validate, use cases are created that may span multiple requirements but tell a story on the behavior of the system. Each use case will trace back to the requirements that it will satisfy to ensure that all requirements are met.

Table 6.4 shows a typical set of use cases for the requirements we've reviewed.

ID	Requirement IDs	Use Case
1	1.0	As an admin, have no centralized setup or maintenance
2	1.0	As a user, install and use without a central server
3	3.2	As a user, create a user profile with a picture and an alias
4	3.1	As a user, add or remove a contact to my contact list
5	3.4	As a user, block and accept a contact request
6	2	As a user, send messages to a contact using rich text
7	4	As a user, see new messages sent to me
8	4	As a user, see all messages both sent and received
9	4.1	As a user, delete a message
10	3.3	As a user, set presence information

Table 6.4: Use cases

The requirements are relatively simple for this application so the use cases will closely follow the requirements one-to-one, though in some more complex projects, a single use case may cover multiple requirements. A use case should tell a story about something a user should be able to do. You often see them written out as a story, such as this:

As a user/admin/seller/customer, I can perform some action.

This provides context as to what you are solving and creates a test plan item as well! For use cases that trace back to a top-level requirement, such as in *requirement 2*, the use case covers all sub-requirements from that requirement as well. You may notice that the use case order doesn't necessarily match up with the requirement order—for instance, use case 10 traces to requirement 3.3 but isn't next to the use case that traces back to 3.2. The story being told is the important part here, and traceability is added to aid in ensuring that all requirements are covered, not that they are covered in a particular order. However, it may be useful to group user stories together under large themes such as *user profiles* or *user capabilities* to help set the context even further.

Task breakdown with estimates

We'll take the requirements as written, treat them as more or less final, and move on to the start of the project plan itself. We'll take the requirements and use cases we've defined and break them down into tasks. *Table 6.5* shows this in detail.

ID	Use Case ID	Task	Estimate (Weeks)
1	1, 2	Design P2P network	4
2	1, 2	Implement P2P network	6
3	6	Build API for text message request/response	4
4	7, 8	Use an Ack tag to track message status	2
5	6	Ensure Unicode support in API payload	1
6	5	Text message to new contact initiates contact request	1
7	4	Add/remove API using message protocol/API	4
8	4	Import/export of the address book	4
9	4	Import/export of an address entry	4
10	-	Support search/discovery for members of network	4
11	3	Create user profile CRUD	1
12	3	Create user alias CRUD	1
13	3	Create user bio text CRUD	1
14	10	Create user availability status key-value pair	1
15	10	Create user location key-value pair	1
16	10	Support full Unicode including emojis in values	0.5
17	5	Build mechanism to accept or deny contact request	1
18	8	Maintain message list for both sent and received	2
19	9	Allow deletion of sent/received messages from list	0.5

Table 6.5: From use cases to tasks

Each of these tasks expands upon one or more of the use cases and provides an estimate of the number of weeks. As you can see, many of these are still high-level *design* and *implementation* tasks and are not grouped yet into features or user stories. The level to which you break it down depends on the expectations of your team as well as your ability for a given use case or high-level task to be broken down further. For example, I suggest the data type for the presence object to be a key-value pair, but in the user profile object, I merely specify that a **Create, Read, Update, Delete (CRUD)** model should be used but not how or any specific behaviors.

At this stage, before moving on to the project plan, I will add buffers for the estimates and then review the task list and estimates with my project team. The team should all agree on what they are agreeing to accomplish and the effort that it will take. If you don't have the information about the estimates (ambiguity and confidence), now is when you work with your team to get those gaps filled in.

Whether you add in buffers at this stage or not is more preference than anything else. For the teams I currently work with, there is a lot of overhead on a developer's time. As such, I've found that a buffer can help account for the overhead and unpredictability of if or when a developer is pulled away from a task for a few hours. In most estimation systems, we use the task that is meant to be estimated as if it were the only task the developer was working on. This helps ensure that the estimate is a measure of the complexity of the task and not a reflection of their working environment. The TPM's job is to take the environment into account, and this may require a buffer.

There's also a discussion in the *Critical Chain* book about whether adding buffers on each task accomplishes any meaningful outcome. The book looks at contract and sales-based software development and found that the tasks always took up the amount of time that was quoted, even when for the same task, the amount of time was adjusted between projects. Their theory for this came down to procrastination, and when that is the main contributing factor, reducing the estimates was better at keeping the project on track than adding more buffers! I personally believe that it depends on the culture of the company and team, and so how estimations are handled should vary depending on the context of the project.

Assembling the project plan

The project plan is a living document that goes through multiple phases during the life of the project. In the beginning, it is strictly a plan—it marks the planned path to get to the end. However, as the project starts, it will start capturing real-time data in the form of actuals: actual start date, actual completion date, as well as actual resourcing. For now, we'll focus on the starting point of the project plan as this form of the plan is what leads to the later forms.

There are a few key pieces of data that you need to gather for any project. Aside from the standard items of the task description, duration, and predecessors, you'll want to capture the requirements that it satisfies. Though I showed this as a separate chart—and it can be a separate exercise—I have found that having a central sheet to see all of the important data is best and reduces the churn of cross-referencing, which can lead to mistakes.

Depending on your company and how you handle resourcing, capturing the crashing capability of a given task is very beneficial. **Crashing** is the act of having multiple people work on the same task at the same time. This can be in the form of overlapping sub-tasks such as quality assurance and the actual implementation or splitting the development up among multiple developers. The crashing count is the maximum number of *resources* that the task can handle but doesn't represent the actual number of people you might assign if everything is going okay. I have found that having this available ahead of time speeds up my ability to react to changes where I can speed up a task that is in danger of missing a milestone or that impacts other work from being able to start on time.

Last but not least, the **start date** and **end date** round out the remainder of your basic plan. Your situation may compel you to add more than this, but these are what I have found are a good starting point for every project. I use a template for the fields I use to ensure that I don't forget them!

Table 6.6 shows the requirements and tasks we've covered in this chapter as a project plan with all of the fields we have discussed:

ID	Req Id	Task	Duration	Crash #	Predecessors	Start Date	End Date
1	1	Create P2P network	16				
1.1	1	Design network	6	1		2-Jan-23	6-Feb-23
1.2	1	Implement	10	2	2fs	13-Feb-23	24-Mar-23
1.3	1.3	Create a network ID to tie a message to a given network instance	3	1	2fs	27-Mar-23	14-Apr-23

2	2	**Text message send/receive API**	**13**					
2.1	2	Set up API for request/response	6	2			2-Jan-23	20-Jan-23
2.2	4.2	Use an Ack tag to track message status	3	1	6fs		23-Jan-23	17-Feb-23
2.3	2.1	Ensure Unicode support in API payload	2	1	6fs		23-Jan-23	3-Feb-23
2.4	3.4.1	New text message to new contact initiates contact request	2	1	6fs		6-Feb-23	17-Feb-23

Table 6.6: Excerpt of Windows Rollout Project plan

The plan is relatively straightforward, but we'll discuss a few points to illustrate how these fields are utilized to build out a project plan. The ID column has been updated to use an outline numbering format to reflect the grouping of tasks into stories. For instance, the *design and implement a P2P network* tasks were grouped together in a story called **Create P2P network**, so these tasks are now part of this story and are a subset of story ID 1. Next, the duration here may look different from the duration first shown because I applied buffers to these numbers. In short, no estimate is perfect, and buffering protects your plan from reality. We'll discuss this in more detail in the next section. For the crashing number, most of these tasks are straightforward and granular in nature so adding additional people likely won't work out, so most are given a value of *1*. A few that are implementation-focused received a *2*, as a lot of development can be paired up so long as more than one code package is being touched. Your developers and software development managers should be able to assist you in determining the maximum amount of crash you can handle. If you know the systems well enough, don't hesitate to use your own judgment.

For the start and end dates, I used the crash here as an actual resourcing count, so the duration is split by the resource count. A duration of four weeks but a crashing count of *2* would end up at two calendar weeks. I usually capture the planned resourcing as well, but for brevity, I used the **Crash** field for both.

The last field to discuss is the predecessor. Though this is a default column in all project management tools, we'll discuss it as a refresher. There are a few different types of predecessors you can have. The most common is the **finish-start** relationship, shown as **fs**, where the task number listed must finish before the given task can start. **Start-start (ss)**, **start-finish (sf)**, and **finish-finish (ff)** all exist as well and follow the same paradigm. I use finish-start the most—it being the most common relationship is likely why it is the default relationship in most tools. I've also found it very useful to include lags, for instance, the implementation of a design doesn't always have to wait until the design is completely finished. There may be aspects of the design, or a key point such as an API definition being ready, where implementation can begin, which allows you to fast-track the implementation. Additionally, you can break the task apart and have the API definition be a separate task and list it as an ff, with the rest of the design as an fs. Similar to crashing, I like to list these areas ahead of time as well—it doesn't mean I will fast-track, but I know that I can, and the sooner I know, the easier it will be to quickly adapt to changes. Catching these optimizations in the plan that are based on how to fast-track and how a particular story might be broken down into smaller deliverables is a key way in which a TPM brings value to the planning process. These optimizations are only possible to catch when you have a technical understanding of the requirements and the structure of your services, including how the code packages are structured.

We've discussed the four main steps to take when building a plan, and it can take some time to do each one separately. Since time isn't always on our side and, sometimes, we just need to get moving, let's see how we might be able to speed this up.

When project planning has to be quick

Even when you have the time, using time-saving tricks can help you focus on the tasks that have no real shortcuts or just need more attention. Planning can be repetitive from project to project, especially when working with the same teams on domain areas, as the themes of the type of work, the people, and the resourcing available will be the same, and over time, knowing how well the people work together can help with estimations. When moving fast, removing repetitive work is the highest-value place to focus your energy to reduce effort and increase productivity. Here are the areas with highly repeatable effort that we can reduce the time spent on:

- Repeatable high-level estimates
- Management checklists
- Project plan templates
- Buffering

Let's explore each of these.

Repeatable high-level estimates

In many environments, there are repeatable tasks that continually come up across projects. These often relate to configurations and data modeling. Keep a list of these tasks, their descriptions, and the typical effort estimate. I typically use a range for the estimate to give some room for quick tweaking. If you feel a specific instance of a task is more complicated, just use the upper range; if standard or simpler, use the lower ranges.

When building out your project plan, consult this list to easily knock out the repeatable items and move on to where your attention is needed. As a bonus, this list is also a good place to pull from for software improvements as repeatable work is the best to automate as it tends to have a high and guaranteed **return on investment (ROI)**.

Management checklists

Just as some tasks are repeatable, there are management artifacts that are repeated from project to project. Generically speaking, each key management area and process in the project management life cycle has repeated actions: reviewing requirements, building use cases and then a task list, analyzing risks, and building a stakeholder communication plan. The list can be very long as there is a lot to project management, and it is also fungible to a specific scenario. Certain tasks may be reduced to a static list—your stakeholders, for instance, might be the same in a small company or team and may not change from project to project.

As you work on your projects, look at the items you are repeating the most and start creating a list of these items along with standard operating procedures for them. When you are in a hurry on the next project, run down the checklist.

Project plan templates

Many of the portfolio management tools out there offer the ability to create and deploy templates for various aspects of project management. These templates are great for when a particular aspect of the project is standardized for your company or team. They can also take parts of your management checklist and delegate them to others as the template with needed or pre-populated information is already there.

For a project plan, tasks such as requirements gathering and verification, creating functional specifications, and launch plans are tasks that are present for every project. In software development, tasks such as code deployment, integration testing, and end-to-end testing are also always present. These may be added at the end of the project plan, or per feature or milestone, depending on how your software landscape operates.

Buffers

Part of your project plan is adding in task estimates. Aside from the repeatable work I mentioned previously, estimates typically come from subject matter experts, usually developers. As a TPM, you may also be in the position to estimate these items yourself. This depends on your company and team's needs as well as your own abilities.

In either case, you will have a set of estimates for each task; however, that is not often added directly into a plan. One of the responsibilities of a PM is to analyze an estimate and project plan and apply buffers. Nothing ever goes exactly according to plan, and it is our job to account for that. To aid in this, I often apply a matrix when determining the right level of buffer. This might take some trial and error to come up with as each person estimates differently, and each company has its own overhead that feeds into standard buffers. *Table 6.7* is an example of what this might look like:

Level of Ambiguity in Task	Confidence of Estimate Accuracy	Team Overhead	Buffer
Medium	Low	10%	35%
High	Low	10%	40%
Low	Medium	10%	25%
Medium	Medium	10%	30%
High	Medium	10%	35%
Low	High	10%	20%
Medium	High	10%	25%

Table 6.7: Estimation buffer matrix

In this example, the team has a modest overhead of 10%. This accounts for standing meetings, recurring training, and other team activities that take a set amount of time. Each team should have its own overhead, which should be revisited often to ensure it reflects the current realities of the team.

The level of ambiguity and the confidence of the estimate work together as a scorecard to determine the buffer. In increments of 5%, high ambiguity adds 15% with low at 5%, and the reverse for confidence, with high confidence at 5% and low at 15%. This added to the team overhead gets you the percent increase for each estimate.

Notice that none of these is 0% because estimates and real life never agree! There is always a buffer for the estimates you have, even if you came up with the estimate. Adding buffers, though intuitive and most of us do this, is not the textbook approach to estimations via the **Program Evaluation and Review Technique (PERT)** methodology. This method is closer to the critical chain method. I've added a resource in the *Further reading* section of this chapter that details the critical chain method.

Refining buffers

Table 6.7 makes adding buffers formulaic or straightforward. However, as was alluded to, there is nuance involved here. I've spent the better part of my career refining the buffers I use, and I always scrutinize my percentages when there are changes to the team or organization or I'm simply starting a new complex project.

As PERT is what is taught in most project management courses, it is worth covering here. For each task, three estimates are created—optimistic (O), pessimistic (P), and most likely (M) to happen—and this formula is applied:

$$Buffered\ Task\ Estimate = \frac{O + (4\ x\ M) + P}{6}$$

This is a weighted average between the three estimates, where weight is given to the most likely estimate. This is useful and can certainly be added to a spreadsheet or project management tool to automatically adjust, but asking for three estimates on each task can quickly become cumbersome. This is why I prefer the table approach, as it allows me to use a single estimate and weigh against factors that would make the task more or less likely to hit the target estimate. The critical chain has a similar approach to adding buffers but restricts buffer additions to only items on the critical path.

We've taken a detailed look into what it takes to drive clarity into requirements in order to produce a working project plan. Now that we have a plan, let's look closer at defining the milestones and feature list for the project.

Defining milestones and the feature list of a plan

As with many terms in the project management space, milestones and feature lists can have different meanings from company to company. This largely depends on the methodologies they follow, if any at all. One of my struggles early on in my career was reconciling that these two terms are often used interchangeably, even though they do have specific definitions.

If you find yourself disagreeing with a definition, that's okay; regardless of what you call something, what it is doing is the important part.

Milestones and feature lists are different measurements that a TPM has against the health of their project. Milestones are often predetermined and, in some organizations, are exactly the same for every project. These are goals during the project cycle that the project is moving toward. A few common milestones in a software development project would be design completion, implementation completion, user acceptance testing completion, and launch, as examples. For any given software project, these milestones would all exist to some degree and make it easy to compare project health across a program.

In many cases, this definition of milestones is rigid and doesn't match with day-to-day usage of the word. When used in this manner, I see it more often in consultation or integration projects and programs where the project plan in and of itself is largely predetermined. This makes having preset milestones a good way to measure one instance of an integration to another. However, in most large tech companies, this isn't the type of project being run and, therefore, this definition doesn't often get used.

Somewhat in contrast to this, a feature list is specific to a project. As the name suggests, it's a list of features that are being built that can be deployed independently. This is what most companies mean when they use the term milestone. From an agile methodology, a feature could be synonymous with the sprint demo at the end of a sprint where the tenet for each sprint is to deliver value. It is an effective way to share when a specific feature will be available to your stakeholders and makes communicating dependent work easier by grouping tasks together that deliver a feature. These features usually correlate to the top-level stories or tasks in bold in my project plan. For instance, the presence object for location and status is a feature that can be delivered alone and be usable, as is the ability to send a text message. As you can see in *Table 6.6*, the top-level tasks, or features, also correspond to use cases, and this is often the case.

Table 6.8 represents the feature list from the project plan:

Feature	Start Date	End Date
Create P2P network	2-Jan-23	14-Apr-23
Build text message send/receive API	2-Jan-23	17-Feb-23
Create address book	17-Apr-23	9-Jun-23
Create user profile object	20-Feb-23	3-Mar-23

Create presence object	27-Feb-23	13-Mar-23
Create access control	20-Mar-23	24-Mar-23
Build message library	20-Mar-23	7-Apr-23

Table 6.8: Feature list

Though the information is available in the project plan, it is often useful to list it separately as these are key metrics to follow the health of a project. As I covered in *Chapter 1*, different stakeholders require different levels of information, and most stakeholders don't want to sift through a full project plan to discern what is happening, so this provides a concise snapshot of the project's trajectory.

You should now have a better understanding of the different ways TPMs drive clarity while executing plan management. We used the *Mercury* program to build out from requirements through to a project plan. We also discussed some tricks to lighten the work during this phase. Next, we're going to discuss resourcing and how it may look different in a technology company compared to other business domains.

Planning resources in a technology landscape

Every industry has its own unique challenges to project and program management and the tech industry is no different. There are two main aspects to resourcing that are consistent across the tech industry and are worth exploring in more depth: prioritization and team overhead.

Prioritization

From my experience, and through the interviews I conducted for this book, tech companies don't follow a **projectized resourcing model** where a project is formed, resources are assigned, and the project keeps the same funding throughout the life of the project. Instead, these large companies utilize **capacity-constrained prioritization**, where they perform multiple prioritization exercises throughout the year to align their existing capacity to the most strategic projects. The frequency of these exercises varies from company to company and, in some cases, team to team, but can happen as often as monthly, quarterly, yearly, or some combination of these. This cyclical prioritization relationship is demonstrated in *Figure 6.1*:

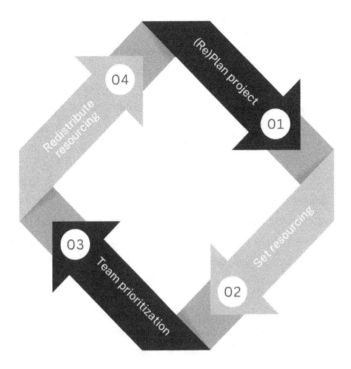

Figure 6.1: Cyclical prioritization

The preceding diagram shows the relationship between the project plan and the capacity-constrained prioritization process used in tech companies. This is essentially a specialized version of the **Plan, Do, Check, Act (PDCA)** process. Once a project is planned and resourcing is set, a team prioritization cycle can then change the number of resources for your project either up or down. Either way, this leads to replanning based on the new numbers you have. This is why I front-load a lot of preplanning work such as crashing counts for a task, adding in a buffer, and fine-tuning the predecessors so I know quickly how tight a finish-to-start relationship actually is.

Team overhead

We briefly discussed overhead when talking about shortcuts to use while project planning. In the example, I used a 10% overhead buffer. In reality, I've seen anywhere from 10% to 40% overhead on various teams I've worked with. Let's talk about a few of the major components of overhead that you'll want to keep track of.

On-call rotations

Many software development teams have on-call rotations where a software developer will listen to ticket queues for problems. If a severe problem occurs, a developer may be asked to look at the ticket at any time of the day or night. Most on-call rotations are a week in duration where the daily duration may be all 24 hours or split up into shifts to cover the full day or the working day, depending on the criticality. During the on-call shift, the developer is often not available for project work.

Depending on the size of your project and the number of teams you are working with, on-call rotations can be a constant source of resourcing loss that can be much worse than other sources of loss such as vacation. A vacation is usually known well in advance and impacts a single person's tasks. On the other hand, on-call responsibility jumps from person to person, can impact multiple resources in the same week, and developers may not remember they have an on-call rotation coming up (it's not nearly as exciting as a vacation, so I don't blame them).

To help alleviate unexpected churn on your project plan, the buffer time for your project should look at the teams involved and their rotation schedules to ensure you have enough slack to cover the intermittent stoppages in work. Check with the **Software Development Managers (SDMs)** and **Software Development Engineers (SDEs)** to understand the time expectations from their on-call rotation. In some cases, the ticket queue may be low and the impact is less than times when they have a higher volume of tickets.

A quick note about on-call and overhead is that I have heard the argument that on-call is separate from overhead and should be tracked separately. To me, this depends on the team(s) you are working with. I usually start with a generalized buffer for overhead that includes on-call and may add explicit on-call items into my project as I know more about the rotation schedule. Calling it out explicitly takes more of your time but can reduce the churn you face in your day-to-day conflict resolution. I have had some teams where they were short-staffed, so each team member was on call more often than usual and I ended up losing one week per person for several months straight. This reduces your effective workforce by an entire headcount for a given month. In these cases, I worked with the SDMs to map out all expected non-project work over the next few months so I could do a single adjustment and set clear expectations with my stakeholders.

Training and team-related work

Like many other industries, technology evolves constantly. To keep up, developers (as well as SDMs, TPMs, and others) attend training to learn about new advances or to brush up on known skills. These are a bit harder to track as they require constant vigilance on the schedules of your developers and can be as painful as on-call. When a popular course such as **Design Patterns** becomes available for our office, a large number of developers will take the course and are all gone at once.

Most companies have a schedule of classes that you can use to ask about availability with your team during sprint planning if running agile or some other planning forum. It's also good to ask SDMs about training quotas for their team and see whether they know the current trend in attendance to help you determine a good buffer.

Team-related work and offsite meetings have a similar impact on the project as training does. Many tech companies have started a trend of hackathon weeks, availability weeks, or improvement weeks. These all are geared toward allowing developers to work on projects that directly impact their services' maintainability or add some quality-of-life features. During these workshops, the entire team may not be available. The same methodologies apply here in terms of a buffer and consultation on the frequency of these events.

Company or organization-wide outages

In larger tech companies, there are often company-wide events that can restrict code deployments. The events may be internal, geared toward reliability checks or security, or they may be externally motivated such as a sales event or a press conference for a new product. Though these are not team-by-team or resource-by-resource, they do need to be considered in the overall project plan.

Team meetings

Most teams have some number of standing meetings that range from operations to team-building exercises. This number is often set and the SDMs should have a good idea of what the impact is here. As a note, when discussing overhead, it isn't too unlikely that this bucket is the only bucket people think about, so be sure to probe when discussing an overhead number so that it covers all of these topics.

Project versus non-project hours

All of these components add up and are subtracted from the project hours available to a specific team. As each team may be different, there may be different degrees of overhead that you will be tracking in the project. *Figure 6.2* demonstrates the breakdown of project and non-project hours:

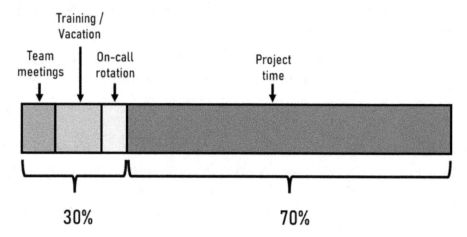

Figure 6.2: Showing overhead, non-project, and project hours to determine available hours

In this scenario, the team has an overhead of 30%, leaving 70% of the team members' time to work on project tasks. The 30% is inclusive of the three sections discussed in the previous section: team meetings, training and vacation, and on-call rotations. The 70% is likely to fluctuate month to month based on actual team meetings, whether or not a particular person is in the on-call rotation for the month, as well as vacations and training. The *law of large numbers* states that with a large enough dataset, the results will be close to the expected outcome. This means that the overhead percentage of a team will equal the expected amount over the course of a project. When this doesn't happen, it's usually because the expected overhead is wishful thinking—ensure that you and your team are being honest when determining this number. The discussion may uncover a need for process improvement.

Resource overhead

The overhead mentioned here is illustrative and will change from team to team. When I discuss overhead, it references the type of overhead that there is some control over. If absolutely needed, I can request that an SDM take an SDE out of the on-call rotation or pause training for a limited time.

Now let's move on to discuss the tools that you will use for resource planning in a technology landscape.

Tooling for resource planning

Just as with project planning, most tools on the market cover resourcing in the same way: non-crashing and projectized. For some industries, this practice is fine and follows how they approach resourcing. However, as discussed in this chapter, tech companies tend to use capacity planning, which may shift due to priorities over the life of the project.

The lack of crashing capabilities means that a task timeline won't automatically reduce when you add additional resources; it will actually reduce the time each resource works on the task and keep the duration the same. Some tools allow you to change this behavior, but it isn't consistent. This means any time you need to crash—or even want to know what the impact of crashing would be—you need to do it manually either through changing durations or forcing the hours spent to reduce the calendar time.

In prioritization meetings, I am often approached by management asking what dates I could meet with x, y, or z resources. So, instead of me dictating the number of people I need, I help weigh the number of resources against priority based on the best ROI I can provide. In these circumstances, I often export to Excel in a Gantt chart style and manually move tasks around to see the outcome.

The other issue, somewhat alluded to, is that the resourcing provided and the optimized resourcing for a project rarely match. This leads to issues where tasks with no written predecessors will all start at the same time, regardless of the number of people assigned. Some tools, such as MS Project, will warn you that a resource is overbooked but requires step-by-step approval to shift timelines. This is still far better than other tools that completely ignore (or hide under a budget sub-system) the fact that resources are overbooked. Not all tools are like this either, but I have yet to find a tool that can handle all of these issues well, so you are left with manual work in at least one of these scenarios. For this, I'll often use a forced constraint for the start date or create a fake predecessor based on resource availability.

When resource planning has to be quick

When planning a project, ensure that you do not forget about overhead. Either ahead of a project, or through multiple projects with multiple teams, build up tables of standard items per team such as vacation trends, on-call rotations, team outings, or improvement weeks, as well as training.

If building and consulting the tables takes more time than you have, then a quick chat with SDMs on their understanding of their teams' overhead can suffice early on in a project. Usually, a 10-minute conversation with an SDM to talk through the overhead list from this chapter and fill in values is enough time for a rough number. As it is an estimate in and of itself, don't forget to add a buffer until you have enough data to make the numbers more concise.

With regard to vacations, these often vary from person to person; some patterns may exist within your team, especially depending on the type of services they run. Local holidays often play into when people will take time off, such as Christmas, or a simple 3-day weekend that is padded to 4 or 5 days. Watch for these patterns and ensure that they are considered when planning.

Now that we know a little bit more about resourcing in a technology landscape, let's apply this to the project plan for the *Mercury* program in *Table 6.9*:

Task	Duration	Crash #	Resourcing	Start Date	End Date
Create P2P network	16				
Design network	6	1	Arun	2-Jan-23	6-Feb-23
Implement	10	2	Arun, Bex	13-Feb-23	24-Mar-23
Create network ID	3	1	Arun	27-Mar-23	14-Apr-23
Arun on-call	1	1	Arun	20-Feb-23	24-Feb-23
Bex on-call	1	1	Bex	6-Mar-23	10-Mar-23

Table 6.9: Updated partial plan with resourcing

For the sake of formatting and space, I reduced the fields that are visible as well as the number of tasks to be enough to understand the concepts we are discussing. As you can see in *Table 6.9*, Arun and Bex both have on-call rotations during the project. They both fall during the implementation of the P2P network between 2/14/23 and 3/28/23. Notice that the duration is 10 weeks, and with two resources, this should last five weeks on the calendar, but it actually takes six weeks. This accounts for the week that both Arun and Bex are unavailable.

Here, on-call is a separate task on the project so it is easy to track. However, some tools allow you to enter calendar time off in the tool itself, and this can automatically shift work during the time off. Though it is a bit of extra work, I prefer the approach of adding tasks because it explains the gap in the Gantt chart much better. With the resourcing tool, you have to cross-reference other sections of the tool and cannot easily convey this via a plan without additional manual work.

We've discussed project planning in great detail and applied the knowledge to the *Mercury* program example. We then saw how resourcing is different in a technology landscape. Lastly, we'll explore how planning differs between a project and a program.

Exploring the differences between a project and a program

Many of the tools and processes are the same between a project and a program. One major difference is scope. In this case, there is the program scope, which has its own set of requirements in the form of the program goals. These requirements are relayed down to the projects that impact them. Though I've been referencing the *Windows Rollout Project*, these requirements could easily have been for any of the other platforms.

When starting a program, you need to refine the goals in the same way you refine the project requirements. In *Chapter 4*, we stated that the *Mercury* program's goal is to have a P2P messaging application with a 100% user reach. This is an okay goal with enough wiggle room to achieve success, but from a requirement standpoint, it's too vague. What is user reach? How do we measure 100% of that?

There are also technical issues with this statement. Let's say that the user base means all users of a given platform. The P2P network would span across the world, and thus across physical and logical networks. Many devices that have access to the internet do not have a public-facing IP address, meaning there is no way for a direct connection from one device to another when they are on different networks. A relay would be needed to—at the very least—route the call between the devices. This can be done in a way that makes the traffic not readable by the relay and for it to be a dumb router, which would satisfy most **information security** (**InfoSec**) teams at large tech firms. However, this loosely goes against the requirement of no centralized system.

Even if we talk about a private installation of this program for an enterprise client, their network is likely large enough for internal network segmentation that also requires a relay. If the relays were also installed on the local network, they would need to be maintained and essentially centralized. The relays could be public and maintained by the *Mercury* program corporation, but this would force traffic out of the network to travel across network segments.

As you can see, just by probing a bit into two words in the goal, we uncovered several potential issues that the program will need to address before the projects can start their work.

Let's look a bit closer at some of the aspects of plan management that may require some different strategies.

Tooling

The tools used for program versus project planning are largely the same, so long as the tool can handle portfolio management. Having multiple projects under a program or portfolio umbrella allows unique reporting as well as cross-project dependency tracking. Some tools will automatically update a cross-project dependency once a slip occurs while others require an explicit refresh to the cross-project dependency.

The automatic tying of multiple projects can act as a forcing function so that everyone is aware of the dependency as well as any change to it.

Planning

As a TPM running a program, one of your responsibilities will be to find opportunities across project boundaries to optimize time, effort, and scope. This is done by evaluating the technical requirements and possible solutions to optimize the path forward, which can lead to a better architecture by ensuring designs across projects align and are consistent where feasible.

For this program, there are multiple platforms that will have their own instance of the *Mercury* messaging app. When you have the same app across multiple platforms, there are opportunities for shared code. Some operating systems will more easily be able to share code than others.

When I wrote the original Windows application, Microsoft's .NET was around Framework 3.5, and the **Common Language Runtime (CLR)** for non-Windows systems was not robust. This would have meant that only code written in C—a language shared by all of these platforms—would be shareable. Arguably, the pain of writing in such a low-level language would outweigh the benefits.

In recent years, there have been frameworks that more capably span across operating systems. With the proliferation of smartphones and smart TVs, the desire to write once and deploy in multiple platforms has led to better tools to facilitate this.

Mono Project is one such framework. It uses the open-source version of the .NET Framework and has CLRs for all of the platforms that we are targeting in this program. The amount of code sharing possible will depend on the level of system coverage each CLR has on its respective operating system as well as the number of idiosyncratic definitions of network protocols and other lower-level APIs, as these can cause divergencies in implementations.

From a planning perspective, these questions may become initial work at the program level to determine the right path forward in terms of frameworks to use and the target amount of code sharing that balances the difficulties in coordinating and writing with the reduced scope per project. This is yet another example of where a *technical* program manager brings value to the program by evaluating technical avenues to increase the efficiency of the plan.

Knowing when to define a program

As discussed earlier in this section, scope is the major differentiator between a program and a project. *Chapter 1* also discussed that a program often has a longer timeframe than a project. When your company's projects are around half a year to a year in length, a program may be multiple years long. If projects are a few months long, a program may only last up to a year. In any case, though, they are relative to one another.

When you are faced with a set of requirements or goals and are trying to decide whether to spin up a project or a program, there are a few litmus tests you can do to see whether a program is the right fit:

- Do you have multiple goals to achieve?
- Is the timeline fixed or based on achieving the goals?
- How many stakeholders are involved?

If you have multiple goals to achieve, then multiple projects, one or more per goal, would ensure clarity of purpose for each project. In this case, a program to manage these projects would make the most sense. To be clear, by multiple goals, I'm not referring to features or milestones but end goals.

If the goal you are trying to achieve has a deadline, this is often a reason for a focused project to drive toward the deadline. If you have multiple goals and one is time-bound, a program with a project specifically for the time-bound goal may be a good fit.

Lastly, if your goal spans multiple departments or organizations within your company, all driving toward the goal or goals, a program with projects per organization may be the most effective way to manage the large number of stakeholders. Each organization may have a succinct deliverable that contributes toward a goal.

Figure 6.3 takes a close look at the company organization structure and how the *Mercury* program and the projects within it relate:

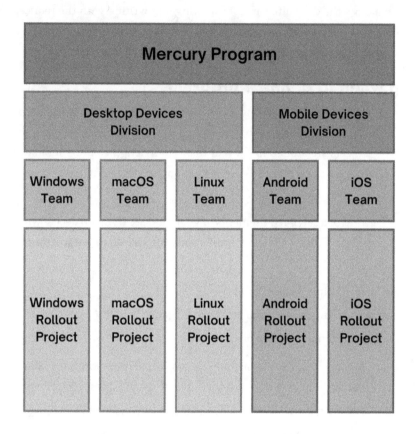

Figure 6.3: Organizational boundaries for the Mercury program

The company responsible for the *Mercury* program divides devices between desktop and mobile. Within these divisions, each operating system has its own team with its own roadmap and priorities. The *Mercury* program spans both divisions and each operating system team is responsible for a project within the *Mercury* program to deliver *Mercury* on their respective OS. This can be useful to map out because, at first glance, the number of stakeholders in this example isn't too large, but the way they are organized and the large vertical slice of the program goal that they each own lends this to be treated as a program with projects as opposed to a single project.

As the earlier questions alluded to, a program will often span multiple organizations and goals. It utilizes the *Mercury* program's company structure to show how the program spans multiple organizations with each organization having a dedicated project.

An answer to one of these questions in favor of a program does not mean that a program is absolutely required but may lean your answer in that direction. For instance, a regulatory compliance project in a company may need to span operations and accounting organizations, but with a deadline and concrete deliverables, a project is likely the best way forward. Conversely, the *Mercury* program has a single stated goal but spans multiple organizations, each with a concrete deliverable of an app that contributes to that goal and with no constraint on the timeline. Though this could be treated as a project, the complexities across the organization and distinct deliverables lend themselves to be treated as a program.

This figure should also look familiar as the device pillars can also be seen as independent product pillars. Each pillar has its own development team and product team. This shows that a TPM is most effective when leading horizontal initiatives.

At the end of the day, these questions and answers are inputs to help you decide what the most effective and easy way to manage your goals will be for you.

Summary

In this chapter, we discussed plan management in greater detail. We drove toward clarity by refining requirements into use cases, tasks, and then a basic project plan. Asking questions during each step ensured that each artifact could be traced back to the requirements.

We covered how a tech firm can add unique challenges to plan management through capacity-constrained prioritization causing mid-project changes in resourcing based on priority shifts. We also discussed the components of team overhead in a tech team, including on-call rotations that service-based teams utilize for service health and stability.

We started discussing the various tools that are available to program managers for both projects and programs and each key management area. Lastly, we discussed how planning differs between a project and a program, which is tied to scope, and that defining a program comes down to ease of management of the goals you are delivering.

In *Chapter 7*, we'll continue the deep-dive discussions and focus on risk management. We'll cover in more detail what risk management is and how driving clarity works in risk analysis, and discuss the unique challenges in technology that contribute to risks you will likely see in your project. We'll also build on the *Windows Rollout Project* plan that we've developed in this chapter and run a risk analysis.

Further reading

- Dr. Goldratt, Eliyahu. *Critical Chain* (North River Press, 1997). This book describes the critical chain methodology that I have discussed under the *Buffers* heading in this chapter. The method is more intuitive to the way we work and gives us a tangible way to handle unknowns by assigning buffers based on complexity and ambiguity.

Additional resources

You can find templates for requirements tables, task tables, work breakdown structures, and project buffer matrices in the GitHub repo related to this book. Please check the Preface for the GitHub link.

Join our book's Discord space

Join our Discord community to meet like-minded people and learn alongside more than 5000 members at:

https://packt.link/sKmQa

7

Risk Management

In this chapter, we'll discuss the risk management process and the type of risks that a TPM may deal with in a technology landscape. We'll dive into the risk assessment process in greater detail and see how to successfully catalog project and program risks and explore methods to reduce or remove their impact.

We'll dive into risk management by covering the following topics:

- Driving clarity in risk assessment
- Managing risks in a technology landscape
- Exploring the differences between a project and a program

Driving clarity in risk assessment

During the introduction to driving clarity in *Chapter 5*, we discussed the cyclical relationship between project planning and risk assessment. Now, we'll drive clarity in terms of what risk assessment is and how we continue to manage risk throughout the project's life cycle.

Risk assessment starts as soon as you have enough information to start assessing, which can be as early in the project as initiation. If you start with a project in a domain that you know very well, a single paragraph about the goal of the project may be enough to start analyzing risks. In other cases, where the domain or project itself is too vague, it may take a full requirements document to start analyzing, which is in itself a risk!

I've been in the same domain area for over a decade, so I know the business aspects of the tax domain very well. I also know our technical landscape and product vision. As such, when new legislation is passed, the legislation itself is enough to start analyzing risks as well as the correct solution.

The key here is recognizing patterns of data flow, user interactions with the system, and trends. In the tax world, for example, once one legislative body passes a new law that increases tax revenue, others will follow and do so quickly. Knowing this allows us to look at a potential solution through a lens that includes other jurisdictions being impacted by a given law. We can think ahead to what the law may look like in 2 to 3 years. This foresight was gained through years of risk analysis of current as well as closed projects.

In a similar vein, some projects are too vague to get very far without a clearer picture. An infamous example is Brexit. The legislation was simply that the UK would leave the European Union but had no concrete details on what this meant, including for import and export behaviors. Though the goal was known, it was still too vague to dive into it enough to gain useful risks aside from missing the deadline!

Regardless of when the process starts, the steps are the same. Part of the process was outlined in *Figure 5.3* in *Chapter 5*, but the full process has two additional steps that *Figure 7.1* outlines below:

Figure 7.1: Risk assessment process

The *track* and *document* steps were added to the existing three steps that were covered in *Chapter 5*—that is, *risk identification*, *risk analysis*, and *update plan*—to round out the process. Each of these steps is part of the assessment cycle, which is a continuous process throughout the project. We'll discuss each of the five steps here.

Risk identification

In *Chapter 4*, we briefly discussed methods to identify risks. These included using a company risk register that contains all past risks from previously completed projects to find risks that fit scenarios in the current project. As an example of a previous project's risk being useful, a project that had risks related to networking communication would be of interest to the *Mercury* program to ensure the same risks are accounted for.

In the absence of a risk register, or in combination with it, working with your stakeholders and project team to discuss potential risks is a good approach as well. The more experience you have to draw upon, the easier it is to identify risks and solve complex issues. Every program that I have run in the last 6 years or so has started with a kickoff meeting with all stakeholders. This is a standardized process in most process management styles, including PMP. The reason for this is because of the valuable information you get from collaborating early on with everyone involved in the project or program. The earlier a potential problem is identified, the easier it is to address. Outside of my professional work, one of my favorite examples of stakeholder collaboration is from the show *MythBusters*. The main hosts, Jamie Hyneman and Adam Savage, were able to see the same problem from different perspectives and find ways to move forward. The show often showcased Jamie and Adam pointing out problems with each other's designs via their perspectives and experiences. In the show's introduction sequence, the narrator mentions that between the two hosts, they have 30 years of combined experience. This is why multiple points of view can be so powerful. Even if two people have each only been in the industry for 15 years, each of their experiences is unique and you get a combined 30 years of knowledge to draw upon. The more people you have, the larger the pool of knowledge.

In this type of scenario, **tribal knowledge**, also called **institutional memory**, can be extremely powerful as it allows for quicker execution within the organization. Tribal knowledge is made up of both documented or documentable knowledge, known as **explicit knowledge**, as well as **implicit knowledge**, which is a person's experience and hunches that can only be conveyed through hands-on discussion and instruction. Tribal knowledge is well understood within the organization and acts like muscle memory, meaning less time searching for documentation for a process or policy and more time executing.

Risk analysis

Searching through registers and discussing with stakeholders and colleagues can lead to a list of risks that need to be analyzed. As with most processes, this can happen organically while having the discussions or it may happen separately.

This analysis is where you determine the level of impact the risk would have on the project should it occur, as well as the probability of the risk happening. Both of these are somewhat subjective and will vary from situation to situation. The same risk that was present in an older project may not have the same level of impact or probability on a new project. For instance, let's say the risk was related to code deployment delays due to a congested service pipeline. As time passed, the reasons the congestion occurred may have improved or worsened. Also, there may be more or fewer code changes for that pipeline than in the older project. Both of these will change the impact the risk has, as well as the probability of it occurring.

During analysis, you might decide to add project tasks to dive deeper into the risk to understand it more. For instance, if you have a risk of using a new framework that your team doesn't know about, you might add a deep-dive task to do a quick proof of concept or find training and get everyone signed up for it, or both.

Some risks may have inherent metrics that you can use to track impact and probability. In the pipeline example, there could be deployment counts and failure rates. Combine this with the number of tasks requiring code changes in that pipeline and you can reliably apply a formula to estimate risk impact and probability.

Other risks will not have metrics or will be indirect correlations, such as developer attrition rates. You can apply an average attrition rate to assess the likelihood of losing a developer, but statistics are about long-term data trends and do not predict immediate behavior.

Updating the plan

In *Chapter 4*, I listed the *plan* step as updating the project plan. Though true for that example, you can't update your project plan unless you have also planned what you intend to do about the risk itself! The risk strategy is often referred to as risk mitigation, but mitigation is only one of four different strategies. I've heard some call the risk strategy *risk optimization* since you are optimizing the strategy for the risk. Each of the strategies has different names, depending on the system, tool, or methodology you use. These are the names that I use:

- **Avoidance**: This is when you create a plan to avoid the risk. For instance, if there is a risk involving a faulty piece of equipment or a vendor with a poor reputation, then avoiding the use of that equipment or vendor is your strategy to avoid the risk. This type of risk is likely one that comes up more often than you would initially think, but you often organically deal with the risk and then dismiss it.

This is true for the example of a known bad vendor. It would likely not even cross your mind to use them because you already know that they aren't a good fit. In these cases, the risk may never make it to your risk log or subsequent company register, but the risk was real and avoided. In some specialties, such as security threat modeling, these are cataloged and still listed in the project risk log, even if they are completely avoided from the start!

- **Mitigation**: This is when you allow the risk to happen—or it just does—and you minimize the impact that the risk has. For instance, let's say that a risk can lead to a 4-week delay in delivering a milestone. You might be able to mitigate the risk by **crashing** (also called **swarming in agile methodologies**) the remaining tasks with additional resources to reduce the delay to 2 weeks. The result of the realized risk causes you to introduce a countermeasure to soften the impact. This strategy is reactionary in nature but is also a good balance for some companies between over-preparing for the unknown and not planning at all. This may also be a good choice when the probability is relatively low.

- **Transference**: This is where you transfer the risk to another group. This may sound cruel or even lazy, but it might make the most sense depending on the risk. If there is a risk of delays in development due to a team not knowing a framework well, contracting a group that knows the framework may be a better course of action. By hiring another team, the risk of delay becomes their risk. This option may not always be available, depending on the company and their willingness to contract out or the expertise existing elsewhere. It's also worth noting that transference may move a risk out of a specific project, but it would likely still exist at the program level. Or, it may introduce another parallel risk in that your project team now has a dependency on a vendor.

- **Acceptance**: This is an option when there is no way to avoid, mitigate, or transfer the risk. Sometimes, the project will just need to take the hit and adjust timelines to compensate. In some cases, there may be ways to avoid, mitigate, or transfer, but the cost to do so is greater than the impact the risk will have on the project. Sometimes, *failure is the best course of action*.

Risk strategy selection

Each risk can have multiple strategies. In the example given for mitigation, you can also have an avoidance strategy where you replan your tasks in a way to add a buffer to timelines. In such cases, the strategy you choose depends on the current state of the risk. If you attempted to avoid it but the avoidance didn't work, for example, then the mitigation strategy would need to be used. If the mitigation can't happen because resourcing isn't available to crash when needed, then acceptance may be the only course. So, it is important to look at each risk and see all the different strategies that you might be able to employ and how they may fall back on one another. Of course, weigh this with the company's appetite for planning, as mentioned earlier; this is likely why many companies seem to prefer the mitigation route as a middle-of-the-road approach to risk planning.

We've analyzed the risk and updated our plan; now we need to track and document it!

Risk tracking

Once you have identified, analyzed, and planned for risks, you need to track them. Risk tracking is cyclical and can lead to re-analyzing, identifying, and planning on the fly as circumstances change in the project. Their impact may decrease as the project gets closer to completion, or the probability may go up as various factors play out—such as attrition causing reduced resourcing.

Also, risks may come to a point where they are avoided or can no longer impact the project. New risks may also come up as the project evolves. For instance, a security flaw could be published that requires internal systems to be updated immediately. This could result in a temporary standstill of all work in a particular area while the vulnerability is being addressed. Though some generic buffer can (and should) be added to unknowns such as this, the risk was still discovered during the life of the project and needs to be added, analyzed, and tracked.

When analyzing the risk and planning for it, you need to include some way of measuring or controlling the risk. Essentially, you need a way to see the risk materializing ahead of time so you can act as quickly as possible. This is why we must continually track for the emergence of risks. For the risk of a stuck deployment pipeline I discussed earlier, you might watch the pipeline health metrics such as the number of deployments per day, the number of changes being merged, and how long it takes a change to make it to production. These metrics will give you an idea of the health of the pipeline and give you a chance to act before the risk materializes.

Expanding on this risk, you can also look at the launch dates of other projects that are committing changes to the same pipeline to see if there are particular dates that are at higher risk than others. All of these actions are taken while tracking risks to help avoid the risks altogether or to be ready to counteract them when ready.

Documenting the progress

As you are tracking, any updates should be included in your communication plan. Changes to risks should be clearly stated so that there are no unexpected changes in status due to a newly impending risk being realized.

Any changes to strategies, closed risks, or newly added risks should be well documented in the project risk log and status updates, and in the company's risk register upon project closure. Documentation is how you build institutional memory that others can rely on in future projects, including yourself! Even if your company doesn't have a risk register, I'd suggest keeping track of your own for future reference and maybe making it available to others. Any additional information from even one other user of the register will improve the chances of success, so don't ignore logging just because the company doesn't have something in place already.

From personal experience, I can say that relying on your own memory to think of risks can only work for so long. Human memory requires stimulation to keep thoughts fresh enough to call upon, and as you add in more and more project experience, the ability to recall specific instances gets harder and harder. This is true when you stay on the same team for a long time as the earlier projects begin to fade. But this is also true when you switch teams and is usually much more sudden and impactful. The brain is great at forgetting things that are no longer useful, and switching to a different team or company is a quick way to forget previous projects and day-to-day nuance from the previous team. Keeping a risk register reduces the chance of forgetting about a risk and, often, the written risk will trigger the memory for you in the moment.

Now that we have looked at the risk assessment process in more detail, let's discuss the tools used in risk management.

Tools and methodologies

For a company risk register, some portfolio management tools will provide this functionality. In the absence of these, using whatever centralized documentation tools you have available to capture risks for future reference is useful.

Any project management software has some ability to manage risks at the project level, usually in the form of a risk scorecard and table entry. The scorecard helps you identify the **risk score** or severity of a risk on a fixed scale. The higher the risk, the more closely it must be tracked, as it will likely cause some level of issue. This is part of the typical *PMP Risk Log* system and is the most common for general use.

There are many different scales in use for risk scores. *Table 7.1* shows the scale and scorecard I prefer to use, where **Risk Score** is the sum of **Probability** and **Impact**:

Probability (Score)	Impact (Score)	Risk Score (Score)
Low (1)	Low (1)	Low (2)
Medium (2)	Low (1)	Low (3)
High (3)	Low (1)	Medium (4)
Low (1)	Medium (2)	Low (3)
Medium (2)	Medium (2)	Medium (4)
High (3)	Medium (2)	Medium (5)
Low (1)	High (3)	Medium (4)
Medium (2)	High (3)	Medium (5)
High (3)	High (3)	High (6)

Table 7.1: Risk scorecard

I use the same three-tier scale across both impact and probability, as well as the resulting score. I have found that a four- or five-tiered scale is too nuanced and can lead to nitpicking the analysis of the probability and impact. The difference between *High* and *Very High* is just too subjective. In contrast, the jump from *Low* to *Medium* or *Medium* to *High* is a bit more abrupt when your scale only allows for three levels, and the clarity of whether something is one of two things is easier to classify than whether something is *Medium*, *High*, or *Very High*. A similar strategy is often used in agile sprint planning when the team is collectively estimating the tasks in their backlog. Instead of a linear scale of 1 through 10, the first few Fibonacci numbers are used (1, 2, 3, 5, 8, and 13). This is to remove some debate of what a 3 versus a 4 would be and to add in some critical thought when you need to jump from 8 to 13, as you'll need to have a reason to make that jump.

In the table, I've included the numbers next to the tiered values to help illustrate that the resulting risk score, the right-hand column, is merely the sum of the probability and impact ranks. The reason for a sum is to remove any unconscious bias you may have in assessing the risk score. It's easier to be honest about two discrete scores of how likely something is to happen, and then separately ask what the impact of a risk would be. Then the final risk is a sum of the two direct scores.

The risk score correlates to the amount of attention a particular risk may warrant from you. If the risk score is low, then either the impact or probability (or both) is low, and not much attention is needed to keep track of it. However, for a high-risk score, the impact is either high or it is almost inevitable that the risk will be realized, meaning that you will need to be ready to act upon your strategies and likely need to watch the risk closely.

To examine this a little more closely, I've included a few high-level, first-pass risks associated with the *Mercury* program in *Table 7.2*:

ID	Risk	Probability	Impact	Strategy
1	Cross-platform tooling issues	High	High	Avoidance: Upfront training Mitigation: Resource crashing Acceptance: Shift timelines to account for delays
2	Tight testing timeline	Medium	Medium	Mitigation: Shift timelines to allow for buffer Acceptance: Shift timelines to account for delays
3	App store approval delays	Low	Low	Acceptance: Shift timelines to account for delays

Table 7.2: Risk log for the Mercury program

In this risk log, I do not include the actual risk score as it is derivative of the probability and impact. It also saves space for this illustration. However, depending on your stakeholders and status audience, including the calculated risk score for clarity's sake may be helpful.

For the first risk of cross-platform tooling issues, I have included three strategies to control the risk. I've put them in the order in which they should be acted upon for the best results in the project timeline. If possible, the first strategy should be avoidance and, with this risk, opting to plan for training upfront can keep the risk from being realized. If that isn't enough and the risk starts to show up through delays in tooling work in a sprint, then immediately start to mitigate by adding additional resourcing. If this doesn't work, then adjusting the due date may be the only recourse you have left.

The ability to see multiple strategies for a risk is a key quality I look for during interviews. TPMs should be able to use every strategy at their disposal to solve a problem. To that end, this list isn't exhaustive and the exact situation you are in can change what strategies are available to you. Do your best to find them all and note them down.

For the second risk, I included a mitigation and acceptance strategy. Though both wouldn't necessarily be utilized, depending on the situation when the risk is realized, a different approach may be appropriate. In this case, the mitigation and acceptance strategies are essentially the same—the strategy you use depends on whether the risk is caught early or late. This isn't always the case but was appropriate for this risk. From a planning perspective, ensuring testing has enough room for iteration is the best course of action if you have the space in your timeline to make it work.

The last risk is low impact and low probability, so it is a good candidate for acceptance. A quick search of iOS App Store approval rates shows that they sit at 60% approval within 24 hours and the outlier approval approaches 5 days. This is a small enough impact and probability that the shift in timelines is acceptable. This could be avoided by adding enough buffer to account for the edge cases on approvals as well.

When risk assessment needs to be quick

When timelines are tight, there are methods to use to ensure that risk assessment is not skipped over entirely. Though there are likely to be gaps in analysis when rushed—as the risk in and of itself should be cataloged—capturing some risks is better than running the project completely blind to what may come at you down the road.

The risk register is a real time saver if it is searchable using multiple criteria. The more you can filter the results, the more relevant they will be to your specific needs. The probability and impact change depending on the project context, so they would need to be updated, but the identification can be largely copied and pasted. Then, a quick iteration to determine the risk score is needed. Often, the strategies to solve a particular risk can be reused if the risks are specific enough to the situation. Again, peculiarities in the exact project may require some tweaking but it's better than working from scratch. It's also a good way to get your mind on the task, which can help you think of new risks that aren't in the register because you are focusing on the problem.

I've found that in cases where a fully indexed risk register isn't available, even risks that are grouped into larger thematic buckets can be a good shortcut. Think of this as adding labels or tags to each item, such as *networking* or *cross-platform coordination*. Even project types can be useful categories. For instance, if you have an ecosystem with multiple data flows, based on the type of transaction taking place, each transaction type or use case could have its own set of risks that are common within that use case. The same refinements would apply here to the probability and impact, as well as strategies.

Lastly, doing a working session with stakeholders to talk through requirements as a single pass can provide a lot of value in a short amount of time. Build in time during the session to identify, analyze, and plan the risk strategies; then, you can update the overall project plan for cases where avoidance was the best strategy to follow.

Driving clarity in risk management is your responsibility as a TPM, and like most aspects of project management, it involves the help of others. In the case of risk identification and analysis, the more people that can contribute to your success, the better.

So far, we've discussed some aspects of risk management that you will see, some of which exist regardless of the industry you are in. Next, let's look specifically at the type of risks you will encounter in the tech industry and use these scenarios to drive further clarity into the *Mercury* program.

Managing risks in a technology landscape

There are various aspects of software and hardware development that are common in the industry but less so in other professions. These relate to the development process itself. Let's take a look at a typical **software development life cycle (SDLC)** and discuss the common risks that arise at each stage:

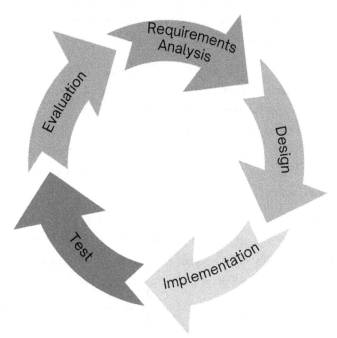

Figure 7.2: The SDLC

The **SDLC** specifies the series of steps or processes involved in software development. This cycle can be adapted to any style of development, including waterfall and agile methodologies. The steps may vary or happen in mini-cycles within the larger cycle, but the steps are still present. Let's explore each one.

We've already talked about the *requirements phase* in various forms in this book. In general, the focus of the requirements phase is to reduce the overall risk by bringing clarity to the requirements. The clearer the requirements, the less room there will be for scope creep in low-level designs and their implementation. In that sense, the main risk in this step is not driving clarity in the project requirements.

The *design phase* is where the high-level and low-level designs are drafted based on the requirements. This process can uncover technical issues with the requirements that were not apparent at first. Aspects that are specific to the technologies being used in a service, or how that service interacts with other services, will come out here in the API definitions, architecture strategies, and release strategy. For **distributed systems**, also known as **Software-as-a-Service (SaaS)** architectures, aspects such as latency and availability play a role in changing or adding requirements and increasing development time, as systems often have specific latency targets and availability goals. If your organization is in this type of environment, these risks should always be listed per your company's practices. While getting estimates for tasks in the requirements phase, you can ask specifically about hot topics such as latency to ensure they are considered in the estimates given. If there is a set process involved in addressing latency at your company, adding a buffer or separate task to account for it may also be an option.

The *implementation phase* is where the code or hardware is built based on the designs. Engineer overhead should be considered in this phase, but this is where a lot of that buffer will be taken up. So, if the team is new or you are new, this could be a risk to watch out for. Track your buffer and constantly rebase your plan as the buffer is taken up. Rebasing doesn't mean you automatically shift your dates, but it gives you an idea of the current trajectory, which will help you decide on the best course of action. Dates may need to be adjusted or milestones crashed if the buffer is insufficient. We'll discuss two specific risks that may crop up here that the design process may not have caught.

The effort of deploying code is often not factored into the effort estimates from developers. During standups, I often talk about the concept of a task being *done, done, done*. In that, I mean that a task, or bit of code, is not truly done until the code is written (first *done*), it is reviewed and approved (second *done*), and finally, the code has made its way to the production fleet and been tested (the final *done*). Knowing your **time to production** (the amount of time post-code-completion that exists until the code reaches production) is a good metric to ensure you are adding enough buffer time. Also, any temporary stresses on the deployment pipelines should be accounted for. As there are always *unknown unknowns*, tracking this as a risk is prudent.

Another risk that isn't always accounted for during implementation is security certifications that need to take place. Every company's **Information Security (InfoSec)** team will have different requirements, depending on the risk aversion of their organization and the nature of the data they work with. These certifications can take up a significant amount of time, depending on what data your service needs to handle, store, and vend. A new service typically takes longer than recertifying an existing service.

The timing of these activities should be known in the company and can be referenced. Regardless of how prepared you are for this process, it is an unknown that is out of your direct control—the *InfoSec* analysis may find an issue your team didn't foresee and delay the process further than planned. Treat this as you would working with a vendor; there are parts of this process for which you are relying on another team and they might have fewer reviewers than they typically would or other reviews that are taking longer than expected. This is a higher risk for a new service as the process is longer.

The *testing phase* is where a lot of the *unknown unknowns* cause issues. These can be problems that only robust testing was able to find, usually in edge cases for your software or service. The level of test framework maturity you work with will determine the level of risk involved here. If you are testing a self-contained software package, then high-test coverage can suffice to greatly reduce the chance of undetected defects. In larger, distributed systems, there may be software states or transactions that are so vast in number as to make full test coverage impossible. Also, when adding new features, there are more chances for unknowns since what you are adding is new. These circumstances all add together to determine the level of risk you may face during the testing step.

The *evaluation phase* (also known as the evolution, iteration, or feedback step) is where you plan the next iteration of your product or service based on feedback from users and stakeholders. Though your product managers should know their product well, there is no better source of feedback than from users, whether the users are internal to the company or external users after release. Products on a release cycle, where new versions of the product are released on a relatively set schedule, will include various testing phases here, including pilots, private previews, and public previews. Even once released for general availability, there is a way for users to provide feedback, either written or in the form of telemetry data like crash reports or use statistics. There are no inherent risks to this stage, though it should include risk analysis while prioritizing which feedback to act upon in the next cycle. This would be a form of high-level analysis; for instance, the feedback may be a good idea but still somewhat vague. This can cause scope creep during the requirements and design phases if the requirement isn't sufficiently clear enough to transform into requirements.

Cross-step risks also exist within the tech industry. These impact your resource availability due to factors outside of the project. Depending on the company and team that you are working with, on-call rotations can impact developer availability. Though this should have been accounted for during planning, things such as sickness or impromptu time off can shift the on-call schedules and cause a developer to be on call more than expected to cover for others.

Another cross-step risk that occurs is also related to security: mandatory software updates. This can come in the form of mundane version updates away from versions that are leaving their support cycle. Though these upgrades are well documented, a project may run into a use case where it can't move forward without the upgrade and needs to take time to do so. Operational teams can help reduce this burden, but upgrades aren't always caught and can be a risk to consider.

Another version of a cross-step security risk comes when an industry-wide vulnerability has been discovered that requires immediate attention. In December 2021, the *Log4j* exploit, referred to as *Log4Shell*, caused industry-wide panic as firms rushed to patch all *Log4j* instances in their services. Naturally, this was an *all-hands-on-deck* situation that diverted a lot of development hours into deploying the patch. There's no arguing, no negotiation of resourcing or payback—projects are just impacted at that moment. These are hard to predict and calling out a risk like this is akin to *crying wolf*. However, it is good to know that these can and do happen. A good amount of buffer can alleviate the impact if everything else is going well in the project. The good news here, if any, is that most stakeholders are understanding of delays caused by industry-wide catastrophes.

Technical risks in the Mercury program

Each project within the *Mercury* program will have technical risks, as will the program itself. We've already discussed the idea of creating a *P2P* subsystem that is shared across the different platforms. As this is cross-project work that creates project dependencies for every project, this would be considered a program-level risk. A separate project may be spun up to handle the subsystem, but the risk merely shifts from the program to that project.

To introduce the subsystem, you can use a cross-platform development environment to organize the shared code and make it easier to utilize in each **operating system** (**OS**). This platform was called out in *Table 7.2* as *Risk ID 1—Cross-platform tooling issues*. *Table 7.3* provides clarity on this risk by breaking it up into multiple risks:

ID	Risk	Probability	Impact	Strategy
1	Cross-platform tooling issues	High	High	Avoidance: Upfront training Mitigation: Resource crashing Acceptance: Shift timelines to account for delays
1.1	New **Integrated Desktop Environment** (**IDE**)	High	High	Avoidance: Training on a new IDE

| 1.2 | New coding language for some teams | High | High | Avoidance: Training on a new language |
| 1.3 | Cross-team collaboration | High | Medium | Avoidance: Daily standups, co-location, or chat rooms |

Table 7.3: Cross-platform IDE risk analysis

Three additional risks were added in the same way you would break down a user story into smaller sub-tasks. I used outline notation to denote that they are related and expanded upon the original risk. This list is not exhaustive of the risks that could occur cross-platform but is used to illustrate diving deeper into a risk to add clarity.

Two of the three risks relate to dealing with new technologies, both the IDE as well as possibly a new programming language. For instance, if the iOS developers are used to using the **Swift** programming language, there may be a learning curve to switch to a *MonoDevelop*-supported language such as C#. This task may be easier for an Android developer who is used to using Java as both **Java** and **C#** are C-based languages and Swift is not. So, the risk to each project may have a different impact and probability.

The last risk is a risk that occurs anytime you have cross-team or cross-project collaboration as this introduces additional communication. The world today is arguably much better at collaborating across different groups (whether that's different teams, companies, or locations) since the pandemic forced new habits. The risk still exists, especially when collaborating with a team you are unfamiliar with, as there is always a **storming phase** where the different groups are working out how to best communicate with each other.

So far, we've learned about the risk assessment process and the cyclical nature of assessing and planning for risks, as well as some unique risks faced in the tech industry. We then demonstrated risk assessment through an example from the *Mercury* program. Next, we'll explore how risk management differs between the project and program levels.

Exploring the differences between a project and a program

Risk management, as a process, does not vary between a project and a program. Instead of thinking about cross-task risks at the project level, you must think about cross-project risks at the program level. Risk registers, risk logs, and scorecards are utilized in both cases.

As for the tools, each one provides risk management forms and templates at the project level. Tracking risks at the program level may require some workarounds in popular tools. Creating a program project within the program to track these concerns is one such way. Transferring risks down to the projects can also work, though this will include some duplication. Depending on the level of cross-project communication, each project team knowing about every risk that impacts them is a way to reduce instances of risks being missed.

When planning the project composition of a program, one aspect to look at is how the project structures can create risk. Cross-project dependencies require a higher amount of coordination than task dependencies within a project.

Figure 7.3 shows program milestones with dependencies between them. We'll look at how this division of work can create efficiencies as well as risks:

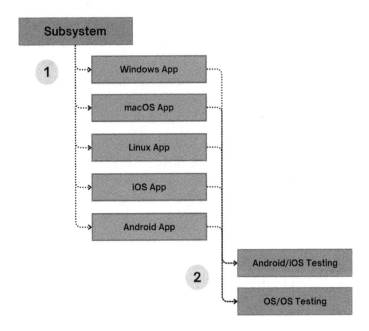

Figure 7.3: Cross-project risks

In this example, the subsystem for the *P2P* network is a separate milestone and is tracked outside of the OS projects. By doing this, we remove duplicative effort across all five OS projects, but we introduce the same number of cross-project dependencies on that subsystem, as indicated by label **1** in *Figure 7.3*. If the subsystem is delayed, it will delay all five subsequent projects.

In label **2**, we can see another dependency that exists between all five OS projects. As each OS needs to test interoperability with all other OSes, this can lead to multiple cross-project delays if testing goes wrong in one OS project.

For instance, if the *Windows Rollout Project* is delayed, then all testing with Windows is delayed, which can delay all other projects as well. Some shifting of tests can reduce the impact of the delay by testing the integrations that are readily assuming they weren't all being run in parallel, or Windows could be completely separated in scope to allow the other platforms to move forward and launch Windows at a later date if more time were needed.

As you can see, just as we would look for and analyze cross-task risks at the project level, we'd do the same at the program level. Each of these risks may be tracked at the project level but should also be monitored at the program level.

Summary

In this chapter, we learned how to drive clarity in risk management through the steps of the risk assessment process. We discussed the different risk strategies available and how tracking risks is a constant process where the strategy that's utilized to address risk may change over time. Then, we discussed some key risk categories that show up in the tech industry. We also dove deeper into the *Mercury* program by driving clarity in terms of the identified risks. Lastly, we looked at how risk management differs in scope from the program to project levels and used the *Mercury* program to illustrate how a program decision can both remove and create risk based on the project composition of the program.

In *Chapter 8*, we'll close our deep dive into key management areas by focusing on stakeholder management. We'll learn how to drive clarity with stakeholders through various stakeholder processes, such as communication plans and status reporting. We'll look at what makes stakeholder management unique in the tech industry and the challenges a TPM will face.

Additional resources

You can find templates for requirements tables, task tables, work breakdown structures, and project buffer matrices in the GitHub repo related to this book. Please check the Preface for the GitHub link.

Join our book's Discord space

Join our Discord community to meet like-minded people and learn alongside more than 5000 members at:

https://packt.link/sKmQa

8

Stakeholder Management

In this chapter, we'll discuss the stakeholder management process, right from determining who your stakeholders are, all the way to building a comprehensive communication plan. We'll discuss what is different about stakeholder management in the tech industry and explore how the communication plan should differ from program to project.

We'll dive into stakeholder management in the following sections:

- Driving clarity in stakeholder management
- Managing stakeholders in a technology landscape
- Exploring the differences between a project and a program

Let's get started!

Driving clarity in stakeholder management

Stakeholder management is the art of managing expectations. Each stakeholder has a different set of needs for the project, and their point of view is based on their personal experiences as well as their expectations for the project. The **communication plan** helps you draft ways to communicate across the entire span of needs of your stakeholders. Knowing how to communicate effectively is the key to driving clarity to (and with) your stakeholders.

There are two aspects to setting up a good communication plan: defining the types of communication you need and discovering who your stakeholders are. We'll cover the different types of communication first because this is usually done only once in the company or team and is reused from project to project, with only minor modifications. These are static templates, whereas the list of stakeholders will vary from project to project. Once the stakeholders have been identified, the communication type templates may require minor tweaks to suit the needs of the specific stakeholders. You *could* do this in the opposite order, finding stakeholders and then defining your plan, but I prefer the consistency of a communication template. It ensures that, from project to project, your communication approach and formatting, styles, and cadences are consistent, with only minor changes based on individual circumstances.

Table 8.1 lists the different communication types that are common across the industry, along with examples of recurrences, owners, and distribution methods:

Type	Goal	Recurrence	Owner	Distribution
Stand-up	Day-to-day collaboration and unblocking progress	Daily	SDE Lead	Sprint board, in-person updates, or email progress updates
Status update	Milestone-level project status	Weekly (*every Monday*)	Project TPM	Email
Leadership review	Leadership-level program status with key insights relevant to leadership	Monthly (*3rd Wednesday of every month*)	TPM Lead	Meeting and email
Senior leadership review	Senior leadership-level program status	Quarterly (*3rd Wednesday of the 1st month per quarter*)	PM-T Lead	Meeting and email

Table 8.1: Example communication plan

The *names* of the communication types listed here may not be the same at every company, but the goals of each type exist everywhere. As called out in *Chapter 1*, there are some instances where the written status report isn't used at all; in those cases, the distribution method may not include sending an email, but the intent of the communication is largely the same. Each communication type satisfies project information that stakeholders at different levels of involvement or seniority will want to see. We'll cover each communication type in more detail in the upcoming sections.

Stand-up

The stand-up type is used in agile and non-agile settings where regular syncs are needed—often with software developers.

This practice can be seen outside of the tech industry where daily coordination across a large team is required, such as in construction. The workers get together, and the foreman or boss goes over the assignments of each worker and the objectives for the day. In the software context, the stand-up allows the developers to talk about what they did since the previous stand-up, what they are going to do that day, and raise any blockers that they need help navigating. The exact protocols used depend on the methodology being practiced, so I won't go into detail on the specifics, but I have included a book to read on scrum practices in the *Further reading* section at the end of this chapter if you are interested. In all cases, the takeaway for the TPM is knowing what the developers are actively engaged in and getting an up-to-date look at any blockers that they may have. Regardless of the presence of a *scrum master* or *development manager*, the TPM's role here is to facilitate unblocking the development team, either directly or indirectly, by getting the right people involved.

Should a TPM run a stand-up?

No. Though the reality is never quite that simple. The way I answer this is to look at what value the TPM role brings to a project or team. Our ability to bridge the technical and business worlds and dive deep into the technical solution while understanding the broader business landscape around us is where we are the most impactful. Running a stand-up doesn't fit into this key value position and, instead, focuses our attention too much on the day-to-day issues facing our team. We certainly need to be present to help unblock but the stand-up should survive and thrive without us being present. A scrum master should be present, whether in the form of a dedicated person or a rotating position amongst the team, to ensure the proper function of the stand-up.

In reality though, there are times when a TPM may need to run a stand-up, and in the short term, this is okay. For instance, when we decided to introduce scrum to our development team over a decade ago, I acted as scrum master across 3 sprint teams for several months until the team was comfortable with the process and we were able to slowly transition the meeting to others. It helped that I was an entry-level TPM at the time, so this was well within my strengths. As a Principal TPM, or even as a Senior TPM, this would be wasted time as my strengths and value-add to the team would be on more strategic opportunities.

Don't be afraid to help out when the team needs it, but also don't be afraid to push back when the value is no longer there for you to be running stand-ups.

The stand-up can also help you craft the status updates as you have the most current task progress as well as projected work for some amount of time (sprint, week, or other, depending on the development methodology). Depending on the team culture or the number of projects you are driving, you may not attend the stand-up, but an update should be produced in some form, either by updating a sprint board, or a written status summary from the developers.

Status update

Most projects will have some form of a status update, either in a written format or via a status meeting. The purpose here is to give a health check on the project at the moment in time with some projection as to the overall health. The focus is on current and upcoming milestones, blockers, and risks with a high-risk score (in other words, risks that have some chance of being realized in the near future). To this end, this type of report tends to be more technical and is meant for the stakeholders who are actively working on the project itself in order to keep them apprised of what is going on around them.

The ownership of the status update is on the TPM driving the project and will include input from all stakeholders (developers, managers, PM-Ts, and so on) who are actively engaged in the project.

In cases where the development managers are not actively engaged in the stand-up, this is a place where they can see how their team is performing and gives them a chance to respond to any delays in a timely manner. This works well for vendors too, where the vendor's management team can be kept up to date with any impacts their team is having on the overall progress.

Pre-communication of status issues

For all communications that involve some level of status dissemination to stakeholders, it is extremely important to be upfront about any issues you are going to raise. This needs to happen *before* the status is sent out so that the impacted stakeholders can have a chance to respond or be prepared to answer any questions. It also helps ensure that your relationship with the stakeholders remains healthy and they don't feel like you are setting them up for failure.

Leadership review

The **leadership review** (**LR**) is a status report whose audience is the leadership. As such, the focus isn't on the day-to-day work or issues but on the longer-term progress of the project, along with risks, issues, and milestones that have a greater impact on the project goal.

These updates often happen with less frequency than regular status updates as the long-term health of the project won't typically change so often to warrant a more frequent update. At Amazon, this review is actually called a **Monthly Business Review** or **MBR.** The frequency of the review is in the name and the audience is implied. I've chosen to reverse that in this edition as the focus should be more on the audience and less on how often it is written.

Beyond these basics, some leadership reviews contain learnings, highlights, lowlights, and other thought-leader types of information. Because of this, the format of a leadership review tends to be company-specific, and sometimes leadership-specific, in the format and information that is expected to be included.

An example from the real world: *Listening to your stakeholders*

In the recent turmoil in the tech industry, there was a period where my senior leadership changed twice in a 9-month period. The leaders had drastically different styles in how they wanted leadership-level reviews to be formatted and even what information to include. This required rewriting leadership reviews that were written for one leader only to be thrown out by the next leader. Though this was very frustrating at the time, it is important to remember that stakeholders are only human and, as such, we each consume information in different ways. Leadership changes or even lower-level stakeholder changes will require you to adjust what you are saying and how you are saying it. This is part of why we are effective leaders.

In all cases though, the intent is to update leadership on the longer-term and broader health of the project.

The distribution of an LR is often in a meeting and may include an email, depending on the format of the report that is used in the meeting. Some companies thrive on PowerPoint or similar slide-based tools to ingest this type of information, which wouldn't be conducive to an email, while others utilize a written report that can be used in a meeting as well as sent out.

Though this is often a monthly review, this doesn't mean that the issues that surfaced are sitting and waiting to be discussed in a monthly forum. Any item that is new in this review should be resolved and is merely being reported if it is important enough for leadership to know about. If your team is blocked, work to unblock them as quickly as possible, and if you need leadership input, don't wait!

The leadership review is usually owned by the TPM, although co-ownership with a development manager, PM, or PM-T is also a possibility. This depends on the company culture and what type of resources the project has. Your company may prefer the PM-T to own this, but if one isn't assigned to the project, it might fall back to the TPM to fill in. *Filling in organizational gaps is part of what a TPM does best!*

Senior leadership review

The **senior leadership review (SLR)** builds on top of the leadership review with a target audience of senior leadership. Not every project will have a need for an SLR, as it depends on the level of visibility the project has at that level in the company. If there is interest at the senior leadership level, a dedicated communication forum is needed to convey details with the right context.

A typical cadence for an SLR is once a quarter. In this case, the SLR combines all LRs from the quarter (or the previous quarter, depending on timing) into a single report with an emphasis on the end goals and major steps, victories, and misses in the time since the last SLR. When combining these reports, not all of the lowlights, highlights, and key insights will be relevant to senior leadership. As such, it is important to think about what is important to this audience to remove noisy updates that don't contribute to the end goal.

As with the leadership review, the SLR isn't a place to surface problems that warrant earlier engagement. At Amazon, there are issues called *Hotly Debated Topics* where consensus cannot be reached amongst the team leadership, and guidance is needed on how to proceed. These aren't blocking issues usually or they are brought up early enough to not cause any impact by waiting for a review. The same guidance applies here as for the LR–if the project is blocked, don't wait for a review to get it resolved.

The SLR is owned by whoever owns the LR–again, in most cases, that is the TPM. There are times though when this can shift due to office politics or company norms. If the only people who get to meet with senior leadership are other senior leaders and the TPM isn't at that level, then the TPM's Director or equivalent might take ownership. Though, in reality, the TPM will own the document, just not present the document!

Decide on your narrative

The key to a good report, regardless of the audience, is to decide what your narrative is going to be. Even if you don't write the report using a narrative frame, knowing what you are trying to convey will help you decide the right information to include or even how to frame the information you present.

Communication timing

You may notice that each of these communication types builds upon the previous. The status report builds on the stand-ups, the leadership review builds on the status report, and the senior leadership review builds on the leadership reviews. Though this may feel like a lot of reports, with good timing, it's not as much as it seems. The key is to time the spacing of each to allow for the collation of information into the next communication level up. I drafted an example in *Table 8.1* where the weekly status reports are sent out on Tuesdays and the leadership review is on the third Wednesday of each month. The third week allows for the weekly status report to be sent on Tuesday and then added to the leadership review before it is sent the next day. Since the senior leadership review is a combination of previous leadership reviews, those are on the same day of the month as the leadership review, and every third leadership review will instead be a senior leadership review. This allows you to focus on the narrative and less on wrangling the data out of your team.

This is just one way to handle timing and it will vary depending on project needs, and the behavior and expectations of your stakeholders. However, I try to not send status updates on Fridays or Mondays. On Fridays, people will miss or gloss over the status before heading out for the long weekend, and in many countries, holidays land on a Monday, meaning you may not be in the office. Sending it on Monday would mean that you would frequently have to send it on the next business day. Even if you stay on top of communication and let the stakeholders know, it will still feel inconsistent, so it is better to avoid this. These are personal guidelines that I feel are useful, but I have come across teams that require a specific day for status reports to be sent, so you'll need to take team expectations into account.

Now that we've defined some potential communication channels and explored when and how often to use each, we need to decide which stakeholders will participate in which communication channel. To do this, we need to determine who the stakeholders are.

Defining your stakeholders

Finding your stakeholders and defining a communication plan is often depicted as a one-time, early-on process. However, like most processes in project and program management, it's cyclical. Depending on the size of the project or company, doing this all upfront may be achievable in a single pass; however, as the project size and company size increase, this becomes something that you revisit often as new stakeholders are discovered. Here are a few ways you can go about finding out who your stakeholders are.

Requirements gathering and refinement is an opportunity to not only understand your requirements better but also determine who the requirements impact or involve, such as the owner of a service.

Talking with the stakeholders you've already identified will give you a different perspective on the requirements and impact. They might know of clients from their services that are impacted by the changes they must make that you aren't aware of. Anyone impacted by the project, no matter how far down the chain or seemingly tangential they may seem, is a stakeholder.

During *project execution*, especially during low-level designs, details may come to light that highlight a stakeholder that you weren't aware of. New developers may also come on and off the project, requiring updates to your list.

The more you drive clarity in your requirements, designs, and risks, the more clarity you'll simultaneously drive in who your stakeholders are.

In your first 90 days on a project

Finding your stakeholders is one of the most important tasks to do in your first 90 days. Ask your manager for the list of need-to-know people and set up time with each one to meet and learn about them. Ask each one about other people that may be of interest to you. Find people that your team often works with, even if they aren't involved directly with your current project, to help build out your network of contacts.

Stakeholder list

In *Table 8.2*, I've drafted a partial stakeholder list for the *Mercury* program to get a better look at what information is essential in tracking your stakeholders:

Name	Alias	Department	Project	Role	Comm Type
Josh Teter	jteter	Mercury	All	TPM	N/A
Arun Ardibeddi	aardibeddi	Windows Team	Windows Rollout	SDM	LR
Danielle Wednesday	dwednesday	Windows Team	Windows Rollout	SDE Lead	Stand-up
Bob Belkan	bbelkan	Windows Team	Windows Rollout	SDE	Stand-up

Vicky Preston	vpreston	Desktop Devices Division	Windows, macOS, Linux	VP	SLR
Cassette Santoro	csantoro	Windows Team	Windows Rollout	TPM	LR
Artem Danyluk	adanyluk	Linux Team	Subsystem	TPM	SLR

Table 8.2: Example stakeholder list for the Mercury program

This stakeholder list gives me enough information to know who the stakeholders are and what role they play in the project. For my projects, I create stakeholder email distribution lists for various communication needs and use this stakeholder table to ensure the lists stay updated. If your company gives you the ability to create directory groups, this can be a good way to manage the project as you will have an email list as well as a group to tie various permissions to if needed.

This table is a snapshot of the Mercury program-level and Windows Rollout project-level stakeholders. For each stakeholder, I list which communication type they will be a part of. The table lists each project as well as the program so that each project TPM can see which stakeholders are important for them as well as how they overlap with other projects.

For instance, *Vicky Preston* is the VP of the desktop devices division, and her involvement is spread across the three desktop projects. So, the Windows TPM, *Cassette Santoro*, knows that *Vicky Preston* would be interested in any risks in the Windows project that may also impact those other desktop operating systems. The point is that your stakeholders can vary depending on the situation, sometimes by level (VPs may not care about a task blocker due to permission issues), but also in the context of the problem at hand and how far-reaching the problem may be.

The communication type ensures that you are sending the correct status updates to the correct people. For me, the status levels are inclusive of the levels below them in terms of who receives the update. This means my development team, who gets the status updates weekly, will also see and know how I am representing the project or program to the higher levels of management.

As people come and go from the project, requirements are refined, and designs are finalized, you will keep this table up to date to ensure the right people are informed and consulted throughout the project. For me, it's one of the most referenced project artifacts that I produce, as I look at the list on an almost daily basis.

Roles and responsibilities

Now that we have our stakeholders, the last component of the communication plan is the roles and responsibilities. Understanding the expectations of every stakeholder in the project is important to ensure work gets done smoothly. It also helps inform natural escalation paths if a task is delayed or otherwise in trouble. *Table 8.3* lists a portion of an example **roles and responsibilities** chart. Let's look at it in more detail:

Step ID	Name	TPM	SDM	PM-T	Lead SDE	SDE	Bus.
1	Requirements refinement	A	C	C	C	C	R
2	Project planning	R and A	C	C	C	C	C
3	High-level design	C	C	C	A	R	I
4	Low-level design	C	C	C	A	R	I
5	Sprint planning	R or A	R or A	I	C	C	I
6	Daily stand-ups	C	C	I	A	R	I
7	Status report	R and A	C	C	C	I	I
8	Leadership review	R	C	A	C	(I)	I

Table 8.3: RACI chart

There are many different styles of roles and responsibilities charts, and like the communication plan chart, this is often static as it refers to the role of the stakeholder, not the actual stakeholder. The style of chart used in this table is also referred to as a **RACI** (pronounced *race-y*) chart. It's an acronym for the roles represented: **responsible, accountable, consulted,** and **informed.**

The *responsible* role is where the person or group is responsible for the step or activity. It does not mean that they are the sole contributors or owners but are the ones responsible for its delivery. For instance, the TPM may be responsible for delivering the MBR (*Step 8*) but will receive input from the rest of the project team.

The *accountable* role is similar to the responsible role, but the accountable party is who ultimately deals with the consequences of something not getting done. In this example chart, the *Lead SDE* is accountable for the daily stand-ups – a sort of scrum master role.

They are where questions go if a stand-up does not occur or if there are questions or concerns. Another example to differentiate responsible and accountable is that the TPM is accountable for delivering a milestone on time, but the developers are responsible for doing the development to complete the milestone.

Tip on varying responsibilities

There can be cases where a single person is both responsible and accountable for a single deliverable. As *Table 8.3* shows, the TPM is often both responsible and accountable for the project plan as well as the status report.

In other cases, the responsibility may shift depending on the project size or team dynamics. In cases where a service team runs its own sprint, the SDM may be accountable for the deliverables and the TPM is responsible for requesting that the correct tasks are worked on and delivered. In some cases, the TPM may be running the sprint and is both responsible and accountable.

For every project, ensure that you discuss the roles and responsibilities with the team. Don't assume that everyone knows what their role is just because they've worked with you or on the team for previous projects. Especially for the roles that are adjacent to the TPM, the exact responsibilities can shift across the Venn diagram of overlaps from project to project.

There have been times that I was working on multiple projects with the same service team and the roles between myself and the SDM varied for each project due to the complexities of the project and where our strengths aligned.

Never hesitate to verify!

The *consulted* role involves the different roles that should be involved in a step but are not accountable or responsible for its completion. For example, developers are consulted during sprint planning because they help determine task estimation and capacity, but they do not own the sprint plan itself. Business partners can be consulted during planning on requirement clarification and their perspective on the priority of tasks or features. A similar role, called *participated*, can take the place of *consulted* or you can even leave both to differentiate a participating **subject matter expert (SME)** from a non-SME.

The *informed* role is for all parties that only need to know of the outcome of a particular activity. In the example here, the business teams are informed about the designs, sprints, and work being done. The mechanism for informing can be the status report or meetings and does not need to be dedicated to each task.

If you have a large number of stakeholders that span many different disciplines and aspects of the project, an additional role of *optional* can be added, or using parenthesis around *informed* or *consulted* to indicate *optional*, as you can see in *Step 8* for the SDE. This is in lieu of leaving the cell in the chart blank, which would leave the role down to interpretation. It allows for a stakeholder to be optional for a particular activity where their active participation is not required but they may choose to participate if it makes sense in a particular situation.

Exploring the dos and don'ts for status reports

There are many types of communication that exist, but the most common and influential is the project status report. This may be in written form, in a meeting, or via a slide deck, but the purpose and content should largely be the same across these formats. I'll be using a written format as it is common and the easiest to work with in a book, but the concepts are translatable to whichever format you or your company use.

First up, here's a quick inventory of what items should be included in a status report:

- **Executive summary**: This is a high-level leadership-focused summary of the progress that is easy to digest and clearly states the trajectory of the project. The traffic-light status is included here, as well as the items contributing to the current traffic-light color the project is on.

- **Project milestones**: There are two schools of thought on milestones. They are either a list of predefined phases or steps that every project goes through, such as implementation, testing, deployment, launch, and post-launch, or they are used as shorthand for the deliverables of the project. I use the former as it provides good metrics that can be used across all projects (such as how often a project's deployment takes longer than expected) and separate this from the feature deliverables.

- **Feature deliverables**: This is a list of deliverables, usually synonymous with the top-level tasks (also called **epic tasks**) in a task list. This lets the stakeholders know when to expect a specific feature or group of features and varies with every project.

- **Open and recently resolved issues**: This is a list of issues that are currently being tracked. These are separate from the known tasks and the known risks but will include realized risks as they move from being a potential issue to an active issue that is currently being dealt with.

I usually have a separate table that I move resolved items to after they are shown as resolved in a status update. This reduces the size of each table and makes it easier to focus on the information that matters—the currently opened and in-progress work.

- **Risk log**: This is a log of the risks as discussed in *Chapter 7*. If the number of risks is large, I usually just include the high-risk items in the status report with a link to the full risk log. The goal here is to show the most relevant information to your stakeholders.

- **Contact information**: In case of issues or concerns, a reader of the report needs to know who to contact.

- **Project description**: Not every stakeholder will remember what the project is about, especially in large organizations and email distribution lists, so including a blurb on the project helps set the context of the status update.

- **A glossary of terms**: This won't make or break a status report, but if it is included, you will receive praise. Tech companies are large, and the number of **three-letter acronyms (TLAs)** that are in use can quickly become daunting. Just as not everyone will know the project, not everyone will know all of the terms being used. Be kind and don't assume. There are also cases where the same term may mean different things to different groups so this will help ensure everyone is using the same definition for this project.

Now that we know the basic elements that should go into a status report, here's a list of things to consider that turn an okay status report into a great one:

- Every action must have an owner and date
- Define your traffic light and stick to it
- A non-green status must have a path to green
- Keep important details above the fold
- Format and grammar matter

Let's go through each of these in detail.

Every action must have an owner and date

The number one rule for any status is that for every action, an owner and date must be identified. This helps ensure the right people are accountable for actions and that the stakeholders know when to expect a resolution. This conveys that you, as the TPM, are in control of the situation and are proactively engaged in all issues.

In some cases, an action item may not have a date at the time of a status report; in these cases, a date should still be supplied as a **date for a date (DFD)**. This lets people know when to expect a concrete plan of action.

Define your traffic light and stick to it

A traffic light, in this case, is a convention of using red, yellow, and green to denote different conditions of your project. It's easy to understand as the meaning of an actual traffic light closely matches how it is used in project management. That being said, every company is different, and even within a company, the thoughts behind how each should be used can be different. Diverse personal backgrounds including culture, as well as diverse professional backgrounds with people working at other companies, introduce varying preconceived notions, which can cause confusion. For this reason, I define my usage of the traffic light status to make it clear why a project has a particular status. This largely aligns with the company definition, but as not everyone is familiar with it, I reiterate it. Let's look at the definitions I use.

Green

The project is meeting current milestones and deliverables and is on track to deliver *on schedule*. Some companies may need to include *on budget* in this status. So long as the currently agreed upon resourcing and scoping can get the project to the scheduled date, I consider it green.

Yellow/amber

For a yellow (or amber in some countries) status, there are active issues that may impact the ability to deliver on schedule. It is not definite that the date will be missed at this stage, but it requires changes to get back on track.

There is ambiguity still – it is a cautionary status and lets your stakeholders know that you are on top of the situation and being proactive to keep the project from going *red*.

As a note, the issues here should rarely be new or unexpected. The project risk log should include all risks that may become realized. Ideally, the *yellow* status will be short-lived as risks have defined strategies to deal with them.

Life does happen, and things come up, but keep this ideal state in mind so that when unexpected issues come up, you can have a retrospective to see whether they could have been anticipated, and then add them to your risk register for future projects.

Is your project seemingly always in a yellow state?

Remember that the advice in this book is largely best practices with some dashes of realism. Though the ideal state is to reduce how often and how long a project is yellow, there are cases where this just won't be true. This doesn't mean you are an ineffective project manager. Projects that run hot and fast often don't have proper time to plan for everything and issues will constantly crop up. The sections where I talk about needing to be fast or quick will help you develop strategies to reduce these issues. But don't let the ideal state bring you down.

Find strategies that work for you and your situation and if the project launches by turning green at the last possible moment, that's okay!

Red

A *red* status means there is no current way to meet the scheduled delivery with the current resourcing and defined work. This is the status that I've seen the most contention in its definition in my career. If a project, left unchanged, cannot meet the due date, it is *red*. This does not mean that the date is impossible to meet but there is *no ambiguity* at this point in the project that something must change.

Contentious topic—when to change the status color

As a TPM, my preference is always transparency on status, even when it makes you or another stakeholder look bad. It's better to be honest and upfront than to sow distrust by reporting a **watermelon status** (*green on the outside, but red on the inside*)!

There are also cases where an event occurs, such as a risk being realized, where it may not be perfectly clear as to whether a status should change. I try and use the status definitions as my guiding principle: if a risk was successfully mitigated and didn't impact your ability to deliver, then the status can stay green (or whatever status you are on, as it does not shift the status).

Sometimes a problem occurs and is resolved in between status reports, but a stakeholder may wish to change the status to flag that an issue happened. This can get very political and may require some negotiation. With a clearly defined status scheme, it will be easier to convey the right message and diffuse tension. Use transparency as your goal and you will find a path that works for your circumstance.

A non-green status must have a path to green

Both *yellow* and *red* statuses must have a **path to green (PTG)**. This is the set of actions that need to take place in order to get a project back on track. Just as with every other action, these require an owner and a date.

For a *yellow* status, the PTG is often well understood with no ambiguity, which is why the project is *yellow* and not *red*. In these cases, there are open issues that introduce doubt about your deliverable dates but the options available are well understood and have a good chance of succeeding in bringing the project back on track.

However, there are cases where the issue's impact isn't well understood and requires some investigation to determine the impact and the right path forward. Though this may seem ambiguous and warrant a red status, I find that, in these cases, yellow may be more appropriate. This is because it isn't clear whether there is an impact to begin with or what the path forward would be. Saying you are red at this stage adds more certainty than is warranted based on what is known. A date for a date may be required instead of a resolution date because the action is pending investigation. It may be tempting to put the date of the investigation's conclusion, but the date should reference when the status will shift to green, which isn't known. In a situation like this, there should also be a clear understanding of a point of no return. That is, if the investigation into the issue takes so long that the project delivery date cannot be met regardless of the outcome, then the status must change to red. This will be a situation to track closely.

For a *red* status, the PTG is often exploratory. Most paths look to understand the impact so that the right action can be determined, first focusing on scope and resourcing. You might look at adding more resources to reduce calendar time or you might de-scope or reprioritize requirements to different milestones or phases of a project. Worst case, moving the due date may be the only way to get a project on track. What this looks like depends on your company and the ability for the project's due date to change. External drivers like a customer promise or regulatory date may make that option not feasible.

Keep important details above the fold

Above the fold is a concept in media that refers to information that is immediately available to the reader. The term comes from the printed newspaper industry where the page is folded in half on the newsstand. This makes the top half of the front page visible at a glance, so this was reserved for the most important headline. The practice is still in use in newspapers today and has moved on to digital media where the content available without needing to scroll is considered to be *above the fold*.

The reasoning behind the delineation is that the content above the fold is the only content that is guaranteed to reach your audience. The concept is often applied to executive leadership at a company where the general consensus is that leadership will read the content above the fold and then stop reading. Even in this case, there is no full guarantee that your stakeholders will receive the information, or read it, but this puts the most critical information at the top and increases the chance of it being seen.

This means that your most important information–project status, path to green, and the executive summary–must always be first and foremost in a status report. Senior leadership may not need to know all of the details of how something is being accomplished, but they need to know that the project team is being proactive and that they have the situation under control.

Once you are below the fold, the information becomes more granular, with updates on the sprint schedule, project burndown, and risk and issue logs. This is where the team leads and development managers will get the most value in knowing what the day-to-day is like in the project.

At the bottom, you place information that is static or near static, such as the project description, project contact information, and the communication plan. The communication plan will technically change every status, as it conveys when the next status will be sent and may mention related communication dates for project leadership and senior leadership reviews, and a stand-up schedule. Even so, I usually have this at the bottom as it is expected information and not pertinent to the status of the project. However, for critical projects or during critical phases of a project, I repeat the next status date above the fold as well.

Format and grammar matter

A consistent format that is easy to follow and understand is important. The more time that the reader has to spend on understanding what you are trying to say, the less they will spend reading in the future, and instead will just send out emails or meetings to discuss the status. When working with new stakeholders, impromptu meetings may occur as they don't understand your writing style or the full context of the project. They might have a different way of consuming information. *Listen to your stakeholders* and work to find ways to format your status to make your stakeholders comfortable with how the status is presented. It will save a lot of time during moments of high-stress movement in the project to not have to go over misunderstandings because the status format didn't make sense. In the same vein, grammar matters – to an extent. I'm not suggesting that perfect Honors-English-level grammar is required, but clear and concise sentences and correct word choice can also improve comprehension among stakeholders.

Format ahead of time

Once I have built my project plan and found my stakeholders, I spend some time working on the format of my communications. In the same way that you line up communication schedules to have an easy flow of information, you can format your status reports to make it easier to refresh things such as milestone tables and current issues and risks. Spending time upfront to find a format that reduces day-to-day work can quickly add up in times of high churn in a project and allow you to put your effort toward more critical work.

Run the format by your stakeholders to see if it makes sense to them. If the flow of information makes sense, the grammar will matter less.

The following is an example status report, broken up into two pictures- *Figure 8.1* with information that is *above the fold*, and *Figure 8.2* with information that is *below the fold*:

Windows Rollout Project Status: Oct-21-24

Next Status: Oct-28-24

Executive Summary

Status: Yellow for *Jan-15-25 launch*

Summary: A delay in the Text Message API definition has caused a day-for-day slip to starting the User Profile Object work as the same person is working on both stories. With the available project buffer and the early stage of the project, this is expected to be recoverable.

Path to Green: Cassette Santoro to work with Danielle's SDM to move her upcoming on-call rotation to later in the year to make up for the lost time. This will add buffer back into the project lost by the delay. **ETA Oct-9-24.**

Risk Log

Id	Risk	Probability	Impact	Strategy
1	Cross-platform tooling issues	High	High	**Acceptance:** Shift timelines to account for delays **Mitigation:** training and crashing
1.1	New Integrated Desktop Environment (IDE)	High	High	**Mitigation:** training on new IDE
1.2	New Coding Language for some teams	High	High	**Mitigation:** training on new language
1.3	Cross-team collaboration	High	Medium	**Mitigation:** daily stand ups, co-location, or chat rooms

Figure 8.1: Status report above the fold

The information above the fold is the most pertinent to understanding the state of the project and no additional information should be needed. This includes the status color and target date for the status, the summary of where the project is at, and the path to green. Since the project isn't green in this example, the status conveys why the status is yellow and includes the PTG with an owner—Cassette Santoro as the project TPM—and the date, October 9th, 2024.

The risk log doesn't always have to be above the fold, but in this case, it conveys high-risk items that can be relevant for upcoming status reports that shift back to yellow based on these risks. If other more important things are going on in the project like open issues, they'll take priority here.

Figure 8.2 shows the remainder of the status report and represents the data below the fold:

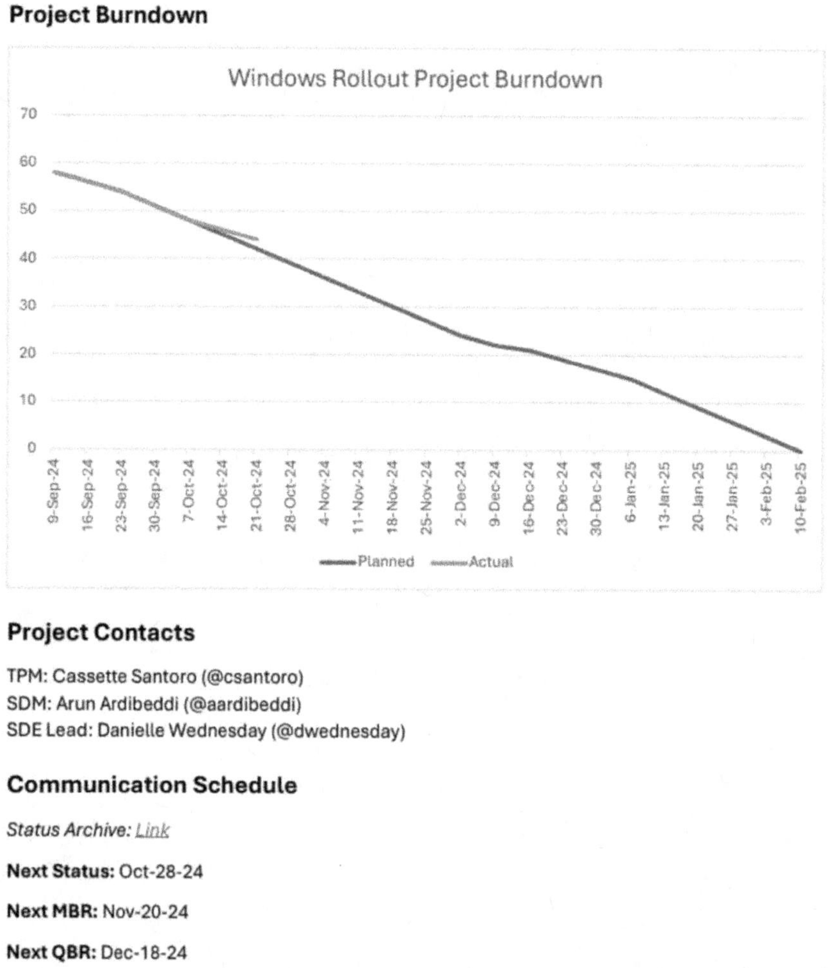

Project Burndown

Project Contacts

TPM: Cassette Santoro (@csantoro)
SDM: Arun Ardibeddi (@aardibeddi)
SDE Lead: Danielle Wednesday (@dwednesday)

Communication Schedule

Status Archive: Link

Next Status: Oct-28-24

Next MBR: Nov-20-24

Next QBR: Dec-18-24

Figure 8.2: Status report below the fold

In this example, I chose a project burndown to convey the week-by-week status of the project. The dip in *actual versus planned* here coincides with the delay called out in this report. Over time, it will act as a visual reminder of the delays incurred. A milestone or feature list table can also be useful here. The **Project Contacts** section is static in this case and gives context as to who to reach out to in the project. Lastly, the communication schedule lists the next weekly status and the upcoming leadership reviews. These dates all follow the dates laid out in the communication plan in *Table 8.1*.

Where are the metrics?

We've been discussing status reports for quite a few pages now but I haven't talked at all about metrics. This is because metrics come into play more often at the LR and SLR levels of communication. Program-level metrics don't change enough on a weekly basis to track them, and the audience at the status level is less concerned with overall program health and more concerned about the day-to-day work. If a metric is changing that often, there's a good chance that the measurement may not be what you are actually looking for anyway and needs some rework!

 Key Performance Indicators (KPIs), metrics, and product telemetry are used to measure the success of something. Every program is measured by metrics or KPIs, which measure the goal of the program as well as monitor the health of existing features. For an API, this could be a metric showing the transactions per second the API is taking in along with a target TPS for a given time frame. A product is measured through metrics or product telemetry such as page hits, clickthrough rate, installations, and even in-product usage data if enabled.

At Amazon, we use the term **Page 0 metrics**, which means a set of metrics that are shown at the top of an LR or SLR before any other information—including the actual status of the program. It's on page 0! This is how important metrics are to measure the success of our work.

We've explored the artifacts used in stakeholder management and how and when to use them and explored the content of a good status report. Next, we'll see how managing stakeholders in a tech world can offer unique challenges.

Managing stakeholders in a technology landscape

Most of how you manage stakeholders is not unique—all disciplines need a stakeholder list, a communication plan, and roles and responsibilities. However, there are some aspects of working in a technology company that can add some additional constraints to how we move forward. We'll take a look at three aspects of how managing stakeholders can be different while working in a tech environment:

- Communication systems
- Tooling
- Technical and non-technical stakeholders

Communication systems

Working for a technology company means you get to work with cutting-edge software; however, this can also be a burden. During the pandemic, many companies scrambled to update and add additional ways to communicate while workers were remote. Companies have since transitioned into a seemingly permanent hybrid model of working from home and the office, and it's hovering around the 50/50 ratio—at least in the US.

With all of these rapid changes from fully in-person to fully remote, and now hybrid, the technology landscape of available ways to communicate has grown, with a myriad of messaging systems such as Slack, Microsoft Teams, Amazon Chime, and Zoom, as well as other productivity tools such as Quip, OneNote, and Evernote. In some cases, a single company may be using multiple systems that have the same or partially overlapping purposes. Adding to the list of stakeholders, their roles, and which communication types are appropriate for them, you may find that you need to track what systems are available and widely used for each stakeholder.

If your company follows a standard here, then this can be a one-time exercise, but if you are like many tech companies right now, knowing which tools to use can save a lot of churn as you move from phase to phase in the project.

In addition, your communication plan should specify which tools you will be using to communicate. If you can standardize your communication tools for your project, it will reduce churn and facilitate effective communication to and from your stakeholders.

In a recent presentation on effective campaign management where mass client communication is required, the presenter consolidated the forms of communication to ensure that all 5,000+ clients could be managed.

The campaign used a ticketing system, similar to Jira, to reach out to the impacted teams. The tickets had their own built-in comments tab, which is great for a single ticket or even a few tickets, but at a larger scale, communicating on each ticket would take a full team of people doing nothing but responding to tickets. Instead, the TPM running the campaign mentioned several times in the body of the ticket that the comments would not be monitored and provided a link to their Slack channel. This allowed the team to monitor a single channel, instead of 5,000, and greatly reduced email noise and SLAs on responses. As you can see, tailoring your tools and their usage based on the needs of your project can greatly increase stakeholder efficiency.

Tooling

When using tools to manage a project or program, you'll want to look into how a given tool can help in distributing the various communication plans that you need. Do this as early on in the project as you can to ensure its benefits help you as early as possible. Some tools offer built-in dashboards that can be used to show the real-time status of a project. This can include upcoming milestones, feature dates, overall status, and more. These can be great tools as they reduce the need to craft a status, but it does mean that status is immediately and always available. However, being able to control how the update is consumed by stakeholders can be a valuable asset to help manage expectations and keep panic and escalations at bay.

When using a portfolio management tool, I use it to aggregate updates to make it easier for me to craft the right message. This is a good middle ground of using tools to save time, but still applying your understanding of the situation and drafting a compelling update yourself.

Tooling permissions tip

If you do use a tool, you'll also need to verify permissions to ensure that everyone who needs access has it. On a related note, you'll also want to check default permissions in cases where there are non-stakeholders who shouldn't have access to ensure they cannot get in.

Technical versus non-technical stakeholders

In the tech world, you are building technology, but you are also in a business that needs to make money. As such, you will run into plenty of non-technical teams that are your stakeholders. In most cases, there is a business team that is driving the work being done. This highlights your superpower as the communication bridge between these worlds. If you have a lot of non-technical stakeholders, an improvised communication plan may be needed to ensure you have a format that will fit their understanding.

To do this well, you need to know your audience while drafting a particular communication. Make sure you have met your stakeholders and taken the time to understand their needs in the project. This can also be a time to lightly assess their technical proficiency as well as their business acumen. This is useful as not every stakeholder will fit into either the business or tech side of the conversation. For instance, you may need to involve a legal team in sensitive decisions in the project. In these cases, the legal team might not be well-versed in the specifics of the project from a business or technical perspective. As an added bonus, I have found that the exercise of re-articulating a problem for a different audience can bring more clarity to the problem as it forces you to look at it from a different perspective.

Exploring the differences between a project and a program

For stakeholder management and communication plans, as with most key areas of management, the difference between managing a project and a program is about scale. The number of stakeholders increases and the number of concurrent communication plans that are being utilized increases. Instead of a single stand-up, you may have at least one per project, and the same goes for status reports and leadership reviews, depending on the complexity of the project.

This isn't to say that you, as the TPM running the program, are directly responsible for each of these communications, but you are accountable for them. If a project is falling behind on statuses, or the TPM isn't meeting with stakeholders enough to keep them in the loop, as the program manager, you are accountable for keeping the project TPM on track. Luckily, there are some additional tools you can use to help keep the program's stakeholders happy and communications flowing freely. Let's look at a few of those next.

Scheduling communication for natural accountability

In *Table 8.1*, I sequenced the communication schedule to allow lower-level communications, such as a weekly status report, to flow into the leadership review. This reduces time running around to get up-to-date information from team members. The same concept can be used at a program level; the only difference is that the level of status you care about will just start out at a higher level. Ensure each project's leadership review is published or takes place prior to the leadership review for the program. If a project doesn't need visibility at the leadership level separate from the program, then just ensure the weekly status reports are published on a day of the week that is earlier than the program leadership review to give you adequate time to collate information.

This may lead to a case where an issue's status has changed between the status report and the leadership review, in which case, updating the appropriate stakeholders out-of-band is important to ensure that there are no unexpected updates.

The same can be done at the program level, as the program's status report will include details from each project, and ensuring the project status reports are sent out prior to the program will ensure a natural flow of information.

Leadership syncs

In a project, there are multiple ways you get information – from daily stand-ups with your development team to project management syncs including development managers, PM-Ts, and key stakeholders. At the program level, you still need avenues of information, but the information you need will usually be at a higher level. As you will have multiple project teams to work with, a leadership sync is a concise way to get project information passed on. This is akin to a scrum of scrums, where the scrum masters from various scrum teams meet to discuss each scrum's sprint to ensure they all stay in sync. Bringing each project TPM into a combined forum not only keeps you informed but also gives each TPM a chance to understand what else is going on in the program.

The sync should flow very similarly to a sprint stand-up. Going round robin from TPM to TPM to get a quick status on the project, including any blockers or concerns, is all that is needed. No doubt, if there were major issues, you would already be aware prior to this sync, so it's really to ensure everyone is aware of the high-level progress being made as well as to ensure all cross-team impacts are well understood by everyone.

Projects tend to use the weekly status report and leadership syncs as their main ways to communicate with a wider audience. With a program, the senior leadership review will become more prevalent as the impact of a program will be large enough to warrant meeting with senior leadership. This may mean that all of the communication plans I listed in this chapter will be utilized when working on a program.

Summary

In this chapter, we covered the artifacts used in stakeholder management, such as the communication plan, stakeholder list, and roles and responsibilities. We looked at how the different communication types allow you to convey information in a specific way based on the needs of your stakeholders. We also discussed how you can discover who your stakeholders are.

We learned what elements go into making a good status report and how clear and concise language and status definitions reduce churn during the project when trying to convey a status.

We discussed the types of challenges you face in the tech world with a highly diverse set of communication tools, along with the varying levels of technically minded stakeholders you need to communicate with.

Lastly, we explored how stakeholder management differs at the program level and how to utilize leadership syncs to collate information across multiple projects.

In *Chapter 9*, we'll wrap up the section on program and project management core principles by discussing how to effectively manage a program. We'll discuss when and how to define a program and how to track the program across all open projects.

Further reading

The Professional Scrum Master Guide: The unofficial guide to Scrum with real-world projects, by Fred Heath

Additional resources

You can find templates for requirements tables, task tables, work breakdown structures, and project buffer matrices in the GitHub repo related to this book. Please check the Preface for the GitHub link.

Join our book's Discord space

Join our Discord community to meet like-minded people and learn alongside more than 5000 members at:

https://packt.link/sKmQa

9

Managing a Program

In this chapter, we'll discuss in more depth how to manage a program. As discussed earlier in this book, program management builds on the foundations of project management by utilizing the same key management areas. However, there are some differences due to the larger scope and broader impact that a program has compared to a project within it, so both of these concepts play a substantial role in defining the differences in management techniques.

We'll explore how to manage a program by doing the following:

- Defining a program
- Deciding when to build a program
- Tracking a program

Let's begin!

Defining a program

In order to effectively manage a program, we need to understand what a program actually is and what sets it apart from a project. The key differentiators between a program and a project are the scope and impact of the goals involved. Let's look at what each of these means in the context of program management:

- **Scope:** The scope of a program or project is the set of requirements that will be satisfied by the completion of the goals. It's easy to dismiss this as being the same as the full set of requirements that exist for an initiative, but that isn't always the case. Going back to the project management triangle in *Chapter 2*, in *Figure 2.3*, both time and resources can impact the scope.

It is a negotiation process between the TPM and the stakeholders as to what the right balance is going to be. Other factors, such as technical feasibility, may also hinder the ability to meet a requirement. This is especially true in cases where those setting the requirements are not technically inclined; they may ask for a feature that sounds feasible but is not something that can be achieved. In the case of a program, the scope is grouped into smaller goals that are then met by projects within the program. So, the full set of requirements for any initiative isn't necessarily within just a single project.

- **Impact:** This refers to the set of stakeholders and systems that are affected by achieving the goals of the program or project. Every service, application, or device that the scope will involve is affected by the changes. Going beyond that, any client of those same systems is also affected and must be considered when making the changes. These clients may be internal as well as external, such as users. The impact can also refer to a financial gain that a program may bring in sales. However, this is often directly related to the stakeholder breadth of impact. For the purposes of this book, we'll focus on the impact on stakeholders. Take, for example, a goal that scales a product to handle 10M transactions in a day from its current ability to handle 1M transactions per day. The goal of a 10x increase can be seen as the impact but that is just the financial impact of increasing scale. The full impact comes from how all systems involved are changed to meet that goal. Let's say the increase requires a change to an API to allow for batching and pagination for bulk requests as part of the 10x requirement. This API change will impact internal clients who may not need the 10x capacity but may still need to update their integration to account for the signature change. On the positive side, there may be a team that wanted to be able to call your service more but was capped by throttling due to system limitations. This API change now allows that team to re-prioritize high-value work on their end to increase their own scale in response. All of these together are the collective *impact* of the program and are all aspects that you, as the TPM, must keep in mind while running the program.

Figure 9.1 uses the *Mercury* program to illustrate where the scope and impact exist:

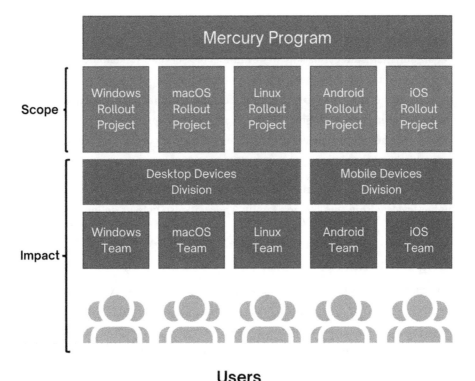

Figure 9.1: Scope versus impact

Within the *Mercury* program, the scope is the combined work of the projects within the program; this is essentially the five operating system applications. The scope will cover all of the requirements across the projects and thus the requirements for the program.

Impact includes both the internal teams as well as external users that are affected by the project's deliverables, either directly or indirectly. For example, in the Windows rollout project, the stakeholders are the desktop devices division management, the Windows team itself, as well as the expected user base for the Windows client. The mobile devices team is impacted by the Android and iOS rollout projects, but this does not affect the Windows team or Windows users, so there is no impact on those groups. Though Windows users might also have smartphones, and thus also care about iOS or Android releases, the Windows and smartphone releases won't intersect – they are by and large users in multiple groups. In contrast, the *Mercury* program's impact includes every stakeholder and affected system from every project within the program.

In some organizations, the impact may also be measured by a dollar amount. You may hear colleagues referring to themselves as managing a $2 million program or portfolio, though arguably, the dollar amount has a direct relation to the number of users and stakeholders impacted as well. Similarly, the impact could be expressed through adoption rates (increased market share leading to higher dollar value) or usage rates within the current customer base (higher usage can lead to more money spent in the ecosystem). These are all ways to express the value of the program to the company and indirectly measure the breadth of change incurred by the program across the organization and stakeholders.

Scope and impact come up all throughout your career as a TPM. Both become broader as you reach higher levels within the TPM job family. They will also help us define proper boundaries in both programs and projects.

Defining boundaries

The boundaries of a project or program are simply its goals and, by extension, the requirements that it will deliver. For a standalone project or program, these are just the goals themselves. For projects within a program, however, it's a little more nuanced. Defining the boundaries of a project or program can help ensure scope creep is monitored and addressed and that the designs that fit the requirements stay within the bounds of the project. This also helps you see which projects should be part of a particular program. Without a clear boundary, a program can stray from its purpose.

To understand how to define the boundaries within a program, let's first talk about how we set the boundaries within a project. At this level, it's fairly straightforward – we define milestones and features. As discussed in *Chapter 6*, *Plan Management*, milestones are often the same across projects and break the project up into phases, such as design completion and user acceptance testing completion. The features are where some work is done as they are specific to the requirements. Looking at the Windows rollout project feature list in *Chapter 6*, in *Table 6.8*, you can see that there are several self-contained deliverables, such as the user profile object and the presence object. Each feature groups together a set of requirements into a cohesive deliverable.

This same methodology is used at the program level, where a feature is represented by a project instead. Looking at the *Mercury* program as a whole, the goal is to make the *Mercury* application available to 100% of users across all platforms. As discussed in *Chapter 4*, *An Introduction to Program Management Using a Case Study*, an easy way to break this apart is by drawing boundaries around each operating system. Each project would then have a well-defined boundary within a single operating system but would also line up well with the stakeholder boundaries of the *Mercury* company.

From a feature perspective, there is an additional boundary that can be created that further restricts the platform scopes that we introduced by carving out the P2P subsystem as a separate project. This has a well-defined boundary of delivering the P2P functionality in a consumable library by the operating system teams. In this way, each project is a feature, albeit a large one.

Now that we've learned how to drive clarity at the program level using the scope and impact to define boundaries, we'll use this knowledge to discuss when and how to define a program.

Deciding when to build a program

Now we know what a program and project are, but the discussion has involved defining the boundary using a pre-existing program as an example. As a TPM, one of your jobs will be deciding when a program needs to be created and whether it is appropriate to the needs of your organization to do so.

From a project perspective, knowing when to create one is straightforward – you receive requirements to deliver a new application or service, a new feature, and so on, and you create a project to deliver on those requirements. Projects can be done standalone and do not need to be part of a larger program. In many industries, this is how almost all work is done: through independent and discrete projects.

However, knowing when a program should exist is a bit more nuanced and depends on the situation. There are two avenues through which a program is created: from the beginning when requirements are determined and during project executions where a need arises. Let's explore both scenarios.

Building a program from the start

Deciding to form a management program around a set of requirements is how most people perceive program formation as it fits the form that project creation takes and is familiar. To make this decision, you need to first clarify the requirements as this process will require analyzing them closely to define appropriate boundaries.

Chapter 6, Plan Management, went in-depth into driving clarity in requirements, so I won't repeat much here in that regard. The biggest difference between driving clarity in requirements for an existing project compared to before project and program formation is that your clarity helps you categorize the requirements. You are looking for deliverable chunks of requirements like a specific feature or function – much like determining features in a project.

When examining requirements, look for scope and impact cues that may serve as logical delineations between multiple projects to deliver on the requirements you have. *Once a set of requirements is broken out into more than one project, a program is needed to ensure the full requirements are met.*

Using the *Mercury* program and project list as an example, *Figure 9.2* illustrates a typical project and program boundary:

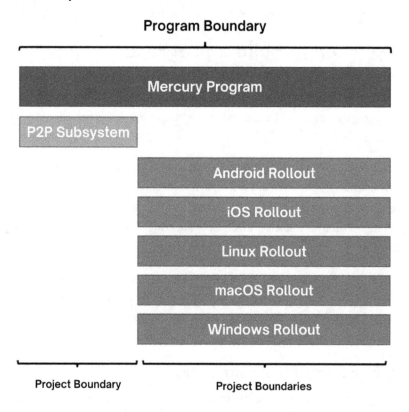

Figure 9.2: Program versus project boundary

The *Mercury* program goal requires that the P2P application is available to 100% of the user base. In *Chapter 4*, we examined the ways of achieving this and concluded that making the application available on all five operating systems was the best approach. Looking at the requirements with this in mind, a natural delineation would be to carve the requirements apart by the operating system. Though these would have been treated as features in a single project, the stakeholders were different for each operating system, and thus the impact on these stakeholders rarely overlapped. These impact cues are what helped us decide that creating multiple projects is the right way forward. As there is more than one project, a program is also needed to ensure that these projects keep the program goal in focus, as well as facilitate cross-project collaboration.

Had we decided to just deliver to the desktop operating systems, as an example, then a single project with multiple feature deliveries may have been appropriate as the stakeholders all roll up within the same desktop devices division within the *Mercury* company. So, the combination of what to deliver to meet the program goal requirements and the organizational structure of the company helps form the decision to build a program. Each company has its own organizational structure, so whether or not a program makes sense for you depends on your company as well as the requirements you are working with. The only hard and fast rule for when a program should exist comes down to when multiple projects are needed to get the requirements met.

Though building a program from the beginning is natural, it is not the only way a program may need to be formed. Let's explore what types of scenarios will lead to creating a program mid-execution.

Constructing a program mid-execution

When I say mid-execution, I'm referring to any point after one or more projects are in flight and a program is created to encompass them. *Chapter 5, Driving Toward Clarity*, introduced the perpetual skill of driving clarity, and this goes beyond the requirements and issues at hand. TPMs are adept at looking at the bigger picture and piecing together when one project may impact another. It is our job to ensure the health of our projects and programs across our organization.

In this constant state of analyzing, a pattern much like the one you look for when given new requirements may emerge. As an example, my current team is working on several projects that impact customer experience. Each project came to life separately out of different needs and different stakeholders; however, looking at the requirements for each project, a common end goal could be discerned relating to the ultimate end state for the customer experience. I did an exercise where I combined the requirements across the projects to see how they would align together. This showed that a common goal existed across the requirements, which also led to realizing that one of our unfunded projects fit into the program as well. Not only that – it was essential for the end goal that these individual projects were attempting to achieve. I took the findings to leadership and pushed for funding for the unfunded project by showing them the larger program goal and how each project fit into the end state we were trying to achieve. They agreed and the project was funded in the next cycle.

Without the program, the projects would have been successful on their own, but the program brings cohesion and purpose to the group of projects and helps uncover value that wasn't obvious on the surface. The program also highlights gaps in the goals for the individual projects where they believed they were holistically solving a customer experience problem; they were only solving it in a single dimension.

When combined, all dimensions are addressed, and the solution is complete. This combination will lead to a better outcome in aggregate than each project could deliver on its own.

Figure 9.3 illustrates the construction of a program from existing projects across multiple existing programs:

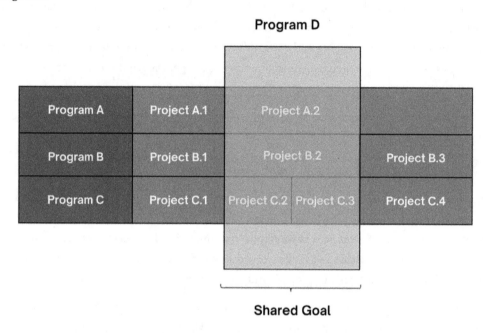

Figure 9.3: Defining an in-situ program

In this figure, multiple in-flight projects, each part of their own program, are combined into a program to align their goals to a shared desired end state. In this case, *Program D* is the new program created to encapsulate projects *A.2, B.2, C.2,* and *C.3*. The program is temporary and will end prior to *Program B* and *Program C* concluding.

This brings up an interesting concept of a project existing within multiple programs. If project management tools are to be believed, this should not be allowed, but there is value in allowing overlap as the overlap highlights different aspects of that project's goals and helps ensure the wider organization is moving together in the same direction while ensuring singular goals are also achieved. In a sense, this overlap is natural and feeds into the TPM's ability to see both the forest and the trees without getting stuck in one or the other.

Using the visualization from the product versus program where products are vertical slices and programs are horizontal, it can be easy to dismiss this new program as just a vertical slice, or product. This is merely a limitation of representing a 3D problem in 2D space.

A better representation of this concept would be where *Program D* was along the z axis, cutting across 3 programs on the x axis. *Program D* in this case is still a horizontal slice but it is cutting across different programs, as well as products, simultaneously.

It's also good to note here that *Program D* is not necessary as each program will deliver on what is needed and hyper-communication across programs can ensure the right solutions are reached. However, a formal framework of the program can solidify goals and team direction and make collaboration easier than trying to drive consensus outside of the framework.

Now that we've driven clarity at the program level and learned when to create a program, we'll move on to look at the different aspects of tracking a program.

Tracking a program

If you have tracked projects before, you will find a lot of similarities between project and program management. A program has the same key management areas as a project and each area has additional aspects to consider given the larger scope and impact. We'll touch on each of these key management areas:

- Program planning
- Risk management
- Stakeholder management

Program planning

Regardless of how the program came to be, the key requirements in the planning stage remain the same. The reason that a program exists is to facilitate multiple projects in achieving a common set of goals. The most important step for a program is to define that set of goals.

If the program is being created from the beginning and no project has started, this is a straight-forward task as the requirements as a whole will tell you what the end goals will be. Each project would then take a subset of these requirements to form its own goals. In the case of the *Mercury* program, the requirements stated that the *Mercury* application needed to be available to 100% of the user base. This became the goal of the program, and the projects took the subset of requirements needed for their given operating system.

In the case where the program is being formed from projects that are in flight, this exercise can be a bit more abstract. This is because it is easy to assign items to known categories at the start of a program and yet hard to determine what categories should be given those same requirements once a project is in flight. In other words, it is harder to see a pattern across in-flight projects than prior to the projects starting.

Let's pretend that the *Mercury* program doesn't exist, and instead, each operating system team is independently creating a P2P messaging app. Each application will look very different in terms of the user interface as each operating system has different conventions to adhere to. Looking at each one individually, it's harder to see where a cross-platform P2P subsystem could be utilized because you are looking at the application as an isolated idea. However, if the potential opportunity for de-duplication of effort and assured cross-platform capability is seen, then a program goal can be created from this opportunity.

It may be that the program goal is written in a way that makes this preferred synergy part of the goal and states that a common network layer component is part of the end state. The result of looking at the program as a combination of existing projects compared to a goal split into projects can change the nature of the goal to ensure alignment and understanding, though the end state will be the same. Writing a goal to be too specific as to how a goal is achieved carries its own risks, so it is best to strike a balance between adaptability and setting a clear intent for the program.

Now that we have the goals laid out, we can specify the boundaries of the projects and then plan each project as you normally would. The difference here is that you will have cross-project dependencies that will need to be accounted for during planning.

Now that we've planned the program, we need to look at how to manage risk.

Risk management

In *Chapter 7, Risk Management,* we looked in-depth at risk management practices and touched on how risk assessment and management at the program level is about a difference in perspective. The program will focus on cross-project dependencies and the risks involved, whereas the project will focus on cross-task dependencies, as well as risks associated with a given task itself.

At the program level, we need to examine how a project's deliverables may overlap with another project's deliverables. These intersections will always include some risk. *Chapter 7,* in *Figure 7.3,* talked specifically about the risk of project delays due to the subsystem component that was required for each operating system project to complete. Aside from scheduling risks, there may be inconsistencies in APIs and the behaviors of the APIs from one operating system to another. The intersection of the subsystem with all five operating system projects represents a risk that the subsystem API capabilities don't align with the needs of one of the operating systems. Any change to the API contract can lead to issues in the other OSes, which could lead to a cyclical risk given the high number of touchpoints. This is certainly solvable as this isn't the first application to have a shared API across multiple systems, but the risks are still present and need to be given due attention.

For cross-project dependencies such as these, the TPM running the program would own the risk and ensure that the risk strategies are followed within the impacted projects. The project lead for the subsystem will also have a stake in the cross-project dependencies and should work closely with all project leaders.

Sometimes, a risk that exists at the project level may be important enough to be tracked at the program level as well. In these cases, the owner may still be at the project level, but the visibility of the risk is elevated to the program level and usually a larger set of stakeholders. Ensuring that risk strategies are followed still falls on the project TPM but will require scrutiny from the program TPM due to the high-profile nature of the risk. As stated above, the subsystem component falls into this category. As another example, the Windows rollout project may have a risk that impacts its ability to enter into cross-platform testing on time. Though this is solidly a project risk based on task slippage, it has the potential to impact the other projects' ability to finish cross-platform testing. As such, the program TPM will report on the risk to the program stakeholders – which includes all operating system teams and divisional management. The Windows rollout project TPM, *Cassette*, would own the risk, with the program TPM watching closely and providing help as needed.

Sharing risks from the project to the program level and aligning program goals across projects requires strong communication strategies. This additional overhead of a program coordinating across projects adds risks related to dependency delays and longer design times to allow for syncing across teams. To reduce the impact of these risks, let's look at stakeholder management to see how we can provide a strong communication foundation for the program.

Stakeholder management

The role of the program TPM is to set the projects up for success. They are there to ensure that each project TPM understands the role of their project in relation to the program. As a project TPM, they should already understand the goal of their project but may not realize how it fits into the larger picture of the program. The program TPM also needs to ensure that the stakeholders are aware of all of the projects and the interdependencies that may concern them. To accomplish these tasks, there are multiple ways to engage your stakeholders throughout the program to offer proper guidance. We'll explore each in the following subsections.

Kickoff

Once a program is created, either at the beginning along with the associated projects or in flight, a **kickoff** meeting is needed. This meeting is where all stakeholders come together to discuss the program and its goals, as well as the role each stakeholder will play in the management of the program.

Just like at a project kickoff, this is where the communication plan is shared with the program team, including expected deliverables used in the communication plan.

The kickoff sets the stage to ensure that everyone is aware of the end goal of the program and not just their respective project goals. Each project lead gets an idea of how their project may impact other projects in the program and each stakeholder has a chance to raise concerns and point out potential new stakeholders.

Leadership syncs

In *Chapter 8, Stakeholder Management*, we discussed the concept of leadership syncs to help co-ordinate across the projects. Not all programs will necessarily require the use of leadership syncs, but in cases where cross-project risks are involved, this is a valuable line of communication to get up-to-date information on the risks the program is tracking.

The leadership sync should flow very similarly to a sprint stand-up. This means going **round-robin** from TPM to TPM to get a quick status on each project, including any blockers or concerns. This continues the theme of the kickoff by not only informing you as the program TPM of the current status but also ensuring all project TPMs are aware of what each other is doing. If a new major issue surfaces, address it after the round-robin is complete so those not impacted may leave. This concept, known as the **parking lot**, is also used in sprint standups to ensure the efficient use of everyone's time.

Roles and responsibilities

As covered in *Chapter 8*, every project should have its own roles and responsibilities chart. In most cases, it is the same for every project. This is also true at the program level. *Table 9.1* is a RACI chart for the *Mercury* program:

Step ID	Name	Program TPM	PM-T	Project TPM	Business
1	Program Planning	A(/R)	C	C	(R)
2	Project Status Report	A	C	R	C
3	Program **Senior Leadership Review (SLR)**	R/A	C	C	I

Table 9.1: Program-level roles and responsibilities

The roles at the program level are usually fewer than at the project level as there isn't as much day-to-day work involved in tracking a program. However, it is still important for everyone to know their role in the management of the program. The program TPM is *accountable* for the program plan. Also, depending on the involvement of the business, the *responsibility* may be with the business team or the TPM. This also outlines the project status reports and lists the project TPMs as responsible. Since a program exists, the accountability is with the program TPM. Lastly, the program's SLR is owned by the program TPM, and the project TPMs are consulted. Though this may seem obvious, it sets up the communication strategy for the program.

Communication strategies

Projects tend to use the weekly status report and **leadership reviews** as their main ways to communicate with a wider audience. With a program, the SLR will become more prevalent as the impact of a program will be high enough to warrant meeting with senior leadership. This may mean all of the communication plans listed in *Chapter 8* will be utilized when working on a program.

As the program SLR builds on the project status reports, ensuring that every status report is on time and that the schedule of reports is set up properly falls on the program TPM. *Figure 9.4* illustrates a reporting timeline for the *Mercury* program that allows for timely feedback to the program TPM:

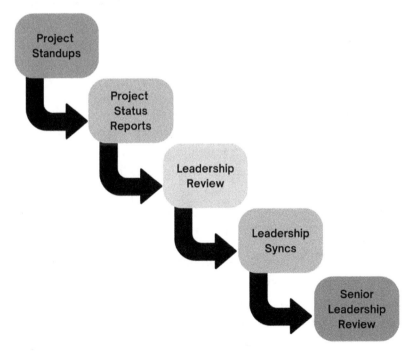

Figure 9.4: Aligning communication

As mentioned in *Chapter 8*, *Stakeholder Management*, the key to effortless communication is setting up a schedule that naturally feeds the right information into the right reports at the right time. Here, all project weekly reports are due prior to the SLR so that it can have the most up-to-date information to draw from. Any clarifications needed can come about during leadership syncs, or directly if urgent enough.

We've discussed the ways in which we can engage with our stakeholders, and how to pass along information. Next, let's dive into when the program TPM may need to dive a bit deeper into a problem.

The art of intervention

The program TPM is a force multiplier to the project TPMs, just as the project TPMs are force multipliers to the project team. In most cases, project-level issues are delegated to the project TPM, and the program TPM is informed or consulted if necessary. However, cases may arise where more involvement from the program TPM is necessary.

The program TPM is accountable for everything in the program, and this is especially true for project risks that impact the program. If a risk is close to being realized, thus has a high-risk score, or a risk has already been realized and risk strategies are underway, closer involvement of the program TPM is warranted. This is to facilitate faster communication and not a means to take away control of the project from the TPM. Attending project-level standups to understand the day-to-day or even hour-by-hour concerns will reduce communication times and allow the program TPM to coordinate cross-projects faster if the need arises.

As the program TPM, it is important to know what your project teams are doing, including when key meetings are occurring. To facilitate quick intervention, having the project sync on your calendar will allow you to easily drop in when needed and reduce the churn of getting the invite while an issue is at hand. It can also facilitate passing along information at the right time to ensure it's addressed when appropriate. For instance, you may have an issue that a project team needs to tackle. Giving the project TPM a heads-up prior to their next stand-up can ensure it gets addressed quickly.

Intervention should rarely be a case of taking control, but rather offering a lending hand to resolve the issue more rapidly, help identify cross-project impacts, and ensure good communication with all impacted stakeholders. If cross-project communication is not required, or the issue isn't being reported at the program level, intervention is not required. That is the job of the project TPM.

Summary

In this chapter, we learned that scope is the set of requirements, and the impact is the group of people affected by the scope. We learned how to drive clarity at the program level by discerning the scope and impact of the requirements.

We then discussed how to use the scope and impact to define boundaries around the requirements. The boundaries can make up both the boundaries of a project and the deliverables within that project, which brings shape to the program.

After that, we learned that a program should be created when sufficient impact and scope dictate that multiple projects are needed to complete the goals. We also discussed how seeing patterns and goals across existing projects may align and warrant the creation of a program to track them as a whole.

Lastly, we discussed various aspects of tracking a program through program planning, risk management, and stakeholder management. Each of these key management areas builds on the management styles used at the project level but with increased scope and impact, necessitating some change in strategies. This includes planning the composition of the program, as well as the program goals, and deciding which risks need to be tracked at the program level. We also dove into the various communication techniques used in managing stakeholders, such as a kickoff meeting and leadership syncs, all used to facilitate the success of the projects in the program.

In *Chapter 10*, we'll discuss emotional intelligence, which is a leadership trait that has recently risen to the top of the list due to the resurgence of generative artificial intelligence. We'll discuss what it is, how to become more emotionally intelligent, and how and why it will be the differentiator that allows TPMs to thrive in the coming decades.

Join our book's Discord space

Join our Discord community to meet like-minded people and learn alongside more than 5000 members at:

`https://packt.link/sKmQa`

10

Emotional Intelligence in Technical Program Management

Since the first edition of this book was written, our world has evolved quickly, with the sudden spike in generative artificial intelligence, or GenAI. This has led to many people contemplating what this means for their jobs. Although some will most certainly be replaced by GenAI or simply made irrelevant, I do not see this as the case for technical program managers. However, it will change what encompasses our day-to-day work, and this comes with an increased emphasis on the aspects of our job that GenAI cannot replicate, which are our soft skills, chief among which is our emotional intelligence.

In this chapter, we'll walk through emotional intelligence with these topics:

- Identifying the components of emotional intelligence
- Developing emotional intelligence
- Applying emotional intelligence in technical program management

Let's get started!

Identifying the components of emotional intelligence

Emotional intelligence is the ability to recognize, understand, manage, and use emotions. It is most often initialized as EQ, which may seem strange, but understanding where this came from is useful in understanding what emotional intelligence is. EQ was coined in 1987 by Keith Beasley when he developed the concept to measure emotional intelligence, and he called the measurement the Emotional Quotient.

Since then, EQ has become synonymous with the concept that it measures and has supplanted EI as the shorthand for emotional intelligence. Beasley chose EQ because it was similar to the measurement term for intelligence, which was called the **Intelligence Quotient (IQ)**. IQ measures a person's relative intelligence to others in their age group by dividing their personal score on an intelligence test, known as their **mental age**, by the average score of people who are the same age (down to the month), known as the **chronological age**; this ratio is known as a quotient. Here's shows the written-out form of this early IQ formula:

$$IQ = \left(\frac{Mental\ Age}{Chronological\ Age} \right) x\ 100$$

Modern versions of the test incorporate a normalized IQ of 100, with standard deviations of 15 to more evenly distribute IQ and ensure that the relative values remain the same over time. However, the general concept is still the same. Unlike IQ, Emotional Intelligence (which is the most often-used term) is not a measurement but a state that relates to your ability to understand and control emotions.

Interestingly enough, when Beasley coined the phrase Emotional Quotient to denote the measurement of emotional intelligence, he did not devise the measurement itself and just used it hypothetically. Measurement of emotional intelligence didn't come until later papers offered various ways to measure it. A common method used is the **Mayer-Salovey-Caruso Emotional Intelligence** test, which defines EQ in four areas and measures each one separately. These areas are your ability to perceive, use, understand, and manage emotions. If you are unsure of your own EQ and where to focus your attention, a self-assessment of your EQ can be a good way to determine where to start. We'll go into the top five assessments later in this chapter.

For TPMs, EQ can help you adapt to a changing environment with controlled emotion and intent. To achieve this level of adaptability, there are four components you need to learn about and grow for yourself: self-awareness, self-regulation, empathy, and social skills. *Figure 10.1* illustrates the relationship between these components:

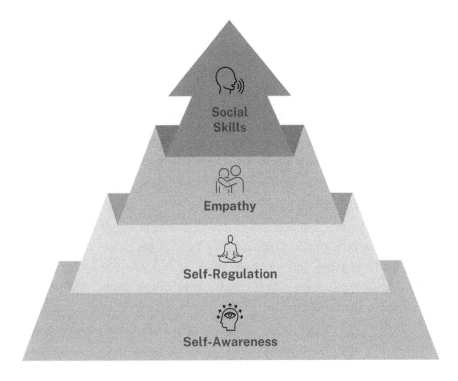

Figure 10.1: The four components of emotional intelligence

The pyramid signifies that each layer is a foundation for the next. It's also indicative of what most people see and think of when they think of emotional intelligence, social skills, as those are at the top and most easily visible. However, in order for your social skills to be effective, empathy and self-regulation are needed, and these all rely on self-awareness in order to identify, foster, and grow these habits.

Let's explore each of these components in more detail.

Self-awareness

As with most other self-improvement systems, the first step is self-awareness. Before you can learn to regulate your emotions and use them to effectively communicate during change, you need to understand what emotions you have and what triggers them. This is not a simple task and will take some reflection, but there are a few things that can help you on this journey:

- **Learn and be curious:** This is a leadership principle at Amazon for good reason. Although it often refers to external curiosity, it can also refer to internal curiosity. In order to be more self-aware, you must be willing to be curious about yourself. Open up to yourself.

- **Be vocally self-critical:** For long-time Amazonians, this is an older leadership principle that can translate into your personal life as well. This may sound like you need to criticize yourself, but being critical and critisizing are different things, and being self-critical does not need to be negative. You need to be able to look at your actions, analyze them, and be constructive and honest with yourself. This is hard, as our natural instincts have us immediately close ourselves off to criticism. The bonus here is that the better you become at being self-critical, the better you can help others with feedback and growth, as empathy will be a natural consequence of your own self-improvement.

- **Practice mindfulness:** You can do this in many different ways, but it centers around paying attention to yourself throughout the day. Notice the positive things happening as well as your emotional responses to your activities and events. The key is understanding what actions trigger the positive and negative emotions to help you better understand them. Writing in a journal is a good way to enforce intention and reflection. Research from the University of Tokyo in 2021 and the Norwegian University of Science and Technology in 2024 has shown that the act of writing, as opposed to typing, increases memory retention as well as creativity. A meta-analysis of 191 studies from the Brazilian Academic Consortium for Integrative Health on meditation concluded that meditation is a helpful practice for focusing on your intentions, which is key to mindfulness, among other health benefits. Although we often think of meditation as involving longer sessions, meditating for just 5 minutes has been shown to help reduce stress and allow us to focus more easily. All of these studies are listed in the *Further reading* section and are freely available.

- **Step outside of yourself:** When you are in conflict with someone else, try looking at the situation from the outside looking in. We often talk about being in the other person's shoes, or looking at a situation from their perspective, and this is really helpful when trying to bridge the gap between two perspectives. However, in this exercise, we are trying to look at our own actions, so look at the situation from a bystander's perspective.

How do you perceive your own actions from this perspective? Do they come across differently than they do from your own internal perspective? Combine this with being self-critical to start making positive changes in your reactions and emotions. This has the added benefit of building an emotional connection, which often leads to longer-term collaboration and mutual benefits.

- **Strive for more human connection:** Let's face it – we are on conference calls a lot as TPMs. Sometimes, even when we are in the office, we take calls from our desks. The best way to build empathy is to spend time with others. Our mind naturally mirrors other people that we are with, and mirroring builds stronger empathy. This can be hard for some people, including me, who are naturally introverts. So small steps are helpful here, which can be done with a bit of effort. Do you have a meeting that takes a while to walk to, or one that is back-to-back with another meeting? See if you can leave a few minutes early, or switch to your phone, and walk to the meeting room to be in person rather than taking the meeting online. Close your laptop if you can, and focus on the meeting and the people in the room.

Now that we have a basis for our emotions, and reactions to our actions and events, let's start building on this with self-regulation.

Self-regulation

Self-regulation is the ability to pause between an emotion and a reaction. Highly reactive responses can lead to behaviors that are against our core values, as we don't take time to evaluate the emotion before acting. It's easy to see this in kids who are developing self-regulation for the first time. This is often called acting out, where we physically react to negative emotions, such as hitting a friend or family member when frustrated. As an adult, it may manifest as speaking over someone when frustrated or yelling. We may have learned to not physically respond, but the response may still occur before we have had a chance to think through our actions.

Thankfully, with the self-awareness exercises we did in the previous section, we have the tools to work through this. We know our emotions and what triggers them, and now we need to control our impulses. Anticipate your emotional response based on the triggers you identified, and preempt the response to give yourself time to pause before acting.

Controlling your impulse and redirecting your response also builds your adaptability to change. Adapting to external change or imparting change is a key skill for TPMs while executing programs.

So far, we have focused on ourselves with self-awareness and self-regulation. Now we'll apply these skills outwardly in our empathy.

Empathy

Empathy is the ability to understand the feelings of someone else. This is why we focus on empathy only after being able to understand our own feelings because if you can't understand your own, it would be extremely hard to understand another's feelings. We discussed this earlier and imagined being in another person's shoes—that is empathy. Practice thinking about a situation as another person to gain their perspective and understanding, and although you may not agree with their point of view, you should be able to start understanding where their point of view comes from to find a path forward.

Another way to build our empathetic muscles is to use active listening techniques in discussions. We talked about this in *Chapter 8, Stakeholder Management*, so I'll only briefly review it here. The key to active listening is that you listen to understand instead of waiting to respond to what you believe is being said. You do this by:

- **Being present in the conversation:** Give the conversation your undivided attention. Put your phone down or in your pocket, and make occasional eye contact if you are able to.

- **Utilizing non-verbal cues:** While actively listening, pay attention to non-verbal cues in the other person's speech, such as their speed. If they are talking unusually fast, they may be nervous, for instance. Folding your arms, furrowing your brow, and pacing can all have negative impacts on a conversation and change the responses to something more confrontational or defensive.

- **Using open-ended communication:** Avoid asking one-word-answer questions. Phrase your questions in a way that allows for elaboration, so instead of saying, "Did you like that?", which will lead to a yes or no answer, try, "What did you think about that?" This allows the other person to elaborate and explain why they feel the way they feel.

- **Remaining neutral:** During the discussion, try to keep your responses neutral without any blame or judgment. This includes non-verbal stances, facial expressions that can express distaste or disappointment, and passive-aggressive breathing or rolling of your eyes. These behaviors will trigger the same defensive or confrontational responses and shut down open communication.

Being an effective active listener increases your empathy for others, and it shows them that you are interested in their problems, not just a resolution that may or may not have their best interests in mind.

Let's take our newfound empathy and apply this on the job through social skills.

Social skills

We've been building toward the methods that we most often think of when discussing emotional intelligence. Social skills are the outward-facing result of our own emotional awareness and control. A person with high emotional intelligence is an effective communicator, both verbally and in writing. Leaders who can use positive emotion to affect change in their company, or even in their shareholders, are a great example of emotional intelligence.

Jeff Bezos is the founder of Amazon, and he was the CEO until 2021 and saw the company through tremendous growth, as well as downturns. It was in the latter case that his emotional intelligence really came through. During calls with shareholders, Bezos would be upfront that the company was going to spend more than it brought in to facilitate growth and ensure long-term success. In most companies, this type of outward admission to revenue loss would be met with high stock turnover, but his energy and use of emotion, as well as a positive outlook, kept shareholders at bay and the stock and company on a strong footing.

Conflict occurs a lot in our daily lives, which is why we focus on conflict resolution a lot. Emotionally intelligent leaders are adept at resolving conflict by leading a conversation to a resolution, instead of demanding a specific outcome. Asking open-ended questions and allowing the conflicting parties to come to a resolution together is a key strategy for successful resolutions.

Sheryl Sandberg, the former COO of Facebook (now Meta), is known for her empathetic and self-aware leadership style. These are two of the top qualities of emotionally intelligent leaders. Empathy toward her team invites inclusive thinking and fosters team building by providing a safe space for people to express their ideas.

As Satya Nadella, CEO of Microsoft, said in an interview, "EQ trumps IQ." Emotionally intelligent leaders will always prevail over those who are smart but lack the soft skills needed to reach their team and affect change.

We've covered the components of emotional intelligence and gone over the basics of how to develop each one. Let's review some tools available to you to dive deeper into each aspect of EQ.

A quick note on motivation

Some accounts of emotional intelligence include sections dedicated to motivation. In my mind, motivation comes as part of our social skills and requires all of the foundational components of emotional intelligence. You will see examples of motivating your team throughout the chapter, as it is an essential aspect of using emotions.

Discovering your emotional intelligence

Self-awareness is the first step to developing a strong EQ. To determine where you need to focus your growth, you'll need to assess your own personal EQ. Although there are many EQ tests out there, there are currently 5 that are the most common:

- **Emotional Quotient Inventory 2.0 (EQ-i-2.0):** Developed in 1997, this tests environmental behaviors relating to emotional intelligence in the areas of self-perception, self-expression, interpersonal skills, decision making, and stress management. This test is available online.

- **Mayer-Salovey-Caruso Emotional Intelligence Test (MSCEIT):** This test has the tester perform tasks that measure the four branches of emotional intelligence: their ability to perceive, identify, understand, and manage emotions.

- **Profile of Emotional Competence (PEC):** This test looks at five areas of emotion: the ability to identify, understand, express, regulate, and use your emotions.

- **Trait Emotional Intelligence Questionnaire (TEIQue):** This test is based on the work of K.V. Petrides' trait emotional intelligence theory, developed in 1998. It consists of 153 questions that use a Likert scale (agree completely to disagree completely) to assess different areas of emotional intelligence.

- **Wong's Emotional Intelligence Scale (WEIS):** This test was developed in 2002 and has two components, each consisting of 20 questions, or scenarios. The first set has you picking the scenario that most represents you in a scenario. The second set has 20 paired abilities, and you pick which one best represents your strengths.

Table 10.1 summarizes these tests in a side-by-side comparison:

Assessment	Emotions					Stress Management	Availability
	Identify	Understand	Perceive	Regulate	Use		
EQ-i-2.0	✓	✓	✓	✓	✓	✓	Scheduled Online Workshop
MSCEIT	✓	✓	✓	✓	✓		Scheduled Online Workshop
PEC	✓	✓	✓	✓	✓		Online Self-Assessment

TEIQue	✓	✓	✓	✓	✓	✓	Online Self-Assessment
WEIS	✓	✓	✓	✓	✓		Self-Assessment

Table 10.1: EQ assessments and areas evaluated

The names for the areas tested have been normalized to show that all common assessments review the same areas. While some tests may break down results at differing levels of granularity, they all cover the same high-level concepts. The exception to this is the inclusion of stress management markers in two of the tests.

While some of these tests are available for self-assessment, most are given as part of a larger workshop. The point of the workshops is to assess and then improve your emotional intelligence. As you can see in the table above, most of these have online assessments and online (albeit live) workshops—this makes sense in the post-COVID world and offers convenience. However, if possible, find an EQ coach who can come to your workplace for an in-person experience. In-person workshops are useful because you get to develop your emotional intelligence while working alongside others on the same journey. Many companies offer reimbursement for EQ courses, as the value of heightened emotional intelligence is recognized as being as important as any other functional skill your job requires.

In my research across these different tests, no one test stood out as far superior to the others. They are all riffs on the same underlying concepts but package them in slightly different ways, bringing value to the company utilizing that test. To that end, an assessment that covers the high-level areas should be enough to get you started on the right path for your journey. Focus on finding an in-person workshop, if you can, that fits your budget; if not, then an online workshop is a great alternative.

Keep in mind that these workshops will help you discover your emotional intelligence and highlight the areas for you to focus on. You will also get some practice in the workshops on some helpful techniques, but the journey of growing your EQ will be longer than the workshops, as they are just there to point you in the right direction and give you a push forward—not to be the end of the journey.

We now know what emotional intelligence is and how to assess and start the journey of growing our EQ, through assessments and workshops. Next, let's put our emotional intelligence to work!

Applying emotional intelligence to technical program management

Emotions and their management are present in our everyday lives. They impact our ability to focus, make decisions, and influence the emotions of everyone around us. This includes at work, where emotions impact social dynamics between co-workers and influence meeting directions and outcomes. In times of high stress, like a looming project deadline or a risk being realized, emotions are often heightened, and our responses can be redirected toward illogical or reactive actions. The ability to control and direct emotions for yourself and those around you is an effective tool for mitigating issues and resolving conflicts, in a compassionate and empathetic manner.

Emotional intelligence can go the other way too, if not handled well. Steve Ballmer, CEO of Microsoft in the early 2000s, has been depicted as a passionate leader who cultivated a cut-throat and adversarial culture. The adversarial nature was both between internal teams at Microsoft as well as toward competition. According to documents in a lawsuit between Google and Microsoft, Steve Ballmer threw a chair in frustration toward a table. In an exit interview in 2004 with a departing engineer, Mark Lucovsky, Ballmer became angry when it was revealed that Lucovsky was leaving Microsoft for their main rival Google. Ballmer threw a chair while stating, "I'm going to kill Google," among other words. This has been downplayed by Steve Ballmer in recent years, but the infamous confrontation has at least some truth—by Ballmer's own admission. This shows that emotional regulation can not only impact your own actions but also the emotions of your entire team, or even the entire culture of your company.

Specifically, within the TPM role, controlling your emotions and the ways that they impact those around you can turn the tide in key decisions. It can ease tension during a firefighting escalation and can build strong emotional relationships with stakeholders. Take a moment to think about a TPM who inspires you and what qualities that person has. It could be their ability to unblock teams, drive contentious meetings, and wrangle resources out of teams, all while being approachable to those around them. These are all traits borne from high emotional intelligence and are foundational requirements to being a strong TPM.

Let's see how emotional intelligence can help you make better decisions in the workplace.

Making decisions

We often attribute decision making to large meetings at pivotal moments in a project. These are the types of decisions that we envision when we think of the greatness of leaders. However, leaders like TPMs make decisions every day while on a project. Which task should be picked up next?

How do we get to the milestone on time? How do we frame the current roadblock to our stake-holders? Each of these decisions can benefit from strong emotional intelligence.

An important aspect to consider when making any decision is the emotional impact the decision will have on the team. The emotional response from your team can greatly affect the outcome of the decision and either help or hinder its ability to come to fruition.

Emotional impact isn't the only consideration, as you must *balance* emotions with the rationality of the decision being made. Many tech companies employ **Key Performance Indicators (KPIs)** or other metrics when making decisions about the direction of a project or program. KPIs can show a poor-performing feature, for instance, that may lead to the removal or revamping of a feature from a product. What can you do in this type of scenario to reduce the emotional toll on your team that has worked hard on the feature that is being scrutinized? If you are stopping a project, removing a feature, or otherwise impacting work that has already been done, relay the decision with compassion and a strong focus on the vision. If someone understands why a decision is being made and how it ultimately aligns with the vision of a company or product, emotional duress is lessened.

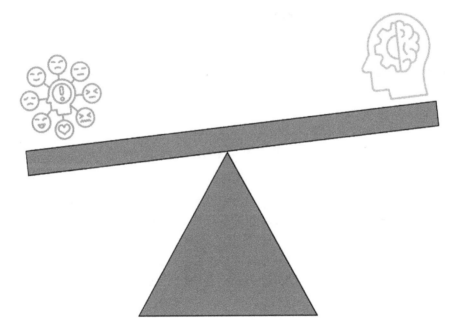

Figure 10.2: Balancing emotional impact with rationality

An example from the real world: *Having high emotional intelligence in a difficult situation*

One of the hardest decisions that a leader can make is restructuring a division. I reached out to my LinkedIn community at large for a story of a leader exhibiting stellar emotional intelligence. Given the large number of recent layoffs in the tech industry, I won't mention the company or team by name, but the story is worth sharing.

In early 2024, a team of 66 developers, managers, technical program managers, and product managers were slated to have their division move continents. When the news came down to the local director that their team was going to lose their jobs, they immediately took action to help their team find replacement positions in the company. They knew, rationally, that the best path forward was for everyone to find a job within the company, as it reduced the churn of looking outside the company and was a smooth transition. At the same time, the division's work needed to continue and transition to the new team. This is never a comfortable ask, as it involved someone training their own replacement, but that was the ask from leadership.

The director put the mental health of their employees first and foremost, and they made it clear that their number one priority was finding them a new position either inside or outside of the company. The second priority was the health of the ongoing initiatives that they were to transition. Focusing on employee health, empathizing with them, and understanding their needs allowed the director to put together a plan to help the team move on. Knowing that the team would be overwhelmed, they created an open list of all open positions and cross-referenced the skill sets of each team member, helping them to find and apply for internal transfers. Ultimately, 60 of the 66 found jobs within the company, and the transition was a relative success.

Another area where TPMs make daily decisions is in risk management. If you have ever stopped to think about whether to delay a milestone due to a realized risk for fear of the consequences from leadership, this is emotional intelligence guiding you on the potential emotional impact. Risk analysis can also consider emotional impact, although we often refer to this as risk attitude, or risk tolerance. This is the level of risk an individual or organization is able to tolerate to meet the desired outcome.

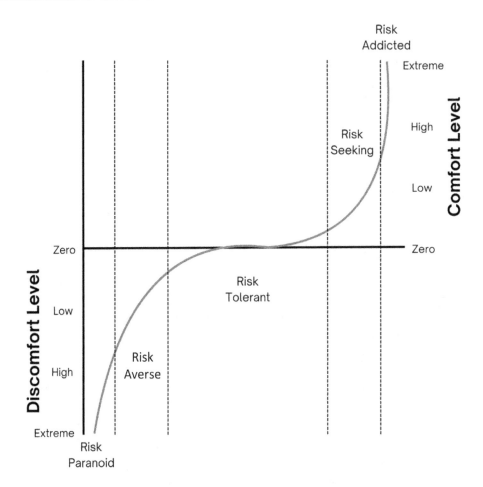

Figure 10.3: Risk attitude spectrum (adapted from Hillson & Murray-Webster, 2005)

Figure 10.3 shows the range of emotional responses to uncertainty. When comfortable with change, someone can range from being risk-tolerant to actively seeking risks, and ultimately, being risk-addicted. The reverse is true when someone is uncomfortable with change. A person can swing from tolerance, via aversion, to outright paranoia.

When discussing the risk score and risk strategies for a given risk, the TPM must manage their emotions and those of the impacted stakeholders, ensuring that the strategies decided upon can be enacted without hesitation if the time comes. While some people are more risk-averse, others are risk seekers. The adage of "no pain, no gain" is an attitude of risk-seeking, where hard work is seen to outweigh the risk of failure without question.

What do you do if you have both risk-averse and risk-seeking stakeholders? These are the scenarios where following a set risk assessment procedure will help smooth out emotional responses. Scoring risks also reduces the introduction of bias and forces discussion on the true inherent risk associated with an event or action. As demonstrated by Sheryl Sandberg, open honesty, transparency, and empathy toward your team ensures open and inclusive discussions that will diminish the impact of an emotional response.

So far, I've mainly discussed emotional intelligence in relation to various conflict scenarios, where emotions are heightened and can hinder change. However, emotions can also be a force that propels progress forward, and an emotionally intelligent leader can use emotional expression to their advantage. Let's see how a high EQ can help you lead your team.

Driving strategic vision

Think for a moment of the most interesting talk you have heard in the last year. What made the talk so interesting? Was it the subject matter? Was it where the talk took place? Or was the speaker very engaging to their audience and full of infectious energy? It was most likely the speaker! Although a good subject and amazing venue can help, without an engaging speaker, the talk just wouldn't be memorable at all.

You can use emotion to motivate your team or inspire a positive work culture. Let's take a look at another leader at Microsoft, Satya Nadella, who took over from Steve Ballmer in 2014. Taking over from Ballmer's culture of cut-throat innovation that often pitted different departments against one another, Nadella introduced a strategic vision that centered on empathy and inclusion as well as a growth mindset. To address infighting, the mantra of "One Microsoft" was created, and many teams utilize the "One" brand in their name. Focus shifted from Windows to cloud- and mobile-first, and the strategy across the company shifted to match this vision.

These principles have transformed Microsoft into a more innovative and stable company with a safer, more inclusive company culture. It should be no surprise that refocusing on inclusion, empathy, and a unified vision also led to soaring profits, often landing it the title of most valuable company in the world and consistently within the top three.

Motivation is a key aspect of leadership, and emotional intelligence is at the root of successful motivation. Leaders regulate their emotions and use the emotional response of their team to propel compelling visions forward.

Stakeholder management

Regulating our emotions and using empathy in our communication is an effective strategy while executing programs. Outside of our immediate team, our stakeholders have high stakes in the success of our programs and require constant and consistent engagement. It's no wonder stakeholder management is its own sub-discipline within the program management industry.

Stakeholder communications like status reports, weekly check-ins, and leadership reviews all benefit from an emotionally intelligent TPM. I've talked about knowing your audience as it relates to including the right amount of detail for senior leadership, compared to a status for your team to consume. This idea extends to any stakeholder's emotional state and understanding how they will react to a status update, a new risk or issue arising, or their team being the cause of a delay. Most of the actions we take center on being emotionally empathetic to our stakeholders—actions like having regular and open communication or reaching out before a status report is sent out to let them know what will be said. These are all instances where best practices are put in place because they show empathy and understanding.

An example from the real world: *Stakeholder empathy*

In a recent program I was running that introduced a new model that impacted 10 teams across 2 VPs, I had a stakeholder who had been with the company for over 2 decades. They really knew their space and the history involved, and they had witnessed many successes and failures in large-scale model changes over the years. Needless to say, their opinion mattered a lot to choose the right direction. We were introducing a new attribute that would tell consumers of the model what the authoring system was of this set of new fields. Knowing the authoring system can help others determine how to best interpret data for their use case. The team wanted a field to be mandatory to ensure that it was used and remained relevant as more teams adopted the model change. The stakeholder had been pushing back vehemently for over a month, to the point of raising their voice in objection any time the subject came up.

In cases like this where a stakeholder is being highly vocal, it's easy to just go with what they want—it's the path of least friction and avoids more confrontation. However, the team knew that making the field mandatory was the right decision. Instead of matching their raised voice, I paused and considered what the risk aversion of the stakeholder might be, realizing that 2 decades' worth of failed projects would put the balance of risk aversion into an automatic negative reaction. I needed to remove the emotion and help them look at this decision from a purely rational standpoint. I de-escalated the conversation by repeating their concerns about possible downstream issues with a new mandatory field, and I acknowledged that they had a lot of experience and valid concerns. The emotions came down in the room, as they felt heard. I was then able to talk with them about the specifics of the problem and the fact that the decision to make it mandatory can easily be removed later if there are unfixable problems, but it would be next to impossible to make it mandatory later if we leave it as optional now. Knowing that I understood the concerns and presented a solution that left room to address the concerns allowed the stakeholder to change their position and move forward with the model changes.

Without recognizing their emotions and acknowledging them, the situation would have likely remained at a standstill or caused an irreversible decision to be made that was not in the best interests of the company in the long term. Emotional intelligence was the key to working with this stakeholder and moving the project forward.

Empathy comes up again and again in examples of strong leadership, and for good reason. Acts of empathy connect you to the people around you and keep the emotional doors open, allowing for more open communication. Openness and understanding lead to better outcomes, as they allow the actual reasons for disagreements to surface and get addressed. Without high emotional intelligence, actions are based solely on your needs or, at best, your internal (and usually unvetted) perception of the needs of others, leading to less long-term collaboration and, often, a less productive environment.

Summary

Emotional intelligence is the most important soft skill that a TPM can have in today's market. Although this has been true for decades, its importance has increased significantly in the shift toward GenAI for more and more of our day-to-day activities. In this chapter, we covered the key components of emotional intelligence, which are self-awareness, self-regulation, empathy, and social skills. We learned that these components build up from self-awareness of emotions, which leads to the ability to regulate them. Once you have control over your own emotions, this extends outward with empathy for others' emotions. These three core components manifest in various social skills that elevate your TPM presence.

We discussed the five common EQ assessments, available either online or through workshops, to help you determine your current EQ strengths and growth areas. Lastly, we discussed how to use emotional intelligence in technical program management and used examples from various leaders in the industry, seeing how emotional intelligence helped or hindered their leadership.

In *Chapter 11*, I'll introduce you to the technical toolset that is fundamental for a TPM. I'll discuss why a technical background is necessary, as well as which areas of your technical acumen are most utilized in the TPM role.

Further reading

- *Emotional Intelligence for the Modern Leader* by *Christopher D. Connors*. If you liked the interjections of EQ stories from leaders in this chapter, this book by Christopher Connors is a great look into how EQ helps modern leaders succeed.

- *Managing Risk Attitude using Emotional Literacy* by *David Hillson* and *Ruth Murray-Webster*. This is a paper that is often cited in the EQ industry. The Project Management Institute has the full paper in its learning library, and it is available to non-members.

- *Handwriting but not typewriting leads to widespread brain connectivity* a high-density EEG study with implications for the classroom by F.R. Van der Weel and Audrey L.H. Van der Meer. This paper showed that handwriting produced more brain activity in the hippocampus, which is vital to memory retention, over typing on a keyboard. Available via Frontiers in Psychology at https://doi.org/10.3389/fpsyg.2023.1219945
- *Paper Notebooks vs. Mobile Devices: Brain Activation Differences During Memory Retrieval by Keita Umejima et. al.* This paper demonstrates higher memory retention from handwriting versus digital mediums. Available via Frontiers in Behavioral Neuroscience at https://doi.org/10.3389/fnbeh.2021.634158
- *Meditation: Evidence Map of Systematic Reviews by Caio Fábio Schlechta Portella et al.* The meta-analysis confirmed several health benefits of meditation, including mindfulness. It's available via Frontiers in Public Health at https://doi.org/10.3389/fpubh.2021.742715

Additional resources

- **EQ-I 2.0 certification:** https://www.eitc.shop/product/eq-certification-online/
- **MSCEIT certification:** https://www.hpsys.com/Training_MSCEIT_Certification.htm
- **PEC online assessment:** https://emotional-competence.co/en
- **TEIQue online assessment:** https://teique.com/
- **W(L)EIS self-assessment:** https://emotivity.my/wp-content/uploads/How-Emotionally-Intelligent-are-You-Wong-and-Law-Emotional-Intelligence-Scale-WLEIS.pdf

Join our book's Discord space

Join our Discord community to meet like-minded people and learn alongside more than 5000 members at:

https://packt.link/sKmQa

Section 3

Technical Toolset

In this section, we will go into greater detail on the intersection between a technical background and project management. We'll discuss the technical skills most often utilized in the TPM role and see how these skills enhance your existing management skills to be the most efficient practitioner you can be. This includes the use of GenAI tools to enhance your project management skills and your understanding of your technical teams.

This section contains the following chapters:

- *Chapter 11, The Technical Toolset*
- *Chapter 12, Code Development Expectations*
- *Chapter 13, System Design and Architectural Landscape*
- *Chapter 14, Harnessing the Power of Artificial Intelligence in Technical Program Management*
- *Chapter 15, Enhancing Management Using Your Technical Toolset*

11

The Technical Toolset

In this chapter, I'll make the case for the technical toolset. Introduced in *Chapter 2, Pillars of a Technical Program Manager*, the technical toolset is a foundational pillar for a TPM. It is the connecting glue between the other pillars (program and project management) and is the foundational pillar that sets a TPM apart from a generalist PM.

We'll continue by discussing the various tools in the technical toolset and how they help you not only excel at your job but also work across job families as the need arises.

We'll explore the technical toolset through the following topics:

- Examining the need for a technical background
- Defining the technical toolset

Let's get started!

Examining the need for a technical background

In discussing the origins of the TPM role, we looked at the role of the PM and how gaps in knowledge could hinder the execution of a project or program. This book has focused largely on the tech industry and the common usage of the word *technical* to refer to information technology. However, if you look at the word as a synonym for *specialized*, then the need for a *specialized* background might be a bit clearer.

Looking back at the pillars of the TPM from *Chapter 2*, program and project management are two-thirds of the foundation of a TPM. This is because these skills transcend each individual project and program management job that you may hold. They are the most fundamental skills needed to succeed.

However, to truly thrive as a TPM, your specialty focus as a technically minded practitioner requires a fundamental understanding of technology. This is what sets you apart and allows you to be more successful than a generalist PM could ever be in this role.

The TPM handles the day-to-day work with the technical teams and must understand what their technical teams are doing. The closer aligned the technical backgrounds are between the TPM and their teams, the better they'll be able to respond to issues and set them up for success. It doesn't end there though, as simple tasks such as planning can be done faster and more efficiently if you understand the work that you are adding to your plan. This power can compound the longer you work with a specific team and understand their frameworks, services, service pipeline infrastructure, and software languages. All of this information can speed up your estimation of tasks and your ability to understand what work can be done in parallel or fast-tracked. Like many professions, the education you get prepares you to ask the right questions, and asking the right questions can mean the difference between a well-laid plan and a late-running, over-budget disaster.

The need for the TPM has become so ubiquitous that subdivisions of the role have started to arise. Let's look at how the TPM role is becoming more specialized in the tech industry.

TPM specializations

The tech industry as a whole is still getting used to the concept of a TPM as a needed role. However, some companies are going a step further and making it more specialized within the technical spectrum. This makes sense given that the reason for the TPM role in the tech industry is to provide specialized knowledge of technology to the PM role. As the market for TPMs becomes saturated, a more nuanced delineation is needed when a simple technical background will not suffice. When you need a TPM specializing in **Application Security** (**AppSec**), then the title becomes *TPM – AppSec*. If you need a TPM that can help you move entire ecosystems to the cloud, you may need a *Solutions Architect – TPM*.

Common path to becoming a TPM

The career path of a TPM was covered in *Chapter 3, Career Paths*, but it's worth noting here that while the discussion on needing a technical background sounds like the path to a TPM is as a PM that expands their technical knowledge, the path is most often a person with a technical background (for example, a software developer, systems developer, or another similar role) that expands their PM skill set.

This is why this book provides a lot of chapters on PM skills that are relevant to a TPM as this is the area of growth for most people coming into the TPM field.

This trend of specialization is similar outside of the tech industry where TPMs are needed. A medical company may need a TPM with specific medical knowledge or a specific software package or device. One such job where this is needed is **Program Manager (Medical Device)**. Though listed as a PM, the role requires an engineering background with knowledge of working with feature launches of medical devices. If the need is large enough, a new title may be created. *Figure 11.1* illustrates a few different TPM specializations found on the *Amazon* job board and how they are related:

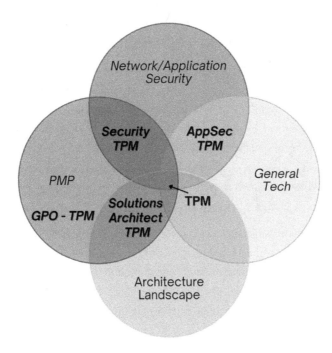

Figure 11.1: Specialized Program Manager overlaps

All of these TPM positions have a basic requirement of project and program management, as well as some technical background. The type of technical background needed is a large differentiator that denotes the nuances between some of these specialties. AppSec and Security TPMs share similar security-related skills. The solutions architect needs to understand the **full stack**, or the services used from the frontend to the backend of a cloud system.

Some of the specializations are not geared toward the technical background but instead toward specialized tools used in that role. The **Global Process Owner (GPO)** role focuses on change management, acceleration, and process improvement skills such as *Lean* and *Kaizen*. The Security TPM focuses on the Risk Management Framework, which is a specific type of risk analysis life cycle based on the life cycle described in *Chapter 7*.

This categorization is not exhaustive of what is out there, nor are the differences between them the same as every company has slightly different needs. However, this illustrates the varying degrees to which a technical background is required to perform the TPM role.

Are these micro-specialties needed?

The TPM role is born out of a need for specialization in order to run a program efficiently. The PM in charge needs to have an intimate understanding of what the team is doing in order to adapt quickly to change. They need to be able to anticipate issues, challenge assumptions, and keep stakeholders involved.

As with any specialty, there is a balance between where the specialization enhances their ability to be effective and when the specialization is too specific to allow the practitioner to thrive. A TPM specializes in technology—largely either software or hardware as a generalist. They can adapt quickly to a specific need through on-the-job learning of specifics needed. This is the same as a software developer or electrical engineer—they don't come out of school knowing the exact language or hardware they will work on, but they have the knowledge and skills to learn and adapt. This is why the TPM role has thrived for so long.

Now, take this specialization deeper, and require your TPM to have a specific skill like knowledge of a Risk Management Framework. On one hand, a TPM with this skill will be able to immediately contribute, but on the other, the pool of available talent is greatly reduced. There may be a stellar TPM practitioner who lacks that skill set but excels in all other aspects of the job but isn't considered.

If the skill is absolutely required immediately and can't be taught along the way, then there may be a need. Or, if the skill required is relatively general, like Application Security, then the balance is still intact.

In general, there needs to be a balance between specialization and the ability to find strong talent that can still adapt to change as needed.

Technical proficiencies used daily

In a specialized TPM role, like the ones mentioned earlier, a generalist TPM can ramp up and perform the job as they already have the pillars needed to be a successful TPM in place. This ramp-up is often costly in terms of both time and resources and isn't always fit for the needs of the organization. So, just as a PM could learn the technical foundation needed for a specific purpose or role, a TPM can do the same.

As we'll explore in more detail in the next four chapters, your technical skills are widely used at every stage of a project or program. We've discussed some of the roles and responsibilities that a TPM has in various aspects of project management. *Table 10.1* provides a list of standard roles and responsibilities that a TPM may have where some level of technical acumen is needed:

Key Management Area	Step	Role
Planning	Refine requirements	Accountable
	Create functional specification	Accountable/Responsible
	Sprint planning	Responsible/Consult
	Review designs	Consult
Stakeholder Management	Draft communication plan	Accountable/Responsible
	Daily standups	Consult
	Status report/meeting	Accountable
	Leadership review	Responsible
Risk Management	Risk analysis	Accountable
	Risk monitoring	Accountable/Responsible
	Issue resolution	Accountable

Table 11.1: Roles and responsibilities of a TPM

Throughout the life of the project or program, the TPM is constantly drawing on their technical toolset to deliver key artifacts, resolve issues, drive clarity, and ultimately deliver on the goal.

During planning, the TPM relies on their technical background to clarify ambiguity in requirements and to ensure they can transform them into a **functional specification (functional spec)**, which is a document mapping business requirements to functionality (APIs, user actions, and features). In turn, the functional spec relies on the TPM's technical background and system knowledge to trace the system functionality back to the requirements. This can be seen as an intermediary step from requirements to the project plan, and in this book, the leap from requirements to plan has been simple enough to not warrant a separate functional spec. However, for more complex projects, a functional spec is needed to ensure all requirements are understood and accounted for in the plan and is a good document for the development team to understand what work needs to be done. Here's an example using a few of the requirements for the Windows Rollout project from *Chapter 6, Table 6.5*:

Windows Rollout Project – Mercury Program
Functional Specification

Change Log

Version	Author	Notes
1.0	csantoro	First iteration

Project Summary

The Windows Rollout project is part of the Mercury Program and will deliver a Windows-based application for the Mercury P2P messaging network. The project is in alignment with the other OS teams and shares some dependent work across the teams related to the P2P subsystem.

Frontend Team

Req. ID	Task	Systems	Estimate
14	Add editable dropdown combo box for availability	Frontend / Message model	0.2
15	Add editable dropdown combo box for location	Frontend / Message model	0.2
19	Delete option for messages	Frontend / Message History Page	0.2

Backend Team

Req. ID	Task	Systems	Estimate
14	Add KVP to presence model for availability	Backend / Presence Data Model	0.2
15	Add KVP to presence model for location	Backend / Presence Data Model	0.2
19	Add delete method for message history	Backend / Message Model	0.2

Figure 11.2: Functional specification for the Windows Rollout project

In the above figure, the requirements are assigned to different areas of the Windows team: the frontend and backend groups. I took three requirements that impact both teams to show that a requirement doesn't necessarily map to a single team's work. In a functional spec, you want to include enough information for the teams involved to understand the breakdown. For this example, I'm tracing back to the requirement it came from in the `Req. ID` column, followed by a name for the task that is specific to that team. The `Systems` column is something I like to add as it shows which areas (services, packages, and classes) are impacted by the functional requirement. Lastly, I give an estimate for the work. I prefer to do a first draft myself and then collaborate with the development teams to get us on the same page, but collaborating from the start is perfectly reasonable as well. I do it this way to reduce the amount of time I'm taking from the development team and I find that people are more productive when they have a document to assess as opposed to creating something from scratch.

I included a change log and project summary as well to add context to the document and give an idea of any changes that may have happened between versions. This document will help the team during execution so they can plan their work accordingly.

During execution, TPMs provide input during sprint planning as to which items to pick up, which draws on the project plan and technical dependencies between tasks that the TPM has identified. In design reviews, the TPM uses their understanding of system design as well as the surrounding architectural landscape to influence the right design choices based on the needs of the project, team, and company.

Stakeholder management is focused on your ability to bridge the gap between business and technical concepts. As the communication bridge between the technical and business worlds, you draft the communications plan and ensure you have the right type of communications in place to bridge the technical gaps in understanding. Status reports, meetings, and leadership reviews all require you to tailor your narrative to the technical proficiency of your audience.

Let's look at a single scenario and see how it would need to be handled differently, depending on your audience. Let's say you have a design that has been delayed because the service interface contract between two services cannot be agreed upon. The sending team wants to treat missing or empty data as null, whereas the receiving team has a technical limitation where their service cannot handle a null value. The receiving team wants the values to be sent as empty strings, or to create default values for every parameter, and the sending team is challenging why the receiving service cannot handle null values for data that is not required to have a value based on the business use case.

If this scenario came up in a project that was building out a platform feature that was not externally facing, your stakeholders are likely all technically minded, and your status reports can stay technical. You would list out exactly what the issue was: a service contract disagreement, and the options being explored—setting default values or updating the receiving service to understand a null value. The audience would understand what was going on, as well as what the next steps were.

However, if your project is to deliver a customer-facing feature or product, you likely have non-technical stakeholders, so the leadership review and status report need to be written in a way that they will understand this issue. In this case, it may be best to state that a design sign-off has been delayed due to a mismatching of requirements and what the newly expected ETA for the sign-off will be. A link to a more detailed rendition of the problem can be added but the details are left at a level that non-technical teams would likely understand: the requirements or implementation steps are not clear, and the team is seeking clarity to close it out.

On the opposite end of translating a technical issue to a business stakeholder, you will be translating business needs into technical requirements or clarifications for your team during daily standups or sprint planning meetings. A common occurrence for this could be in the interpretation of the business requirements as the business teams may have their own jargon that can be confusing to your team. As an example, I worked with tax compliance legislation, where requirements take multiple steps to get to the development team as they are essentially translated from legislation into system requirements and then into functional specifications. On the extreme end, you have the business as the tax legislation that is written. Legislation is often very heavy in legal terminology, which can be hard to translate into system requirements. For instance, one law may refer to the tax owed on a customer's purchase. This may seem straightforward for a brick-and-mortar system but can be complicated when talking about e-commerce systems, where a purchase may result in multiple boxes being shipped out, blurring the line on what a purchase is. Understanding the difference between what the law says a purchase is versus what that means for the e-commerce ecosystem is something I worked on as the TPM when writing functional specifications. Helping the development team understand that a purchase has a different meaning in the business than it does in the technical workflows helps remove built-in assumptions from the developers as to what work is being done. When the same word or phrase has more than one meaning across different teams, it can cause immediate confusion and missed requirements.

In risk management, the analysis will draw on your deep understanding of the technical systems you are working with to identify and classify risks. The more you know and understand the frameworks, network protocols, latency constraints, and availability needs of your system, the more problems you will be able to foresee.

Now that we know why the technical toolset is needed, let's explore how the toolset can help you help your team by helping others in their role.

Using your technical toolset to wear many hats

Wearing many hats means leaning into one technical skill over another to fill in gaps in roles based on need. As such, your technical toolset should be well-rounded in preparation for that need.

In *Chapter 1*, we discussed the need for a TPM to *wear many hats*, or to take on part of a role that is normally adjacent to you but that is missing. If your organization has a product but doesn't have a product manager, you might find yourself prioritizing a product roadmap. Similarly, some TPMs take on the role of a scrum master when one isn't present.

Each of these roles leans on different technical skills and will require some level of proficiency to *wear the hat* effectively. *Figure 11.3* illustrates the interconnection your technical toolset provides to allow you to step into varying roles:

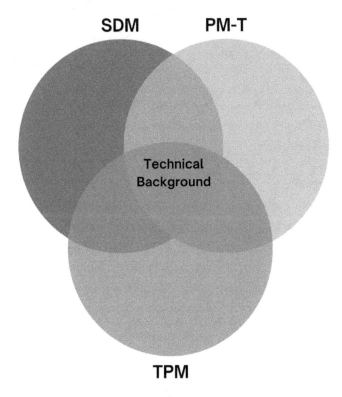

Figure 11.3: Technical overlap across job families

This Venn diagram highlights that, across the adjacent job families of TPM, PM-T, and SDM, all three positions rely on a technical background to succeed. As seen in *Chapter 1, Figure 1.5*, each of these has some overlap outside of the technical background that also helps you wear the hat of a PM-T or SDM. However, without this technical background, the other skills would not be enough for you to step into these other roles to take on service-level projects for the SDM or roadmap prioritization efforts of a PM-T.

Now that we've made the case for needing a technical background and how the technical toolset will help you in your role, let's look into what the skills are in the toolset.

Defining the technical toolset

As we discovered in the previous section, the technical foundation that you have can vary widely, depending on what your role requires.

Each of these tools is an accelerator to your role when your proficiency matches the needs of your team. In cases where it doesn't match, you will need to lean on a specialist that does have that proficiency, such as a specific programming language. This will add time to the project as additional communication is needed to get the same results you would get if you were proficient in the right technical skills.

In this section, we'll discuss three areas that are most widely used across the generalist and specialist TPM roles. We'll touch on the level of code proficiency that may be needed, system design, and the architectural landscape.

Code proficiency

As a TPM, you will rarely be asked to write code. However, this doesn't mean you shouldn't be proficient. You will be working alongside software developers as they are the main resources working on technical projects. This means that your work breakdown structure will largely be high-level coding tasks, or stories, aimed toward your development team to implement. Your estimates, daily standups, and a large portion of issues and risks will be related to code or some part of the software development life cycle, such as deployment or testing issues.

To determine accurate estimates, confirm timelines for tasks, and even help with designs, you'll need to have a basic understanding of reading and writing code. As with most tech jobs that require you to write code, the language you know isn't as important as knowing one. This is because understanding a programming language is more about the capabilities, shortcomings, and problem-solving related to programming languages.

Learning the syntax of another language and ramping up on its weaknesses and strengths is much easier once you know at least one language. This is why many tech companies allow their developers to interview in any mainstream language and this applies to the TPM role as well.

There is one caveat to this, however. There are different types of programming languages and knowing a language of one type doesn't immediately translate to a language of a different type. The most common types in modern systems are object-oriented languages such as *Java*, *C#*, and *Objective-C*, and functional languages such as *Scala* and *Haskell*. *Python* can be used to write in both styles and is popular in technical classes for this reason. Knowing an object-oriented language does not guarantee an immediate understanding of a functional language because they behave fundamentally differently. The same is true for the reverse as well. However, knowing one language is still easier than learning from scratch!

Chapter 12 will go into more specifics about the level of code proficiency expected, along with some examples.

System design

System design involves mapping the components and data flow within a system or service. It is also the most commonly exercised technical proficiency for a TPM. This is because most TPMs are associated with a service team or group of service teams, so knowing how the service components connect, what their APIs do, and which other services they interface with is required to perform your job. You cannot effectively write a functional spec without understanding the system that the functional spec is referencing.

In most cases, your day-to-day experience with system design will involve writing functional specs and participating in design reviews. This means you will mainly be learning existing systems, so understanding how to dive deep into a system is an important skill to hone. You need to learn what APIs are available to clients of the system, what arguments they take, and what information they vend. I find that to truly understand an API, it's best to also understand why it exists in the first place. This goes deeper than the answer that it exists to vend certain data. You need to ask why the API was created in the first place instead of extending an existing API and what service boundaries the API is working within. This can be enlightening in cases where an API was extended to a newer version. The reason a new version was created can tell you a lot about the limitations of the service or its clients as well as how the service has evolved to cope with change over time.

As the bridge between the business team and the technical team, it is important to understand the *why* and *how* of your systems as much as the *why* and *how* of your business. The reason why an API exists—which is often business-related—can help drive clarity to software designs when the developer proposes multiple options based on technical optimizations or needs.

You can rule out proposals based on the business context of the requirements of the API or the needs of the business. Acting as the bridge is where our most valuable contributions come from.

A bridge can also exist between multiple technical teams. In this example of examining an API, I've talked about why the API exists from the service team's point of view and from the business point of view. It is also worth knowing what your customers are doing with the data they get from the API and why they need it. This ensures you have a holistic view of the API from the team that owns it, the team that helps shape it (business), and the team that consumes it. They will all have slightly different perspectives on the API and its use.

An example from the real world: *What happens when system design doesn't bridge the gap?*

A few years back, a relatively junior team was taking over a storage system owned by my organization. The team had a lot of internal user complaints about how hard it was to add new fields to the storage model and a concern about the provenance of some of the data being added. The junior team led a new design effort to rebuild the storage system and centered the design ideas around the internal team's pain points.

As a storage team, the data they were storing was used by upstream services, and the model was effectively owned by those services upstream of them. The storage team failed to check with the team that generated the data to understand their perspective. They also failed to check downstream service teams that read the data they stored to understand their needs.

I came into the project to take over from a TPM who left the company only to find a system that was almost fully implemented but didn't meet nearly half of the requirements of our end customers, nor did it fit with the usage of the team that generated the data to be stored.

The project was paused and reassessed, and though it moved forward, the scope of work was shifted and some data controls that were desired by the storage team were removed to allow for proper use of the data being retrieved by downstream systems.

Almost 3 years later, there's a discussion to scrap the new storage system. This all stemmed from not bridging the gap between all of the relevant teams to truly understand how a system is being used before designing a replacement.

Chapter 12 will also cover system design in more detail and will provide an example of system design, as well as some expectations in interviews.

Architecture landscape

An **architecture landscape** is a map of application and service interconnectivity at an organization or enterprise level. It's similar to a system design but has a wider scope. Whether or not you will need this depends on your organizational structure and how closely you work with systems outside of your team. This also correlates with your TPM level: the higher your level, the wider your scope and impact becomes, which will necessitate understanding periphery systems to your team. Just as a junior developer would only focus on creating classes and methods for an existing system, an entry-level TPM would focus more on the immediate systems they interact with and may not think much about the overall architectural landscape.

Given the broader scope of architecture landscapes compared to a system design, the level of depth you'll be expected to understand is much more shallow. After all, these systems are not your immediate concern, so knowing about their internal data flows is not nearly as important as understanding the input and output of the systems.

When mapping out an architecture landscape, you may focus on different aspects of system relationships, such as system dependencies or data flow. Each of these aspects brings a different perspective of the landscape to light and may aid in answering different questions. For instance, if you need to get access to a piece of data, knowing where that data originates and which systems it currently flows through can help you define and design a solution that gets the data to where you need it. However, knowing the system dependencies can help you determine the impact an API change may have on downstream services so that you can start a campaign to work with potentially impacted clients to navigate the change.

Understanding your architecture landscape is another area where the TPM acting as the bridge between the technical team and business teams is important. Similar to knowing the ins and outs of a system, knowing how your system connects to other systems in the company ecosystem can help you notice patterns or places of concern that others closer to the project cannot see. Understanding how downstream systems might react to a new piece of data or even a new value for an existing field can speed up the design process and prevent undue issues from coming up during integration and testing. Aside from knowing how systems will behave with new data, you also understand which systems are impacted by your requirements and can include them in your initial project plan.

Summary

In this chapter, we looked into the need for a technical background to be successful as a TPM. As a specialized PM, the TPM brings their technical toolset to the table to manage a technical project more effectively. We saw how the trend of a specialized PM is going deeper as the TPM position itself is being refined into hyper-focused areas of expertise, such as `AppSec - TPM`.

Then, we examined the common technical background across adjacent job families and how this allows the TPM to fill in gaps in personnel on their project or team more effectively than PM skills alone.

Lastly, we looked into the tools in the toolset that are most used across the industry to get a sense of how those tools are used.

In *Chapter 12*, we'll dive deeper into some of the technical skills introduced in this chapter. We'll discuss code use and proficiency for the TPM role and look at some of the high-level concepts you should understand.

We'll also discuss system design. As this is a highly used skill and it is often brought up in interviews, we'll focus on good and bad design practices while using the *Mercury* project as a basis for the examples.

Additional resources

You can find templates regarding functional specifications in the GitHub repo related to this book. Please check the Preface for the GitHub link.

Join our book's Discord space

Join our Discord community to meet like-minded people and learn alongside more than 5000 members at:

`https://packt.link/sKmQa`

12

Code Development Expectations

In this chapter, we'll cover code development expectations for a TPM that is working in a software environment. As discussed in this book, there are other specializations of the TPM role, in particular a hardware-facing TPM, that may not find this chapter as relevant. However, the majority of TPMs in the industry are working with software teams, including some hardware TPMs, so this is an important topic to cover. Though programming isn't a core competency that you should expect to see come up in an interview, it is foundational to project and program success. If we don't understand what our team is doing, and if we can't relate, push back, and advise, then we will never have complete control over our project.

Trust is a very important part of being a leader. You need to be able to trust that your team knows what they are doing and are making the right decisions, but you also need to be able to verify progress and be there for your team when they need your input. This is what I mean when I say control; it's not that you are micro-managing every aspect, but that you understand enough to know when to trust and verify and when you need to be in the middle of a problem working toward the solution.

Without understanding the basics of programming, it will be hard to achieve the right balance of trust and verification. With that in mind, we'll go over some fundamental code concepts that are most relevant as a TPM. These concepts are not exhaustive but will provide a good foundation for additional knowledge related to programming. Along with system design and architectural landscape design in *Chapter 13*, these topics are important to any TPM position in the tech industry. Not every TPM has these foundational skills, but the best TPMs I know in the industry do.

This chapter will cover the expectations of code knowledge and give an overview of important concepts and language basics. However, it is not meant to be a single source of truth on programming knowledge. If this is an area in which you feel the need to improve, use this chapter as a guide to know what to dive deeper into and provide a primer. There are books in the *Further reading* section to go into more depth.

We'll explore these code development expectations through the following topics:

- Understanding code development expectations
- Exploring programming language basics
- Diving into data structures
- Learning design patterns

Let's start at the core by looking at code development.

Understanding code development expectations

TPMs are surrounded by software development teams and interact with developers, support engineers, and development managers on a daily basis. They are involved in technical discussions around requirements, release management, and feature and system designs. So, in the midst of all of this software talk, let's explore what level of code proficiency is expected in the TPM role.

No code writing required!

As a TPM, your focus will not be on writing code yourself, but on getting it written through others. Of all of the TPMs I know and have worked with, only two—including myself—have written code as part of their role. I've heard of TPMs writing code in start-ups. This aligns with our need to wear many hats because the number of people involved in a start-up is comparatively small and the need to step up has a higher chance of occurring. In larger companies, roles are usually tightly defined, and the overlap and opportunity to write code has a smaller chance of occurring.

The type of code I've written as part of my role was only to help me perform my job and was not related to project deliverables. In one case, I was doing data analysis (wearing the hat of a data analyst as we did not have one on the team) and needed to take service logs and extract client information from each call to get a list of clients. I started by just using simple text manipulation in a text editor but saw an opportunity to write a script to get the job done much faster, so I wrote it. A fellow TPM wrote a script to pull and format data from a tool into a status report, reducing the time to draft the weekly status report. This wasn't strictly needed to do the job, and no one saw the code, but it made our jobs easier.

Though not required, writing this code fits my style of management, and I also enjoy writing code anyway. I say this to illustrate that though some TPMs may write code, it's by no means a requirement of the job.

That being said, you will be working directly with software developers, and to be an effective leader and communicator, it's best that you understand the basics of at least one programming language. We'll start by looking at basic concepts of programming.

Exploring programming language basics

Most companies lean heavily toward a specific language or set of languages, depending on what the code is used for. Server-side applications in enterprise settings tend to prefer Java, whereas **machine learning** (ML) applications perform fairly well in functional languages or hybrid languages such as Python. Whichever language you find yourself closest to, you should learn the basics of that language. If the team you work with heavily uses a functional language and you only know **object-oriented** (OO) languages, use this as an opportunity to bridge the gap and learn the fundamentals of functional programming. There are books on both language types referenced in the *Further reading* section of this chapter to go into more detail but I'll cover some of the basics here.

As a brief recap, **OO programming** (**OOP**) is a language paradigm where the application is defined by a series of objects that can interact with each other. An object consists of data fields and methods that act upon the data fields. Most OOP languages also support events, which are methods that are automatically invoked based on the state of the application. As an example of an event, in a standard Windows dialog box, the **OK** and **Cancel** buttons on the dialog box are both objects. Both buttons have an event that is triggered when a user clicks on the corresponding button. The buttons also have data, such as the text on the button, pointers to the OnClick event (which points to code to execute once the button is clicked), and even font settings for the text. By clicking on the **Cancel** button, the button's OnClick event will interact with the dialog box—which is the parent object for the button—and have it close with a special state denoting that the dialog's request was canceled. The application that invoked the dialog box will then have the chance to act upon the canceled state. When events are the catalyst of interaction for a program, it is called event-driven programming. In an event-driven program, not all actions are driven by the user, as some events may be triggered by hardware changes, or by other applications on the system, among other reasons, but the concept of objects interacting with each other is the central concept of OOP. The interactions are through a series of written-out procedures to manipulate the state of the application—this makes OOP a type of **imperative programming**.

A primer on abstraction and inheritance

OOP has two key concepts that should be understood before moving on: abstraction and inheritance.

To understand why these are important, we need a quick primer on what a class is. A class is a group of code instructions that define an object, its methods, and its properties. When we talk about calling a method, this method lies within a class on the object we are referring to.

OOP developed a way to write less code and form a model that allows one class to build on top of the foundation of another. One class can **inherit** all the properties and methods of another class and can then add additional properties and methods that are specific to it. A class can also have another class defined within it, called a subclass. This allows for complex modeling of the real world within an object model.

An abstract class, or an abstract method within a class, is an outline of a class or method with no code inside. An abstract class will have properties and methods defined but the methods won't have any code inside them. Classes that inherit from this abstract class must define the content of the methods themselves. What this does is ensure that all subclasses that inherit from a given abstract class have the same methods and signatures on those methods. This makes acting upon an instance of a class easy because you don't need to know the specific subclass in order to invoke it. *Figure 12.1* shows a classic example of a car:

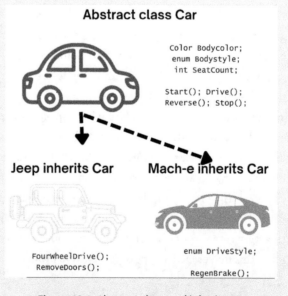

Figure 12.1: Abstract class and inheritance

As an example, think of an abstract class called Car. This would have properties like color, body style, number of seats, and so on. It can have a subclass called Wheels that contains properties like wheel size, number of wheels, and tread type. The Car class has abstract methods for Start(), Drive(), Reverse(), and Stop().

Now you can have a class that inherits from the Car abstract class and call it Jeep. This inherits the properties of the Car class and must define how the car starts, drives, reverses, and stops. It can add a new method for four-wheel driving called FourWheelDrive() that is specific to it and maybe another to remove the doors! Another class, the electric Mach-e, also inherits from Car. It has a new enum property to define the driving style, like eco-mode, sport, or fast. It also has another method for stopping that invokes regenerative braking, called RegenBrake.

Now, with cars that actually drive themselves, those in that industry are probably looking at the example and crying out at its simplicity, but you can understand the general idea, as well as how it can save a lot of needless typing and allow for complex relationships between objects!

In contrast, **functional programming** utilizes **declarative programming**. In a declarative computer language, the code does not describe how to perform an action, only what the outcome needs to be. In the popular declarative language **SQL**, you are stating which data you need in the SELECT clause, which filter to apply to the data in the WHERE clause, and which tables to retrieve the data from in the FROM clause. You are not stating how to retrieve the data (such as running a loop over the data and retrieving specific fields for each object, then sorting the resulting list). The language will determine how to best retrieve the data on its own.

The declarative nature of functional programming puts emphasis on the **function**, which is a method that returns a value, instead of objects and their interactions with one another. Therefore, the data remains local to the individual functions, which reduces side effects by not allowing non-local data manipulation. The data returned by the function is all that has been manipulated.

Regardless of the language type, you should know enough about the language to read through the code and have a basic grasp of what it is doing. This is especially useful in organizations where the code base is accessible to you (not all companies have an open code base or allow non-developers access). Being able to read a method and see what it does instead of finding a developer to explain it can be a valuable time-saver and will give you the chance to understand your services at a deeper level.

A good start to understanding a language, and your own services, is understanding the method, function, and API signatures. To do this, you need to understand the components of the signature as well as what that API is doing. The following code snippet takes a look at an example method from the original source code (in C#) for the Windows *Mercury* messaging app. We'll examine the method signature and discuss the basics of what the method is doing as an illustration of the level of depth that is useful for a TPM to have in *Figure 12.2*:

```
public void SendTextMessage(string message, MemberInfo miTo)
{
    messenger.SendMessage(new MessageInformation
        {
            Member = myInfo,
            MessageType = MessageInformation.MessageTypes.Text,
            To = miTo.ComputerName,
            Text = message
        });
}
```

Figure 12.2: Mercury code snippet

In this example, the method we are looking at is a method in the Member class that sends a text message to another client on the network. This is a method, as opposed to a function, as it is defined within a class and therefore has access to all information within the class. This tells us that the procedure does not return a value and is therefore a method. For a function, the keyword void would instead be an object or data type corresponding to the object or data type that the function returns. This method has two parameters: a string named message and an object of type MemberInfo called miTo.

Inside the method, the SendMessage method is invoked on an object named messenger. This method, in turn, is passed a single argument of a new object of the type MessageInformation, which is instantiated, or created, inside the method.

There are several objects referenced within this method that are defined outside of this code snippet. However, some inferences can be made based on the names of these objects. For instance, we can guess the intent of the method is to send a text-based message from the current user to someone else on the network. Based on the method call to SendMessage on the messenger object, we can make an educated guess that the messenger object is responsible for sending the actual message. This is further reinforced by the payload in the argument being information on the sender, client, and actual message to be sent.

As you can see from this example, a full understanding of every construct in a language is not needed to build a good idea of what is going on. Following through from the method signature to what the method is doing can often build up enough context to understand what is going on. And if you have full access to the code, further investigation into the definition of these custom objects can solidify your confidence in what the method is doing and even where it is invoked from within the application. Though this is a method from within a class, this same exercise works for APIs of services and is extremely helpful in building an understanding of how the services and applications you work with interact with one another and the type of data they return.

Now that we have established the required basic language literacy, we'll move on to some fundamental programming constructs that will likely surround you in your day-to-day dealings with developers and software development managers.

Diving into data structures

Though a TPM is not held to the same level of proficiency as a software developer, we should understand the basic concepts of programming. We'll cover the programming topics that come up the most in your day-to-day activities.

A *data structures and algorithms* class was likely in your first or second year of college if you took the traditional route of obtaining a computer science degree. As with most of the programming fundamentals, you won't use this yourself in your day-to-day work. However, you can think of it as a strong foundation for the language that your development team will use in most conversations you have with them. I'll briefly go over a few of the more common data structures that I come across in design meetings, standups, and general work conversations. I encourage you to read through the books in the *Further reading* section on this topic for a more in-depth review. Even if you've taken the class and remember the concepts, it's always good to refresh your memory.

Space and time complexities

Before discussing data structures, it is helpful to understand the **Key Performance Indicators (KPIs)** that we measure them by. In a computer, **random access memory (RAM)** is where data is stored that is in active use, such as variables in an application. As RAM is a limited resource, measuring the amount of space data takes up in RAM is an important consideration. The other consideration is the amount of time it takes to perform an action on the data such as searching, inserting, deleting, or accessing the data. This is especially true for OOP, where data is often accessed inside of loops that iterate over large datasets. The amount of time it takes to perform an action once is then compounded by the number of times the loop is run and can add up very quickly to a considerable time sink if the wrong data structure is utilized for the task.

Both of these measurements use what is referred to as **big O** (*big "Oh"*) notation. These measurements are essentially categories used for reference to understand the performance of a data structure or method. For this context, big O notation is used assuming asymptotic growth and uses *n* to denote the input that impacts the growth. Essentially, these math functions represent the curve, or behavior, that the space or time performance will start to match as *n* gets larger. As an example, if the amount of time it takes to access a specific element correlates linearly to where it is in the data structure—for instance, the fifth element in a collection—the big O would be *O (n)*. As *n* increases, so does the time it takes, which is referred to as linear time. However, if the amount of time it takes to access an element from a data structure is the same regardless of where in the data structure the element is, then the big O is *O (1)*, or in other words, constant time. As a TPM, knowing where the complexity categories come from isn't as important as knowing the relative costs associated with each big O. *Figure 12.3* shows each big O category on a curve of *operations* versus *elements*:

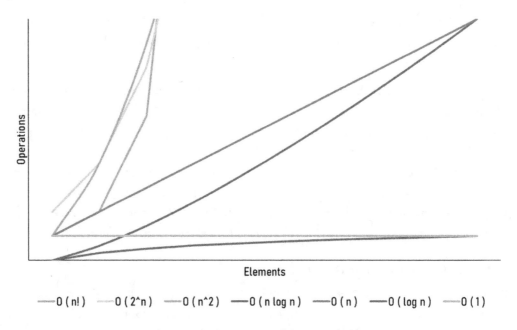

Figure 12.3: Big O space and time complexity

As a TPM and not a software developer, this is one of the instances in which understanding the relative position of best to worst is more important than how and why the algorithm functions. In this diagram, we can see that a *big O* of *O (n!)* (*n factorial*) performs worse once *n* gets large, and *O (log n)* and *O (1)* perform best at near-flat curves. In the *Data structures* section, I'll refer to the big O if it is of particular interest.

It's worth noting that these categories are models of performance and won't necessarily match real-world performance, especially as *n* becomes much larger than expected, as can happen in large-scale tech industry applications.

Data structures

There are a large number of data structures that you will come across in programming, so much so that there are entire books on this topic alone. I've added a good book that covers this extensively in the *Further reading* section at the end of this chapter. For now, I'll summarize a few of the more common data structures that you'll come across as a TPM listening and contributing to design reviews, standups, and various hallway conversations. The goal here isn't to make you an expert, but to ensure you know enough to be comfortable in conversations and make informed decisions when appropriate.

Linear data structures

First up are **linear data structures**. These are a collection of objects that are accessed in a sequential fashion. In OOP, the most common way to act upon a large dataset is to loop through each piece of data and perform the same manipulation on each one. As such, linear data structures are some of the most common data structures you will encounter in OOP applications. We'll discuss the three most common linear data structures next.

Arrays are a sequentially allocated collection of values or objects accessed via one or more indices. The array can have multiple dimensions, the more common being a two-dimensional array, which can be visually thought of as a table with rows and columns. Arrays can be multi-dimensional as well and behave like a one-dimensional array where the value at a given index is an array itself. Since an array is sequentially allocated in memory, accessing a particular index is constant—an $O (1)$ complexity. This is because the index represents the distance in memory from the starting point of the array, so to get to the 50th element, you add 50 to the starting point in memory.

Lists are a collection of objects that are accessed in a linear fashion where you can traverse forward and sometimes backward. Many modern lists also support accessing via an index, essentially making them a one-dimensional array of objects with built-in methods to manipulate the list. As such, they behave similarly to arrays in terms of complexity when an index is involved. Without an index, accessing a specific element has an $O (n)$ complexity, and is constant with an index. In many languages, such as *Java* (ArrayList) and *C#* (List<T>), lists are internally structured as arrays but have built-in methods for manipulation. In this regard, lists are often preferred over arrays unless specific optimizations regarding size are required since arrays can be given a specific size when instantiated.

Dictionaries are a collection of key-value pairs where each key can only appear once in the collection, meaning that dictionaries are hash tables or hash maps—depending on the usage of the dictionary. Since the value is only accessed via the key, the manipulation of the dictionary is O (1), which means it's constant. Though some modern dictionary implementations allow you to traverse the data, the order in which the elements are retrieved is not guaranteed to be consistent, just that all elements can be iterated upon. So, for a precise looping of data, dictionaries are not a good choice.

Figure 12.4 compares these three linear data structures:

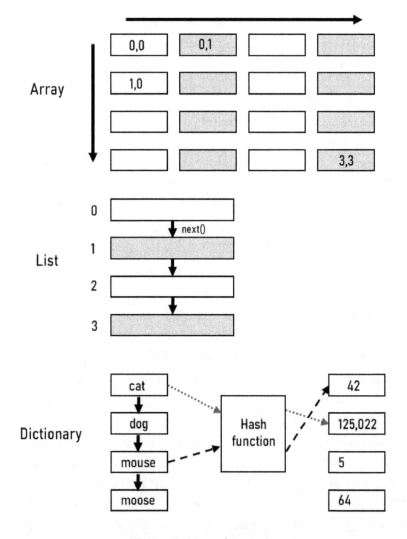

Figure 12.4: Linear data structures

In this diagram, you can see that all of the data structures we've talked about so far are linear in that they have values that are accessed in a linear fashion, forward and backward, or directly via an index or key. As these are all linear data structures, they have a constant $O(1)$ complexity for accessing an element, but varying complexity for searching, adding, and deleting, depending on how each element is connected, or relates, to its neighbor. *Arrays* and generic *Lists* both have an $O(n)$ cost for these actions as all items after the one you are adding or removing need to be reassigned to make room for the new element. If the list is sorted, this can be reduced to $O log(n)$ by using a binary search. But if the list is a **Linked List** where there is no index, and every element is linked to the next element—and the previous element for **Doubly Linked List**—the operation is constant as only the references of the inserted item and previous and next elements need to be updated. The list doesn't need to be traversed in any manner.

Now that we've discussed some of the common linear data structures, we'll talk about non-linear data structures, including trees and maps.

Non-linear data structures

Trees are a collection of **nodes**, where each node can point to a collection of nodes called children. Each child node can only be referenced once and the path between any two nodes is defined as an **edge**. This creates a hierarchical relationship to the data. There are many examples of trees in your day-to-day life, such as an organizational chart at work, or a phylogenetic tree that represents evolutionary relationships between organisms (this likely came up in a biology class!).

Graphs are similar to trees in that they are collections of nodes, and the path from one node to another is called an edge. Unlike a tree, however, a node in a graph can be referenced by more than one other node. Also, a node's relationship to another node can be *bi-directional*. A graph is the computer science equivalent of a map graph in mathematics. The best real-world example of a graph is a road map. If the intersection of two or more roads is a node, then it's easy to see where you can have a two-, three-, four-, and even five-way intersection. In this case, the roads are the edges that define the path between nodes, or intersections. In most types of trees and graphs, inserting, deleting, and searching all have the same complexity of $O log(n)$, or logarithmic time, with a worst case of $O(n)$.

Figure 12.5 illustrates a tree and a graph for comparison:

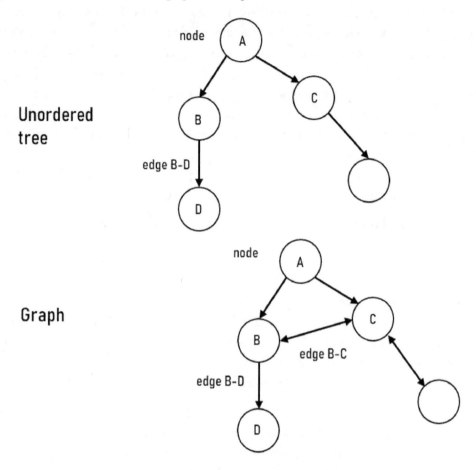

Figure 12.5: Examples of non-linear tree and graph data structures

In this example, we have an unordered tree and a graph. The nodes are in the same locations to illustrate the similarities and differences. The nodes are represented as circles, with the path between nodes as the edges. Notice that in the unordered tree, the paths only go in a single direction and any one node is only referenced once. In the graph, the path between two nodes can be bi-directional, as seen on *edge B-C*. Also, *nodes B* and *C* are both referenced from two different nodes. In these ways, a graph allows for a more complex interrelationship between nodes that a standard tree cannot provide.

These are all of the basic data structures that will be beneficial regardless of the discipline of the software teams that you will work alongside as a TPM in the tech industry. However, just as a TPM may be specialized, so can the development team, so additional data structures that are more closely related to the software being developed may be helpful. The *Further reading* section has an entry for data structures that goes over a larger list of useful structures. Use this as a starting point and dive deeper where needed.

Next, we'll move on to design patterns to wrap up our basic expectations of code knowledge.

Learning design patterns

Design patterns is a class that I see developers take often while on the job, mainly as a refresher as it is taught in college. It ensures a common ground of understanding, which is why I encourage TPMs to take the class as well. Here, we'll explore two groups of design patterns: creational and structural. There are more, but these are the two that I find the most useful for a TPM to have a good understanding of. To learn about other design patterns, check out the *Further reading* section in this chapter.

Creational design patterns

Creational design patterns are related to the creation of objects. By creation, I'm referring to how to create an instance of an object, which is also referred to as *instantiation*. We'll discuss three of the more common creational design patterns next.

Builder pattern

The **builder pattern** separates the construction of an object from the specific composition of that object. As an example, we'll take the *Mercury* subsystem, where you might have two different styles of message you can send: rich text and simple text. A builder will allow you to specify a generic set of building methods that each object type will then provide its specific implementations of. The rich text builder would include additional steps in the method to handle rich text data such as text formatting, whereas the simple text builder would just need to deal with the text itself. In this way, the application can deal with a single builder object where the output can be specific to the type being instantiated.

Figure 12.6 represents a simple builder pattern that is present in most OOP languages today:

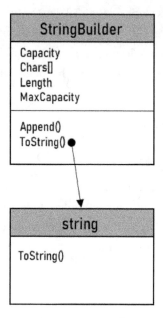

Figure 12.6: Builder pattern

The StringBuilder class allows for the creation of a string from various complex data elements. The Append() method has several overrides that allow passing in every primitive data type to add to the end of the string. The creation method in this case is the ToString() method, which will take all elements appended to the builder and output a single string. Though seemingly simplistic, the StringBuilder class is significantly faster and takes less memory than simple string concatenation. This is because strings are immutable objects in most OOP languages, meaning that they cannot be modified. So, each addition of two strings creates an entirely new pointer and memory allocation. The StringBuilder class, on the other hand, stores all of the data in an array and only needs to update its memory allocation if the array runs out of space.

Simple factory pattern

A **simple factory** is where a class is used to create a specific type of object, usually through the use of an **enum**, which is a list of constant values, to specify the type of object to create. Using the same message example as in the builder pattern, you can have a single create method and use an enum to specify the type of message instead of using different methods.

In the rich text versus simple text use case, after creating the message using a simple factory, you would need to call that object and add additional information that isn't common between the different message types. *Figure 12.7* demonstrates the flow of a simple factory:

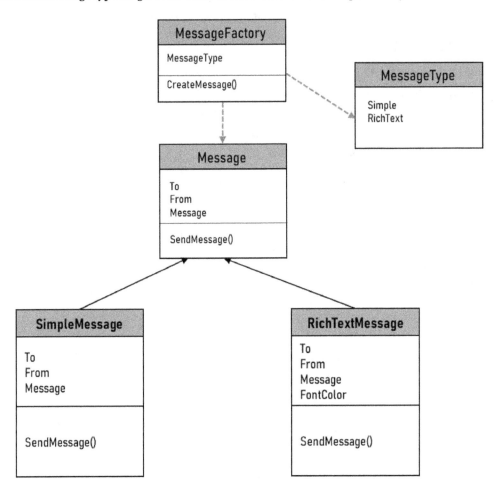

Figure 12.7: Simple factory

The simple factory example in this figure uses the Message class from the *Mercury* application as an example. The MessageFactory class takes in an enum to specify the type of message that you want to create and creates the correct instance. Notice how the RichTextMessage class has an additional property that neither the SimpleMessage class nor the Message class has. That is data on the font color. The number of properties and methods can vary greatly between the objects created within a single simple factory.

Another common example of the use of a simple factory is to create various types of cars (as we explored earlier). You can have a simple factory class with an enum for different car types that can generate a different subclass of an abstract car class and return it. This same example is used to illustrate abstract classes and the inheritance of properties between a class and a subclass.

Singleton pattern

A **singleton** is a pattern that ensures that only a single instance of a class can exist globally. This is done through the use of a static object within the class. A static object can't be instantiated directly, and thus only one can exist. *Figure 12.8* illustrates the behavior of a singleton class:

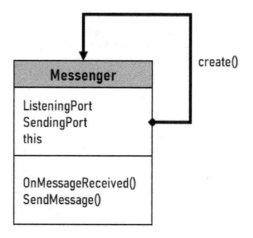

Figure 12.8: Singleton

The Messenger class from the *Mercury* application is an example of a singleton class, as only a single instance of the Messenger class can exist. In this diagram, you can see that the class has a reference set to itself that is returned when the class is asked for the object. If the object doesn't exist yet, an instance is created as referenced.

As you can see, the creational design patterns will be a common occurrence as they relate to the creation of objects. Knowing the patterns and their names will help you interact more smoothly with your development team by having a common understanding of basic concepts so that you can focus on the problem you are trying to solve instead of trying to understand what the code or a design is actually doing.

Let's now look at the other group of patterns that is often discussed in design reviews: structural design patterns.

Structural design patterns

Where creational design patterns focus on object creation, structural design patterns take a step back and discuss how system components are related to one another. Though these do have in-code representations, and that is often what people look to for examples, I'll be using the design approach as these patterns will come up in the system designs and architectural landscapes that we'll cover in the next chapter.

Adapter pattern

The **adapter pattern** is used to convert between different object types, which may often serve similar purposes. From a code perspective, it's similar to an abstract class and classes that extend them. From a system perspective, think of a currency conversion system. Each bank has its own currency conversion system, and you may need to interface with multiple banks depending on the currency you are converting. Instead of custom integrations for each bank, you can use an adapter to take your common data model used by your internal systems and convert it to the specific need of the bank you are calling. *Figure 12.9* illustrates what this might look like:

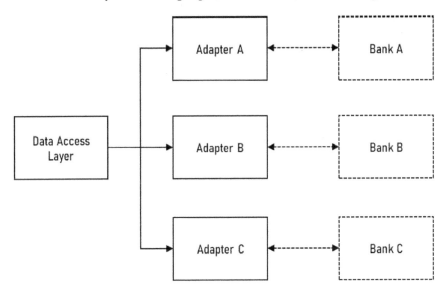

Figure 12.9: Using adapters to connect with multiple currency converters

As you can see, adapters act as a type of bridge between the internal systems and the needs of the external systems. Each adapter takes the internal data model and adapts it to a conversion request that is specific to the bank that it is calling. The data returned from each bank is then converted back into the internal data model. In this way, it encapsulates the details of those differences so that the rest of the system doesn't need to know about them. So, if *Bank A* were to change its API, only *Adapter A* would need to be updated and the rest of the system would not even know a change occurred.

Decorator pattern

The **decorator pattern** allows the addition of new data to an existing object without changing the underlying object. Using the adapter example of multiple bank interfaces, each bank will have a different response that has different data in it. The adapter will fit that data into the internal data model, but you may need to append additional data to this that is not related to the bank call. This might include adding additional context to the data model that isn't available at the time the conversion takes place or wasn't relevant to that call—such as full customer information. Though it shouldn't be sent to the bank, it may need to exist in the model so that a decorator can be invoked to add this information back in. *Figure 12.10* shows how a decorator pattern would work:

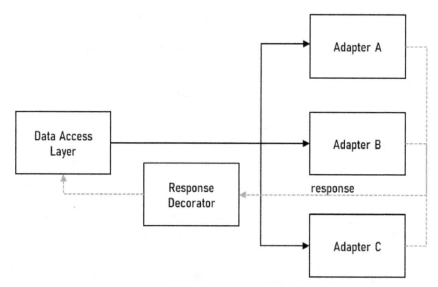

Figure 12.10: Using a decorator to add data to a response

Using the adapter example from *Figure 12.9*, the response back to the data access layer takes a slightly different path through a response decorator. In practice, this may be multiple decorators or a single one that can add data, depending on the adapter that was invoked.

Façade pattern

Last but not least, the façade design pattern is used to simplify component interactions by re-ducing the number of systems that need to be interfaced with by upstream services. *Figure 12.11* illustrates a system map before and after a façade is introduced:

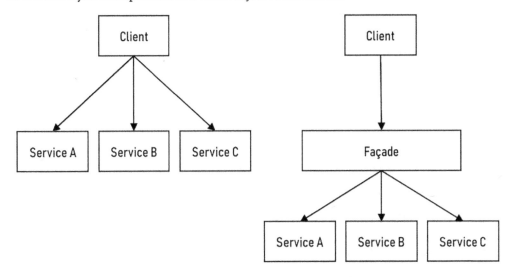

Figure 12.11: Using a façade to simplify client interfaces

In this example, Services A, B, and C are all owned by the same team and have external-facing APIs for other teams to interface into. The client needs to know what each of the services does, and where their endpoints are. The façade on the right side of the figure reduces the number of connections between the components from the point of view of upstream clients. It simplifies the landscape by reducing the amount of information each component (or service, or client) needs to know about the landscape by delegating inter-system calls to a single component. This also has the added benefit of allowing underlying system changes and re-architecting without impacting the calling clients. For instance, Services A and B could be combined into a single service, and clients on the other side of the façade wouldn't know there had been a change. So long as the contract with the façade APIs doesn't change, there is no upstream impact.

Summary

Code development makes up a large portion of the deliverable work in a tech industry project or program. As a TPM, we are responsible for this work, though do not do this work ourselves. In order to be responsible, we must be able to understand the work so that we can properly engage with our team during design discussions and stand-up meetings, and to convey the current progress to stakeholders.

To ensure that we are successful in our role, we discussed the styles of programming that are most in use right now—OOP and functional programming. We learned that many languages allow for a mixture of the two styles in the same code base and that certain styles have benefits for particular tasks.

We learned about data structures that are commonly used and how their performance is measured using space and time complexities expressed through big O notation. We learned about simple list-based structures as well as more abstract structures, such as a graph that represents non-linear, unstructured, and complexly interrelated data.

Lastly, we discussed both creational and structural design patterns, which are foundational to feature and system designs. As such, these patterns will be useful for any design reviews you are a part of as a TPM.

In *Chapter 13*, we'll dive into system design and architectural landscapes. Both of these are technical tools that you will rely upon a lot as a TPM. We'll explore both good and bad system design concepts using the *Mercury* application landscape to dive deeper.

Further reading

- *Learning Object-Oriented Programming*, by *Gaston C. Hillar*

    This is a great introductory book to OOP, starting with a basic real-world understanding of objects and methods. If you are unfamiliar with OOP or want an in-depth refresher, this is a good place to start.

    ```
    https://www.packtpub.com/product/learning-object-oriented-
    programming/9781785289637
    ```

- *Mastering Functional Programming*, by *Anatolii Kmetiuk*

    This book uses both a traditional functional language, Scala, as well as an OOP language staple, Java, to teach the foundations of functional programming. It then goes beyond the basics to get you comfortable using functional programming concepts and styles in your day-to-day programming.

    ```
    https://www.packtpub.com/product/mastering-functional-
    programming/9781788620796
    ```

- *Hands-On Design Patterns with Java*, by *Dr. Edward Lavieri*

  This book gives you a real hands-on approach to learning a large number of design patterns using Java. All design patterns I covered are also covered here at a greater depth, making it a good next step to dive deeper.

  ```
  https://www.packtpub.com/product/hands-on-design-patterns-with-
  java/9781789809770
  ```

- *Everyday Data Structures*, by *William Smith*

  This book discusses data structures as well as algorithms, a cornerstone of computer science, in great depth. It uses hands-on programming in various OOP languages to explore each data structure and algorithm. All the data structures I discussed are in this book, and I encourage you to dive deeper using this book.

  ```
  https://www.packtpub.com/product/everyday-data-structures/9781787121041
  ```

Join our book's Discord space

Join our Discord community to meet like-minded people and learn alongside more than 5000 members at:

```
https://packt.link/sKmQa
```

13

System Design and Architecture Landscape

In this chapter, we'll cover two of the most important technical skills that a TPM possesses: **system design** and **architectural landscape design**. These are the levers we use to influence the technical direction of our organizations.

We start out in our career focusing on system designs in individual projects and influencing the right design for the requirements and services they impact. As we grow, we start looking at the architectural landscape that surrounds our projects and programs to see patterns of opportunity and areas of risk. We start to influence the teams around us and the organization as a whole.

We'll explore system designs and the architectural landscape through the following:

- Learning about common system design patterns
- Seeing the forest and the trees
- Examining an architecture landscape
- Preparing for a system design interview

Let's dive in!

Learning about common system design patterns

As a TPM, you split your time between the high-level scope, which spans multiple systems, and the weeds of a specific feature design. It's due to this breadth and depth that system design is one of the most important technical skills a TPM can have.

It's important enough that it shows up in every interview loop for the big tech companies and is starting to show up in more and more companies across the industry. I'll cover the aspects of system design that you need to consider, ensuring that your design is well thought out.

When we think about system design, we often conjure up a diagram of multiple services, each covering a single function or area of concern, working together to power the ecosystem as a whole, for instance, the entire e-commerce stack for an online store. However, system designs come in many different sizes and complexities. At a small scale, a feature design, such as a feature to add a new contact to your contact list in the Mercury messenger app, is its own system design. Somewhere in between these is a system design for an entire desktop or mobile application.

As a TPM, you need to be prepared to work with a design at any of these levels of complexity. Many designs will comprise more than one design pattern, especially for complex systems. The names and behaviors of these patterns may be used in the designs themselves and therefore need to be understood. Knowing the behaviors and key features of design patterns will also make evaluating them more effective. As such, I'll walk through some of the more predominant system design patterns (often referred to as architectural patterns) that are in use today.

Model-View-Presenter

The **Model-View-Presenter** (**MVP**) design pattern is a variant of the **Model-View-Controller** (**MVC**) pattern. While MVC is popular in client-server applications, MVP is used often in desktop applications:

- The **model** is the data model of the application. All the data manipulation and storage happen in this layer.
- The **view** is the user interface at the top of the diagram. This displays all of the data in the application in ways that make sense to the user.
- The **presenter** sits in between the model and view and acts as the connecting layer between them. The user interacts with the presenter, usually through input fields in the view such as text boxes and buttons, which trigger events. The events live in the presenter and make changes in the model based on the event that occurred.

Let's try to understand this better with the help of an example building off of the Mercury application in Windows:

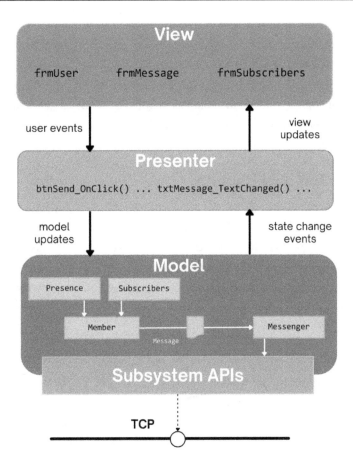

Figure 13.1: Windows Mercury application system design

The model is broken down into three sub-components, the first of which are the business objects. These are the classes that house the data for the user (the member), their messages, their contacts, and their subscribers. The second is the messenger class that handles the sending and receiving of messages across the network. Last is the subsystem that is shared across the operating systems that talks to the TCP network layer (via system APIs) to transport the messages.

The view displays the data model based on the context of the user actions from the presenter. For instance, the PresenceInformation class may be displayed as a colored dot beside the username of the client logged in, where the color represents a specific status. The user may also click a drop-down button to update their status, which would be relayed back to the model as an update to the PresenceInformation class via an event in the presenter on the IndexChanged() event for the dropdown.

This pattern is useful in any instance where you are interacting with a user. This is a basic separation-of-concerns model to ensure that what you are showing the user in a window or form is not directly tied to the underlying data model. The reason for this is that how you display information can change based on operating system norms, changes in trends, and usability needs, but the data itself may not change. This allows changes in both the display and the data model to take place without directly impacting the other. Separation of concerns is a common concept you'll see throughout these design patterns.

Object-oriented architecture

Object-Oriented Architecture (OOA) is where you use objects to model real-world concepts. Though this seems straightforward due to **Object-Oriented Programming (OOP)** being widespread, it does not dictate what the objects themselves are and, in many cases, the objects created are unique to the problem space that the application is in. However, in many industries where the software is a byproduct of or in support of the main business, the software tends to emulate real-world functions that are digitized. Actions such as filling out forms give rise to form-based applications centered around this architectural concept.

Figure 13.2 shows how OOA applies to a form-based application:

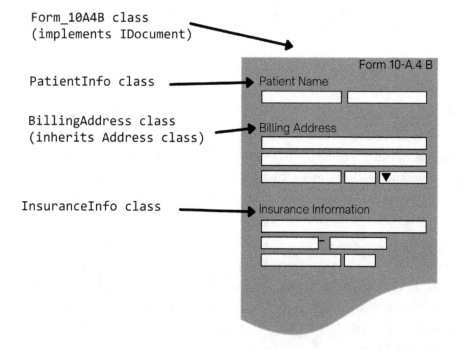

Figure 13.2: Object-oriented architecture

The preceding figure shows a fictional US healthcare form on the right-hand side with typical information, such as the patient's name and billing address, as well as their insurance information. Each of these bits of information is represented by a class, and these are all combined into an object that represents the form. Grouping objects together and inheriting through abstract classes, such as a generic `Address` class, highlights **abstraction** and **inheritance**, tenets of OOP that OOA takes advantage of.

As you can see from the example I chose, OOA is used heavily in business firms that need to represent real-world objects in an application. Some languages, like Visual Basic, go so far as to couple the model and view together. This makes writing an application much faster as dragging a button onto a form will include the business logic behind the button as well and is quick to "wire up." However, it also constrains usage to a coupled model, making it hard to separate concerns without extra work.

OOA in the workforce

I spent most of my first 3 years as a developer maintaining code written in Visual Basic 4 that was ported to Visual Basic 6. This is the epitome of business-driven development and was heavily OOA-based. Objects only existed if they were visible on a form with only a few minor exceptions like a timer object—which is still placed on the form but is invisible to the user.

I was able to quickly write new programs, but each one was its own little application and any code that would have been shareable was instead copy-pasted from application to application. With the end of life for Visual Basic 6 already passed, I knew I needed to move all 45 applications out of that language. Though it was a steep learning curve, I chose C# as a robust C-based language as it was still a "Microsoft shop" and would be the easiest to move to. The migration took over a year and most of that time was getting around roadblocks where Visual Basic's OOA environment made certain tasks extremely simple that are more involved in a standard C-based language.

However, in the end, the resulting applications, when removed from the strict OOA-based Visual Basic, were more flexible and a lot of shared code was able to be put into libraries to share across applications. So, while OOA can be good for getting your application out the door fast, you pay for it in the end with the high cost of maintenance any time large changes are needed.

Domain-driven design architecture

Domain-Driven Design (DDD) is a concept where domain experts work alongside the development team to influence the data model and data flow of an application. This is used in domain-heavy scenarios such as healthcare and financial systems where specific procedures, nomenclature, and protocols need to be followed.

On the surface, this feels very similar to OOA since OOA models real-world objects. However, you can model real-world objects in some cases and then not in others. In the case of DDD, the entire design is based directly on the domain, and, in some instances, the user interface is a direct reflection of the underlying model. This type of stricter coherence is not the goal of OOA.

DDD does not require the use of an OOP language, but there are natural similarities. There are also cases where a **Domain-Specific Language** (DSL), such as **Structured Query Language** (SQL), which isn't an OOP language, is used in conjunction with DDD for a specific use case, like relational databases.

The architecture of a DDD system is often depicted as a hexagon, as it has layers of abstraction between the core domain logic in the center, and the use of adapters for each client to interface with the domain—transforming their data into a common model for the domain. We talk more about adapters later in the chapter, but this is still worth taking a look at here in *Figure 13.3*:

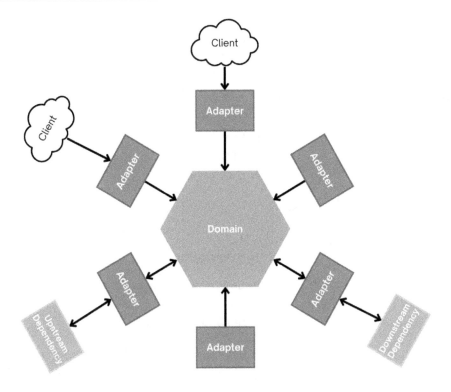

Figure 13.3: Domain Driven Design

The domain is in the center and contains all of the business logic. This core is surrounded by adapters that translate into and out of the domain to various subsystems or clients. The use of adapters means that the domain's business logic can literally be adapted to many different clients without any changes in the domain logic itself. Any translation issues between the client and domain are handled within the adapters. If you have ever had to deal with integrating your business with a customer relationship management system, like Salesforce, then you've encountered a domain-driven design.

As you can see with the use of adapters, the core domain system can be utilized in many different contexts with no changes to the domain. However, this comes at a high cost to the client as each client must have their own adapter, which is often fully customized integration work to map the client system to the domain system. So, essentially, the cost of maintenance is moved to the client instead of the domain system.

Event-driven architecture

Event-Driven Architecture (**EDA**) is where the application's data model is updated through user-triggered and system events, which often signal to change something about the data model state. As we saw in the *Model-View-Presenter* section, the presenter utilizes events that are triggered by actions taken by the user on the user interface (for example, clicking a button). As such, EDA is often associated with OOA and can also be used in conjunction with DDD. As seen in the OOA example above, languages like Visual Basic rely heavily on EDA and OOA to drive the "drag-and-drop" forms that are used in business-driven development.

P2P architecture

This book covered P2P in *Chapter 4* to some degree, but it is worth expanding upon here. There are two types of P2P networks: structured and unstructured.

A **structured network** has a strict topology that is adhered to as hosts leave and join the network. Every host has a list of nearby hosts, or neighbors, so that any one host can easily access another host. This type of network results in a lot of discovery traffic being broadcast but allows you to find a peer or file quickly.

An **unstructured network** has no imposed structure and is resilient to changes in hosts dropping and adding to the network. However, finding a specific host or file is not guaranteed. This is a problem, particularly when using P2P for file sharing, as rare files will be just as rare to successfully find. For a messaging app, the biggest hurdle to this type of structure would be finding your contacts on the network, if you're relying strictly on searching. A way to share direct-connect information between two parties would alleviate some of this pain.

Though many may relegate P2P networks to the likes of file-sharing sites from the 2000s like Napster, Morpheus, and LimeWire, or torrent sites like BitTorrent or Gnutella, there are modern uses for this network type today. Any time you need to share resources between two systems without the need for a central connection, P2P can fit the bill. Notably, Bitcoin uses a P2P architecture, as do some content delivery networks, which are used to deliver content from the nearest local repository for systems like Netflix. Another use is payment systems like Venmo and Cash App that allow payments between two nearby devices. These are all forms of P2P networks that are thriving today!

Service-oriented architecture

Service-Oriented Architecture (SOA) is arguably the most widely used architecture in the tech industry today. SOA is the basis of cloud-based architectures and offers a logical separation of concerns in larger organizations.

Figure 13.4 takes the Mercury desktop application from *Figure 13.1* and re-imagines it in an SOA setting. Let's take a look at how this changes the design and behavior of the system:

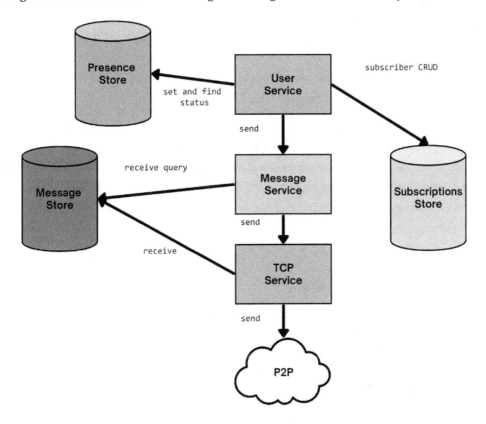

Figure 13.4: Mercury re-imagined as an SOA

In the preceding figure, the three sections of the model from the MVP are now distinct services. **User Service** is essentially the user model objects and controls all aspects of the user. Now that what was a single desktop application is represented by multiple services and is decentralized, we need storage mechanisms to house what might have been in memory or serialized to the local disk in a desktop application. **User Service** connects to **Presence Store** as well as **Subscriptions Store. User Service** connects to **Message Service**, which is an analog for the Message class in *Figure 13.1*. It connects to **TCP Service**, which handles both sending and receiving messages. This is the most important difference between the desktop system design and the SOA design. Since this is a distributed system, a user isn't logged into a specific physical device and thus their location on the P2P network isn't static, so a user cannot reliably be reached to receive inbound messages. **TCP Service** circumvents this issue by storing incoming messages in a data store that a user can query for unretrieved incoming messages.

Although not a practical example given the requirements of the P2P messaging service, this does serve as a good illustration of where certain aspects of a design might change. The lack of a centralized system often leads to a high reliance on centralized or synced data stores to handle stateful data. On the other hand, having individual services allows for scaling to be handled on the pieces of the system that need it and not others. It also serves as a concrete mechanism to ensure the separation of concerns by forcing data contracts between any two services that interact with one another.

Client-server architecture

A client-server architecture is a classic design used to connect a user to a centralized service. This is the architecture used to browse the internet and connect to a specific website. It is also used in mobile architectures where the mobile application (the client) connects to the application's backend on a centralized server to send and receive data.

Throughout the book, I've been referencing a program that builds a P2P-backed messaging system across multiple operating systems. A P2P system is relatively straightforward, so I'm going to expand the program requirements for the sake of a more representative system design. For this example, I'm going to add the requirement of a web-based interface for the messaging application. It will still be P2P-backed, and the operating system-specific applications will still be present, but this design will focus on the web interface.

Figure 13.5 showcases the system design of the web portal interfacing with the P2P network:

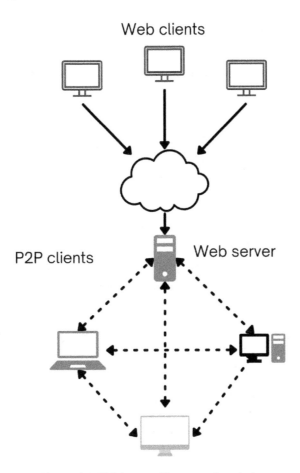

Figure 13.5: Web browser Mercury system design

This system design is a hybrid between a traditional client-server pattern and a P2P pattern, with the biggest difference between this design and the one used in *Chapter 4* being the addition of a **web server**. This server is the gateway for the web-based interface. Once a user connects to the web server, the backend behaves in the same manner as a single host on the network would be-cause the server is just another host in the network. The difference is that this particular host—or fleet of hosts—maps to multiple users instead of a single user on a single host.

This design isn't perfect as it is a first pass at integrating the two patterns. This is a good time to talk about some design considerations that can help when working with any design and then we'll take a second look at this example.

Design considerations

These design considerations will help ensure your designs convey a clear intention, which will reduce project churn and have the added bonus of helping you during an interview for system design. Pay close attention to these concepts:

- *Avoid vague design traits*: You want your system design to be clear, so make sure you are not generalizing aspects of the design so much that you lose your key understanding of the interactions between components. Ensure that pointers between components are directional when direction matters. For instance, a network topology doesn't need to specify directional flow, as data flows in both directions on a network. However, when a component is accessing a read-only datastore, the direction makes a difference and conveys the read-only nature through the data flow.

- *Don't omit key functionality*: Missing out on functionality is usually due to an expectation of familiarity where the missing piece is seen as obvious—or parts of the design are overly generalized, which blurs the functionality between two or more parts of the system.

- *Understand system traffic patterns*: Traffic patterns can refer to the amount of traffic that your system receives on average, at its peak, or even during a cyclical pattern. For example, an e-commerce system will have high volumes of traffic when its user base is awake and within that wake period, it will peak at certain times of the day. This pattern depends on the cultural norms of the customers and so will be different from country to country. Knowing the patterns helps you design a system that can handle the maximum loads as well as to know whether utilizing auto-scaling systems like Amazon's **Elastic Cloud Compute (EC2)** Auto Scaling to dynamically change the number of servers in your fleet based on traffic patterns is a good fit.

When working at the scale of any large-scale software company, there are a few topics that should be considered in every design. In most cases, these are handled by off-the-shelf components in cloud computing systems like AWS, Google Cloud, and Microsoft Azure, but they are worth understanding as they will be present in almost every design at any tech company working at large scales. Let's look at them now.

Latency

As is the case in most companies in the tech industry, **latency**, or the amount of time for which a request and response are processed, is of the utmost concern when creating a system design. Long responses, or even perceived long responses, can turn users away from using a system.

This could mean lost sales revenue through not placing orders, missed ad revenue, or a reduction in market share by driving users to the competition. For these reasons, you must ensure that your system design takes latency into account when it's applicable.

There are a few ways to combat latency that you can consider depending on how they fit with the needs of your system. If you have a lot of microservices, you can minimize network hops by co-locating services onto a single server. If you have a data store, ensure that the right data store is chosen based on the needs of the system. A system that focuses more on reads than writes, for instance, should have a data store that is optimized for reads that will reduce the overall latency of the system. The system design can show the specific database being used to highlight the high read or high write capabilities.

Though not easy to show on a system design, you can hide latency by increasing the amount of asynchronous data processing to reduce the overall time for the call to process. This is akin to swarming a project with multiple resources to bring the calendar time down.

Design patterns have a varying impact on the latency of the system, so the latency requirements both now and projected in the long term should be evaluated when selecting the right patterns to use. This does not mean you shouldn't use a pattern just because it introduces latency, but it means that measures may need to be put in place to counter the latency introduced. These long-term considerations of the requirements and needs of the system are key contributions from a TPM during the design process.

Availability

Availability, or the ability of a system to respond to high volumes of requests without experiencing an outage due to no resources, is a key performance indicator that is tracked in every client-service architecture. As this architecture pattern is utilized to make thousands or millions of connections to a system, ensuring that the system can handle that load and not fail is critical to the success of the system. To mitigate availability outages, you need to increase the number of hosts that are ready to take requests. In order to ensure that the web client doesn't need to know how many hosts you have and where they are, you can utilize a load balancer service that takes all requests to the web client and distributes the requests across the fleet of servers. Most load balancers can detect server outages and switch off traffic automatically to a misbehaving host to reduce the number of bad responses as well. In some cases, a fleet of load balancers may also be needed. Equally, when increasing hosts, other factors, such as concurrent database connections, need to be adjusted as well and may factor into which type of database you use for your system.

Scalability

Scalability, or the ability to quickly respond to a fluctuating call volume, is often discussed at the same time as availability, as they have similar solutions. Once the servers are behind a load balancer, servers can be added or removed without compromising client connections. In many systems, the ability to add and remove on-demand is key to scalability, as it can save on costs to reduce the fleet size in off-peak times so you only have a large fleet when it is needed.

Defendable choices

Above all of these individual design considerations and patterns, you'll want to ensure that the design you have created is defendable. There is more than one way to solve a problem and a system design is no exception to that rule. As such, you need to understand the choices you have made in the design and why you made them. I've found that in most interviews, so long as you understand the trade-offs you are making, the outcome is often favorable. You can always be taught new ways of solving problems, so the goal here is more to demonstrate that you can think critically and adjust as new data comes in that may impact your design considerations.

If you are already a TPM, then you will often review designs from your development team and can use these concepts to ensure that the design holds up to scrutiny. Aside from these high-level checks, you will also look at the designs and see how they hold up to the other projects and programs that are in flight and are there to ensure that other teams, services, and projects are considered in the design.

Now that we've discussed some design considerations, let's take a second look at the client-server architecture from *Figure 13.5* with some of these considerations applied to *Figure 13.6* here:

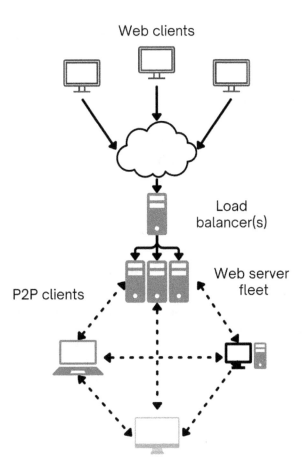

Figure 13.6: System design with availability and scalability mitigations

As you can see, the network diagram now has a fleet of boxes for the web service, all backed by the added **Load balancer** to distribute the requests. As the Mercury application is a single local application, there are no latency concerns that need to be addressed at the system design level, although this will be revisited at the architectural landscape level. The availability and scalability have been addressed through the addition of a load balancer, which supports multiple web servers to ensure enough connections are available during peak demand. As with *Figure 13.5*, this design has a similar issue where a web client doesn't have a persistent connection to the P2P network, so inbound requests won't know which server to send the connection to. A similar database solution that stores incoming messages that the web client can query would be one solution to this.

Now that we've talked about all of the system design patterns and how to make a good and defensible design, let's expand our scope and learn to see the forest and the trees.

Seeing the forest and the trees

The architectural landscape is not often talked about as a standalone topic outside of specific instances such as migrating from on-premises to the cloud. In many ways, it's similar to system design in its intention, as well as patterns. In most cases, the design of a single system within a larger ecosystem will match the design patterns of the systems around it. If the trend at your company is to utilize SOA, then you will see SOA at every level. The biggest difference between the architectural landscape and system design is the scope that the design encompasses.

You can't see the forest for the trees is a proverb that was first published in 1546 in *The Proverbs of John Heywood*. The idea is that from the middle of a dense forest, you can see every tree that surrounds you in great detail from the trunk all the way to the crown of the tree – but from this vantage point, you literally cannot see the whole forest; you don't know how vast it is or the directions in which it flows, as the breadth and depth are lost. This saying has become so common it is now an idiom in the English language.

People often relate to this idiom when they are too close to a problem to see the bigger picture or have been too close for too long to see clearly. Think back to a time when a problem was frustrating you and you worked to solve it with no progress. Then, you stepped away from the problem and when you came back, the solution came to you quickly! It came because you changed your perspective by allowing different information to come into play. Simply put, you saw the forest.

I offer a slightly different version of this proverb as a directive to all TPMs:

> *You must see the forest* **as well as** *the trees.*

A TPM must have both breadth and depth of knowledge. The depth (or the trees) refers to system designs and the breadth refers to the architectural landscape (or the forest). You can extend this analogy further and see where a system design and an architecture landscape are one and the same; when no other systems surround the one that the system design describes, then it is both the system design and the architectural landscape, like a lone tree on a hill. However, you can then zoom out from that tree far enough to see other trees and understand where it fits into the larger picture of the trees around it. That is to say, no modern system is in isolation, but the level at which you focus will depend on the needs of your role. It may be at the team level, organization or department level, or company level.

Important tools we use to see the bigger picture better (the forest) are program, product, and team roadmaps. These roadmaps encompass different components of an architectural landscape. Each one looks into the future deliverables of a group of systems. More importantly, they describe either directly or indirectly the intention of that group of systems, why they exist, and what they are striving to become. The intentions, as well as discrete deliverables, are what determine the picture of the architectural landscape both as it exists today and how it will change in the future. Some companies publish technology directives that give the general direction that the company's platforms are evolving toward, which can include the technologies that will be centralized.

A TPM will be expected to pick up on these cues from roadmaps and directives and point out when there's an issue or an opportunity between multiple projects or programs. A principal TPM is expected to see these issues or opportunities without being prompted, whereas a senior TPM is expected to see these connections as they relate to the projects or programs they run.

On the other hand, we also need to recognize the individual trees. Your contribution to design reviews at the system level will lean on your knowledge of the architectural landscape as you set outside context against the proposed system design. In general, an SDE's focus is on the system design and its interactions within the context of their own software. Just like a TPM, the SDE's breadth also grows as they ascend the corporate ladder. Even so, the TPM's job of looking across projects and a cross the organization is always required.

Figure 13.7 illustrates the varying areas of concern of a TPM, SDM, and SDE across an architectural landscape:

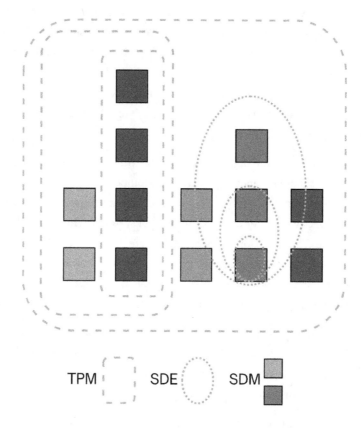

Figure 13.7: Areas of concern across job families

In the preceding figure, each column of boxes represents the services owned by a single **SDM**. These services are the purview of our **SDM**, and they are expected to understand each one in its entirety, as well as how they interact with each other. It's often necessary for our **SDM** to know about the services outside of their team that have a relationship with one or more of their own services. In these instances, the **SDM** area of concern will look similar to the senior **SDE** area of concern.

The circles represent the three main areas of concern for our **SDE**. The smallest inner circle is an entry-level **SDE** who is mainly concerned with a single service. An industry **SDE** will need to stretch to related services, often under the same **SDM** that they report to. They know how these services work and how they interact with one another and are starting to learn about outside dependencies. The largest circle is the senior **SDE** who needs to know about all services under their **SDM**, as well as the services that have a relationship with them from other teams.

The last group is our **TPM**, represented by the rounded squares in the figure. An entry-level **TPM** starts out with the same expectations as an industry **SDE** in that they need to know the complete architecture of their **SDM** (also known as an **embedded TPM**) or the services they are focused on. An industry **TPM** is expected to know about the dependent systems of their focus area as the initiatives going on in that space. Lastly, a senior **TPM** is expected to understand the architecture of their organization—not necessarily to the same level of detail as with the services they focus on, but at least the high-level data flow and interactions.

This illustration is a common example of the areas of concern and how they overlap but is by no means the only breakdown. Highly specialized TPMs may focus more on the depth of their services or certain aspects such as security. In some organizations, the senior SDE's purview may be the same as a senior TPM, especially for a seasoned SDE on the path to principal. In cases where a TPM isn't present, an SDM's area of concern and influence may also need to expand to fill in the gap.

We've focused on seeing the trees through various system designs and how this aligns with your day-to-day role as a TPM. We've also seen how the areas of concern grow as your level grows. Next, we'll take a look at the forest by learning what an architectural landscape is and how it is different from a system design.

Examining an architecture landscape

To get a good understanding of what an architecture landscape is, we'll compare a system design with an architecture landscape. We'll follow this up with a look into the implementation of the *Mercury* messaging application on a corporate network.

There is more in common between a system design and an architectural landscape than not. The design patterns between the two are the same and are often referred to as architectural patterns. They also both describe the relationship between components of an ecosystem that share some relationship either in the data they process and handle or the function that they collectively perform.

Where they can differ is the scope and depth of the design. A system design is limited in scope, as it often covers a single feature or limited data flow between highly related systems. The design may dive into API definitions, as well as illustrate the data model and how it flows through the system.

An architectural diagram usually covers high-level system interactions and multiple systems and features that share a common theme. APIs and data field flows are less relevant at the level of the architectural landscape.

To start, in *Figure 13.8*, we compare a system design to an architectural landscape:

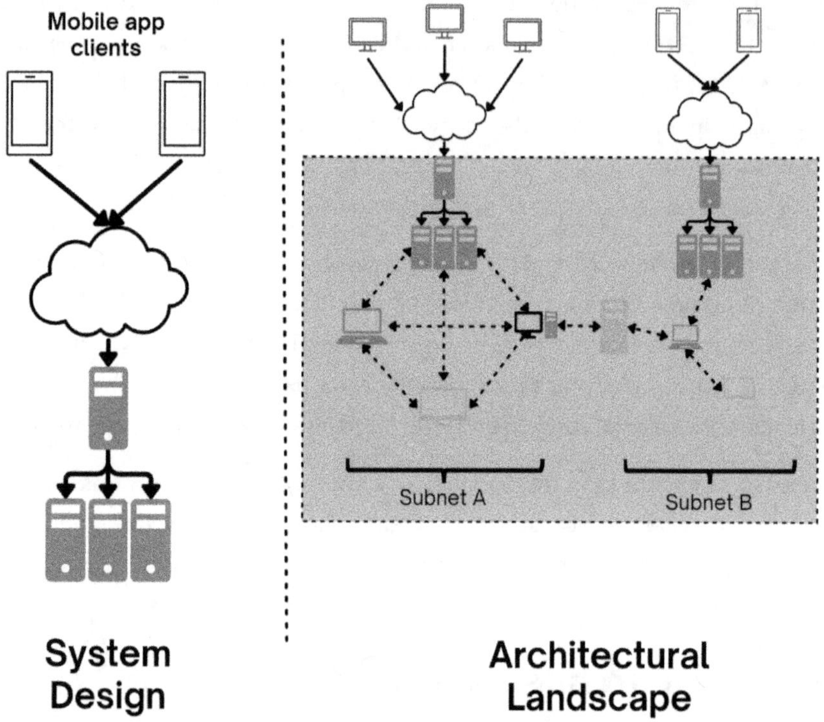

Figure 13.8: System design versus architectural landscape

In the preceding figure, the left-hand side is the system design of a **Virtual Private Network (VPN)**. A VPN provides a secure connection to a specific network as though your device were on that network and is often used in corporate settings to give employees access to the corporate network while working remotely. This design describes a single feature of gaining access to a network through a load-balanced VPN.

On the right-hand side is the architecture diagram for the *Mercury* application implemented in a corporate network. On the upper right-hand side of this picture, you can see the VPN system design within the architectural landscape. The landscape tells the story of the entire *Mercury* system, including all points of entry and network traversals. It does not detail the *Mercury* application as we saw in *Figure 13.1*, but it does include multiple independent system designs, including the web-based client system design from *Figure 13.6*.

Next, let's take a closer look at the architectural landscape, including labels, and discuss the various components. *Figure 13.9* shows the Mercury corporate installation in greater detail:

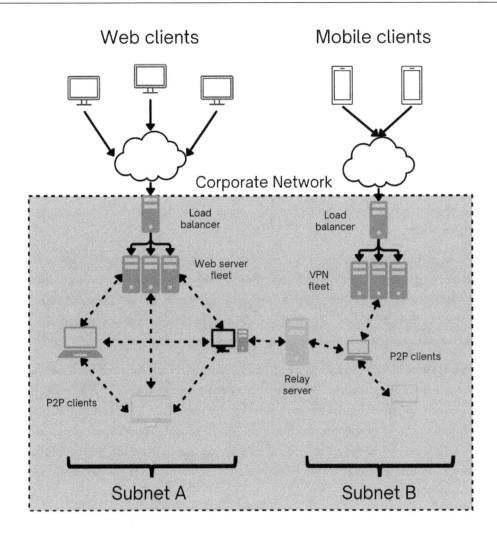

Figure 13.9: Mercury corporate installation architectural landscape

We've seen various parts of this architectural landscape throughout the book, starting with the P2P network on the right-hand side. This is representative of an unstructured P2P network and is contained within the same network as well as on the same subnet—in this case, denoted as **Subnet A**. The web client that we added in this chapter to illustrate a client-server architecture is above the P2P network and connected to the network as **Web server fleet**, where each member of the fleet is on the network.

New to this architecture landscape is the second subnet, **Relay server**, and **VPN fleet**. A large corporate network may need to be segregated into multiple **sub-networks (subnets)** to reduce network collisions by having fewer devices share the same physical wire for data transmission. In a traditional network, routers are used to transmit data across subnets. In a P2P network, all hosts have direct connections to other hosts, which does not include routers. To get around this limitation, the relay server that is part of the P2P network would need to receive a P2P packet and then relay it to the correct subnet to which it is also connected. Lastly, to get the *Mercury* application on mobile devices onto the corporate network, the design incorporates a VPN. Through the *Mercury* application on the device, it first establishes a connection to the P2P network via the VPN. In this sense, it behaves a lot like the web client in how it connects to and interacts with the P2P network.

To be clear, many of these additions to the architecture go against the original requirements of the *Mercury* program, specifically around not requiring any centralized setup or maintenance. On a hyper-local, single subnet network, none of these components are necessary and a simple P2P design would suffice. However, these are good additions to illustrate key design concepts and the overall complexity that can come up when working through requirements.

All of these system designs come together to paint a larger picture of how the *Mercury* messaging system could be implemented. As a TPM, I may be on the Windows team and thus largely focused on the internal system design of the application itself as seen in *Figure 13.1*. I might also be the lead TPM for the *Mercury* program and thus need to understand the full architectural landscape in order to effectively oversee all projects in the program. Lastly, it's worth noting that both the architectural landscape and the system design utilized multiple design patterns to fit the needs of the ecosystem.

Now that we've discussed different design patterns, we can take a look at how to use this information while preparing for a system design interview for a TPM position.

Preparing for a system design interview

Throughout the chapter, I mentioned how various concepts help both in your day-to-day work as well as in interview preparation. Here, I'll go into more detail on what you can expect in a system design interview. Keep in mind that every company will be different, so do some research on the company ahead of time to get an idea of what to expect. The recruiter or recruitment materials often give you some general ideas as well.

There are two main types of system design questions:

- **Building a system or feature from scratch**: This type of question will have you designing a new system or feature on an existing system. The questions often ask you to add a new feature to your favorite app or design a system that meets a specific requirement. In this scenario, they are looking for you to put on your product hat as they are probing for what feature is missing, or how to design a system to meet a specific requirement. Be intentional in your design choices and don't be afraid to ask clarifying questions around the parameters of what they have asked you to design. After all, driving toward clarity is a key trait of a good TPM!

- **Describing a system that you know well**: This often entails you describing a system you are currently working with or have deep knowledge of from a previous project or job. The goal here is to see how well you know a system in real life as this helps them understand the depth of your system knowledge. This is my favorite version of the question because it brings passion to the discussion, as the interviewee gets to talk about something they know a lot about. It also allows the interviewer to go as deep as possible. One of the key aspects to this is understanding why design choices were made, like the type of database being used, or the use of one service or multiple services. Another is seeing how well you can communicate a technical solution to someone who likely has no understanding of the system being described. This shows your ability to bridge the gap and explain both domain and technical concepts in the same conversation, which is another trait that all TPMs should be adept at.

Regardless of the interview question, there are some common considerations to take into account:

- **Prepare as though you are an engineer**: Every company treats the TPM role differently, so assume that the role will lean heavily on tech. Even in cases where your role won't see you in the design reviews often, there may still be an expectation that you can be in the room. I've seen some cases where the interviewer asked about scaling needs based on transactions per second numbers. It's better to have some preparation than none at all for these scenarios.

- **Ensure you know why design choices were made**: Whether you are explaining a new feature or an existing system, you need to know why a design choice was made.

- **Understand the use cases for the system**: This leans on the product side of our job but is also highly relevant to requirements analysis and planning. You must know why your system is doing what it is doing by understanding the user base, the expected traffic patterns, the availability of the service, and the data it contains, among other things.

- **Research the company:** Though not related to the design itself, make sure you read up on the company's interview practices ahead of time. Read all the material they provide and check job boards and sites for more candid information. Some of these are available in the *Additional resources* section below.

- **Practice system design:** Just as you might take a practice exam before a college final or a professional certification, practice system designs for both question types. Don't expect one or the other but have a prepared design for both and write them out a few times to ensure you understand them enough that nerves won't prevent you from designing during the interview.

People often obsess over ensuring that an interview goes well so they can get the job. However, just like with any test, it's important to remember the reason for the test is that the skills tested are meant to be used. So, while preparing for an interview, remember that these skills will continue to be useful in your career once you land your role as a TPM.

Summary

In this chapter, we explored the trees as well as the forest. Just as a forest is made up of trees and therefore trees and forests have a lot in common, so do system designs and architectural landscapes.

We learned about various design patterns that are used in both system designs and architectural landscapes. We discussed the elements of a good design, as well as a bad design. Above all, we discussed the importance of defensible choices, as there is always more than one way to design a system.

Finally, we dove into the differences between a system design and architectural landscape and how this relates to the areas of concern for a TPM throughout their career.

In *Chapter 14*, we'll take a look at how generative artificial intelligence can help you improve your technical acumen as well as your program management skills. This will balance the work we started in the emotional intelligence chapter by ensuring you are ready to embrace the new AI reality in the workplace.

Further reading

- *Architectural Patterns*, by Pethuru Raj, et al.

This book covers all of the system design patterns discussed in this chapter, as well as additional patterns. If this is an area of particular interest to you, this is a good place to start:

https://www.packtpub.com/product/architectural-patterns/9781787287495

- *Solutions Architect's Handbook – Second Edition*, by *Saurabh Shrivastava, et al.*

The work of a solutions architect is a popular field, as it focuses on moving from on-premises to the cloud. To do this, a full understanding of the current architecture is needed in order to determine the right solution for the cloud. As such, this offers a great view for understanding an entire architecture:

https://www.packtpub.com/product/solutions-architect-s-handbook/9781801816618

- *Hands-On Design Patterns with Java*, by *Dr. Edward Lavieri*

This book gives you a real hands-on approach to learning about a large number of design patterns using Java. All the design patterns I covered are also covered here in greater depth, making it a good next step to dive deeper:

https://www.packtpub.com/product/hands-on-design-patterns-with-java/9781789809770

Additional resources

- **Glassdoor.com:** This website contains a lot of useful information about the company's culture including work-life balance, salary expectations, and interview experiences. Users can report their own interview experiences for others to see, including questions asked and even response times, from the interview to the hiring decision.

- **Indeed.com:** This site is mainly a job posting site but has some of the same company background information as Glassdoor. It's always good to check multiple sources for candidate experience and example interview questions, and of the job sites, Indeed has a good amount of user-submitted experiences.

- **System design prep courses:** There are a plethora of courses available online as well as videos that go into various aspects of system design. Many are specific to a company, such as system design at Netflix. I am not listing any particular resource here as there are too many and they are changing too often but a quick query on "system design prep" or "system design prep for *company name*" is likely to give you plenty of results to work through. Don't skip this step as researching the company and learning about the expectations for a given company are all part of successful interview preparation.

Join our book's Discord space

Join our Discord community to meet like-minded people and learn alongside more than 5000 members at:

https://packt.link/sKmQa

14

Harnessing the Power of Artificial Intelligence in Technical Program Management

Artificial Intelligence (AI) has been around in computing for decades, in one form or another. The general aim of AI is to achieve human-like intelligence within a computer or machine. However, intelligence turns out to be a very complex concept and the advances in this area of science have been slow until the last few years. Well before the current surge in AI technology, it's been in your life in various forms and under different names. Most notable to consumers are recommendation engines from sites like Amazon or streaming platforms like Netflix. These utilize machine learning technologies to predict output based on known data or input. If you have ever found your next favorite TV show from the Netflix algorithms, you can thank AI for looking at your watching habits and comparing them to millions of others to help determine what sorts of shows you would most likely like.

Though this type of AI is very useful, its outputs can only come from its existing data: it cannot recommend something to you that it doesn't already know about. This is where **generative Artificial Intelligence (GenAI**, or sometimes GAI, though I'll stick with GenAI here) takes us to the next level of productivity and usefulness. GenAI is a branch of AI that focuses on the creation of new content based on existing data. Arguably, this is the first real instance of AI in the way in which the common person views intelligence.

While the headlines have focused heavily on the artistic creativity coming out of these generative AI systems, there is a lot of work happening on the business productivity side of content generation. As prefaced in *Chapter 10, Emotional Intelligence in Technical Program Management*, the rise of GenAI in the workplace is fundamentally changing the definition of the workplace, including the definition of the role of the TPM: from changing what project artifacts we need to author, to risk analysis, and even tasks as mundane as capturing meeting notes and taking action items. All three foundational pillars I talk about in this book, project management, program management, and technical acumen, are impacted by the advent of GenAI. EQ teaches us to be adaptive to change, and we must do so in order to stay relevant.

We'll explore GenAI as well as other AI tools through these topics:

- Distilling generative AI basics
- Examining current capabilities and limitations of AI tools
- Perfecting prompt engineering
- Exploring AI tools in key management areas

Let's start with looking at understanding the basics of GenAI.

Note to the reader on the fast-paced nature of AI

AI is an ever-changing field where even the definition of AI can change day to day. Scrolling through sites like LinkedIn, you can see a steady stream of posts talking about the top tools available for every line of work. Writing a book is a necessarily long process, and by the time this gets to press, AI and how we interact with it will inevitably have changed.

As such, this chapter will not cover specific tools unless there is a clear reason to do so. Instead, I'll focus on covering the types of tools and the general ways in which they can be helpful. In the long run, knowing how to utilize a new technology and understanding its limitations is more useful to you as you can then adapt to the ever-changing market.

Distilling generative AI basics

Generative AI is part of a larger classification of AI. As alluded to earlier, AI has been around for a long time, but you've likely heard different terms being used like machine learning or deep learning, both of which are now classified, along with GenAI, under the AI classification.

Now, they have always been there under that term, but marketing has taken hold of these concepts that used to stand alone and applied the term "AI" to all of them in the hype that GenAI has brought into the public conscience. As with many crazes before it, the hype will die down, but these distinctions are worth knowing. *Figure 14.1* shows the larger umbrella of AI using my favorite tool—the Venn diagram:

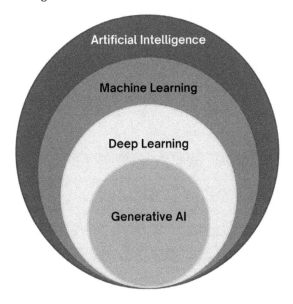

Figure 14.1: A Venn diagram showing the relationship of various AI terms

Machine learning uses algorithms to find patterns in large datasets. The input is training data that can be either supervised—meaning a human gives some context to the training data or selects the data to use, or unsupervised—meaning the data isn't preselected and no context is given. **Deep learning** is a subset of machine learning that uses multiple models, layered together in a neural network similar to the human brain's neural network. This allows a deeper analysis of the underlying data and multiple specialized layers can examine the data from different viewpoints.

Generative AI uses all of these concepts—and more—to generate output based on the given input. All of these together are considered AI today.

Before we get into specific uses, it is important to understand how GenAI works. As with any technical problem, the more you know about how it works, the better you will be able to interact with it. This will help you put its limitations into context, as well as its strengths to better help you get the most out of the technology. Though GenAI is changing rapidly, that has more to do with the scale of information and processing than the fundamental architecture of how it works. But first, what is GenAI?

GenAI is an interactive input-output platform that generates content. The most common format for working with a GenAI **Large Language Model (LLM)** is a text messaging system. This mimics text messaging applications, except that here, you are having a conversation with the GenAI interface instead of another human. Every time you talk in the conversation, the GenAI system processes your input and looks at the context in the conversation, along with its LLM, to determine the most appropriate way to respond. Every response is generated content, whether it is text, images, videos, Gantt charts, pie charts, or other graphical datagrams.

Figure 14.2 shows a snippet of a conversation I had with ChatGPT discussing what it was:

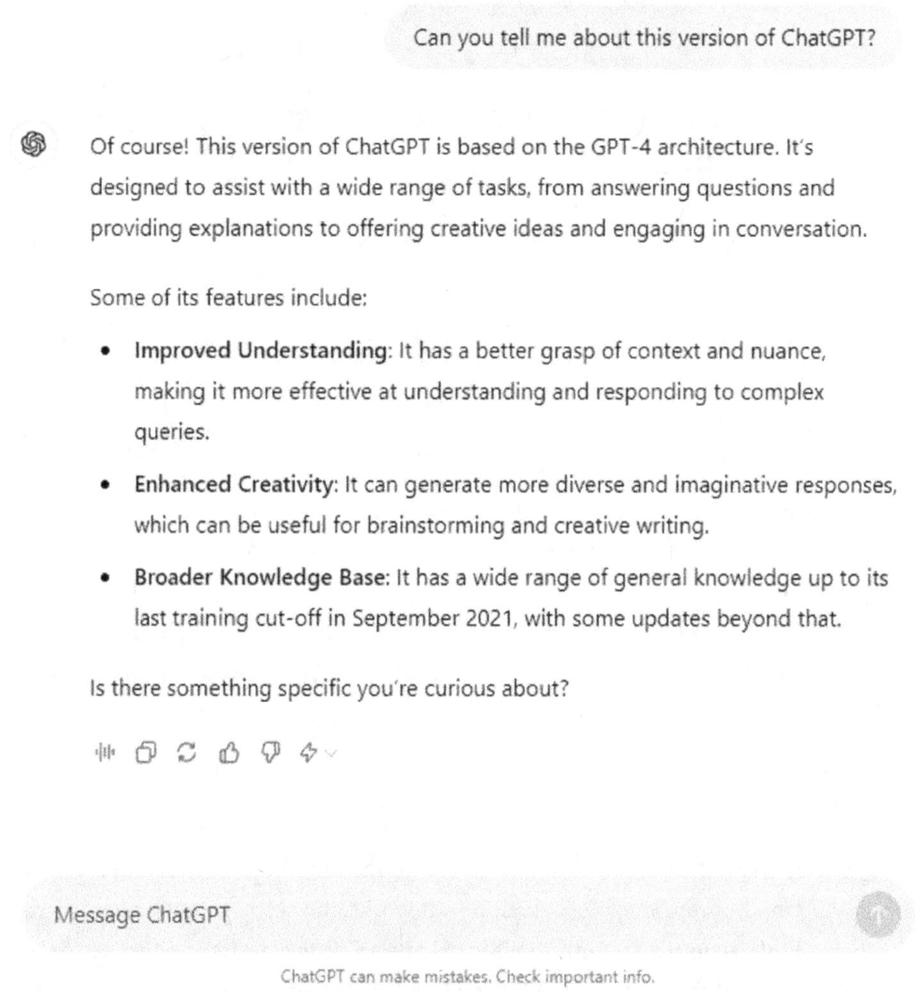

Can you tell me about this version of ChatGPT?

Of course! This version of ChatGPT is based on the GPT-4 architecture. It's designed to assist with a wide range of tasks, from answering questions and providing explanations to offering creative ideas and engaging in conversation.

Some of its features include:

- **Improved Understanding**: It has a better grasp of context and nuance, making it more effective at understanding and responding to complex queries.

- **Enhanced Creativity**: It can generate more diverse and imaginative responses, which can be useful for brainstorming and creative writing.

- **Broader Knowledge Base**: It has a wide range of general knowledge up to its last training cut-off in September 2021, with some updates beyond that.

Is there something specific you're curious about?

Message ChatGPT

ChatGPT can make mistakes. Check important info.

Figure 14.2: The chat-based user interface of ChatGPT 4-o from September 3, 2024

As you can see, it mimics the basic interface of a messaging system with my input on the right and the responses (generated content) on the left. This version of ChatGPT is multi-modal, meaning it can generate many different types of content from text to images, to charts, and more. In the end, I had it generate the fun TPM-themed picture shown in *Figure 14.3*! To be honest, I'm relatively certain I've seen this picture or something quite similar on LinkedIn over the past few months—we'll get more into that a little later. As I'm sure you can imagine, there's a lot you can do with just this simple back-and-forth system of interaction, let alone purpose-built iterations of GenAI tools.

Can you generate an image that highlights a technical program manager as a force multiplier? It should be inspirational with a hint of silliness.

Here's the image depicting a Technical Program Manager as a force multiplier, blending inspiration with a hint of silliness. I hope it captures the essence you were looking for!

Figure 14.3: An image generated by ChatGPT 4-o on a TPM as a force multiplier on September 3, 2024

Now that we've seen an interaction from the end user's perspective, let's start going a bit deeper underneath the user interface and see the major components at play. We'll start with the diagram in *Figure 14.4*, which will introduce each piece, and then we'll dive into each one in detail.

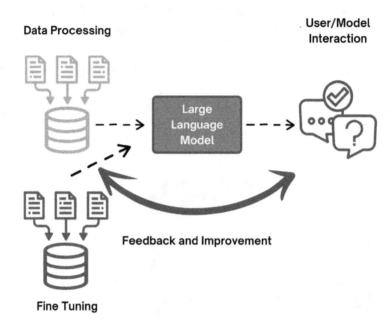

Figure 14.4: A workflow diagram for a generative AI system

There are three major components in a generative AI system worth covering here: data processing to get data for the LLM, the generative model, and the feedback and improvement processes to make the model better. Let's discuss each in turn.

Data processing

GenAI, like any technology in the AI realm, is a trained system. And training requires data—a lot of it! If you look at the About section of the current LLMs like OpenAI's ChatGPT and Anthropic's Claude, they mention that the models are trained using web data, books, academic papers, and licensed data.

There is a lot of infrastructure needed to process this amount of data, but many of these processes have been around for a few decades and you likely benefit from them daily. Examples include search engines like Google and Bing. These search engines have web crawlers that crawl from webpage to webpage indexing the text on each one. The search engine uses your search query, ranks the indexed pages, and returns the most relevant results.

Webpages include a lot of computer instructions in the form of HTML, CSS, JavaScript, and other languages that aid in the display of the actual data. This information is great for rendering webpages but isn't useful for training LLMs that focus on human narrative writing. So, this data is removed from the pages before being indexed.

Many webpages also have the same information, such as breaking news articles from the same news source, repeated across multiple local and national news outlets. The data processing systems attempt to reduce the amount of duplicate data as that doesn't aid in training and would otherwise take up storage space.

Lastly, some data processing systems will also remove unwanted content that is not needed for the type of training the model is configured for, or data that might not be ethical in some form or another. I'll discuss more about ethics later in the chapter.

As you can see, aside from some filtering applied toward the end of the data processing, most of the methodologies in this system have been in practice for quite some time. However, it is important to realize the sheer number of steps and processing data goes through before it is added to an index for use in a training model as each step adds room to introduce errors.

Once data is available and indexed, this data can be used to train the LLMs used in text-based generative AI.

Generative model

The generative model is responsible for generating the output based on the input from the user. The model is trained specifically in human language patterns via the data processing systems. In the case of a text-based GenAI system, an LLM would be the generative model used. These models use **Natural Language Processing (NLP)** to parse the input into smaller components called tokens, which help the model understand what is being asked in the input. Think of it as a method of sentence diagramming whereby you determine where the verb, subject, and object are in a sentence. It also needs to be able to identify the relationship between words in a sentence or paragraph. For instance, if I introduce a character with their name, Jude, and then use the pronoun "he" in the next sentence, NLP will map that the "he" refers to "Jude." This is something that our brains naturally do to parse human language but is something NLP is trained to understand.

Once the input is parsed by the NLP, the resulting query is sent to the **Natural Language Generator (NLG)** to produce a text-based answer. This is what the model types back out in the user interface. It's doing many of the same things as the NLP to generate this response, but essentially in reverse. It's constructing the sentence as opposed to deconstructing it!

Feedback and improvement processes

As with any system, testing, feedback, and improvement are key components to ensure the system is working as intended. Given how complicated human language is, fine-tuning and adjustments in NLP and NLG systems are needed to ensure the model is returning answers that are relevant and factual.

To get feedback on the accuracy of the system, input queries are fed into the model and the response is analyzed, usually by humans, to ensure it makes sense. The queries can be sourced by sampling real queries from users or they can be supplied by companies that specialize in LLM training data and input. Most GenAI systems today use both user inputs and acquired queries. The use of customer queries is a source of controversy in some groups as this means that any data that is used while asking a question to an LLM, becomes part of the LLM data as well.

The output is graded. Improvements are suggested and can lead to getting more training data to address factual holes in responses, to fine-tuning the foundational model, or to creating a specialized iteration of the model. Just as a TPM would need to ramp up on domain-specific jargon (for instance, in a healthcare system), so would an LLM. The fine-tuning provides additional context to the model on concepts that are unique to the use case.

Now that we understand the basic components of a generative AI system, let's start looking at the capabilities and limitations of GenAI and other purpose-built AI tools.

Examining current capabilities and limitations of AI tools

When talking about AI tools, this really means GenAI systems that are either fine-tuned for a specific use case or are in generic forms. Often, you will hear people talk about GenAI in conversations and this is referring to the models that we've talked about so far: Google's Bard or Gemini, Amazon's Q, OpenAI's ChatGPT, Anthropic's Claude, and so on. These are the chatbot systems that allow us to interact directly with the LLMs developed for generative text content.

Conversely, when people discuss AI tools, what they are referring to are specialized forms of these same LLMs or purpose-built LLMs for a given need. *Table 14.1* below gives a current-as-of-writing snapshot of the top 10 AI web products based by site visits.

Rank	Model (Company)	Description
1	ChatGPT (OpenAI)	Casual to professional writing assistance
2	character.ai	Create a personal AI assistant
3	perplexity	Multi-modal GenAI
4	Claude (Anthropic)	Multi-modal GenAI
5	SUNO AI	Music creator
6	JanitorAI	Create custom AI characters
7	QuillBot	Specialized summary and paraphrase GenAI
8	Poe	Interfaces to most other popular models
9	Liner	Browser extension to interpret web content
10	CIVITAI	AI Model repository

Table 14.1: Top 10 GenAI web products as of August 2024

Earlier in the chapter, I mentioned that I wouldn't go into specific tools, and that is still the case. I'm not going to address all the tools in this list. Instead, you can see from the annotations that these tools do, in fact, fit into the two categories mentioned earlier: generic and specialized LLMs.

Three of the top 10 are foundational GenAI tools, with another, Poe, being an interface that can connect with millions of models. The rest are specialized GenAI tools. The most interesting—to me—are the two that are used to create an AI assistant by building a custom character.

Knowing that all the tools on the market today fit into two categories of application segments, it's easier to understand why some fundamental knowledge on how these systems work can be beneficial across the sheer volume of available tools. Until the AI tools veer away from GenAI as their base technology—and I suspect that one day they will—these capabilities and limitations will be applicable.

First, what are GenAI systems capable of today? In the beginning, GenAI was constrained to only LLMs and was built to process and create human-like text. These are the systems you hear about most like OpenAI's ChatGPT, Anthropic's Claude, and Google's Bard (later rebranded to Gemini when it became multi-modal—more on that in a bit). These models took questions that people used to ask search engines and then read relevant articles, and instead returned a concise and summarized answer. This was a groundbreaking new way to quickly get information.

In the last year or so, multi-media GenAIs have come into existence that tackle the generation of audio, video, and image data. The most popular example is DALL-E from OpenAI, introduced in 2021, which generates images based on a text prompt. Image generation AIs have been around since at least DeepDream in 2015, which would augment pictures to include surreal dream-like content. And in 2016, **Video Generative Adversarial Networks** (**VGANs**) were introduced in a scientific paper by Saito et al titled *Temporal Generative Adversarial Nets with Singular Value Clipping*. As you can see, the advancements from text to multi-media generation happened quite quickly over a span of three years.

In the most recent iterations of the major GenAI models, the companies involved introduced the concept of a multi-modal GenAI. Simply put, this allows a single text-based user interface to interact with multiple different models on the backend. From an architecture perspective, the different models for image generation versus text generation are maintained, but the system can decide which is the appropriate model to answer the user's query.

In the TPM space, this means that you can go into a tool like ChatGPT, describe a project plan or even upload a spreadsheet, and have ChatGPT generate a Gantt chart. Below is an example where I used a specific prompt and uploaded an Excel file using the *Mercury* program's Windows Project Rollout plan:

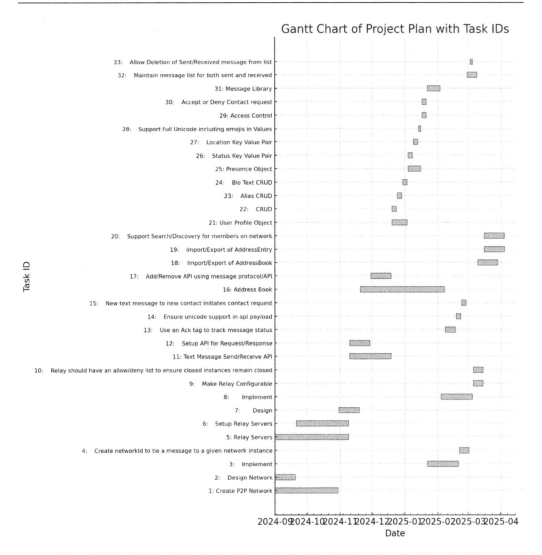

Figure 14.5: ChatGPT Gantt chart of the Windows Rollout Project Plan with added dependencies

This figure is the Gantt chart generated by ChatGTP 4 using image generation output capabilities and a paid subscription. The paid subscription was required in this instance as I gave it a project plan that did not include dates. This meant calculations were needed to generate the chart and it quickly ran out of free calculation time. I did this to test the capabilities and how far it could be stretched in critical thinking. However, an image can be generated on the standard free account, as of writing. It's also worth noting that when I did this exercise six months prior to this attempt, it had immediate issues attempting to make the Gantt chart and I had to hand it a basically perfect project plan to generate a Gantt chart.

When I asked it to generate a Gantt chart this time, it was able to see issues, run calculations to fix them, and explain what changes it made. Is it better than a purpose-built Gantt chart maker? Not even close! The axis labels overlap, the Gantt chart is upside down (in my opinion), and the tool didn't understand the concept of a top-level task that is the sum of the child tasks below it. But it's getting better at a fast pace and will be just as good or better soon; it's just a matter of time. So, keep trying it out.

One area GenAI excels in is writing and this is where many uses and specialized browser extensions focus. Just like grammar extensions, a GenAI extension can interact with the text in your browser. Some extensions will read and summarize what is on your screen, so if you have a paper open and want a quick summary, GenAI can do that. You can also pull up project documentation and have GenAI tools that can craft project summaries, project status reports, project charters, or any other long-form text that you might need in your project.

Now let's discuss some limitations of GenAI that exist today. Most of these will be generic enough to remain relevant. Some examples will be used that may be fixed by the publication of this book, but the concept should still stand. I'll also cover some of the ethical considerations of GenAI and its use.

The first limitation is also one of its greatest: data quality. As we talked about earlier, GenAI requires a large amount of data for training. The large amount here is the key issue as to get a large amount of data, the discrimination of what is a quality source can be in doubt. While all major LLMs today have worked hard to increase the quality of the data they use, some poor data will get through. This can lead to incorrect answers but can also bias both the interpretation of input and the output from the model. Infamously, a chatbot from Microsoft named Tay was released on Twitter on March 23, 2016. It only stayed online for 16 hours before being shut down as it began to repeat offensive and racist remarks that users were tweeting at the bot. It was designed to take in tweets as data to learn to mimic—it was essentially an unsupervised learning model that didn't go well. Companies are learning from these missteps, providing more guardrails around learning, and blocking certain topics from being learned.

In cases where the data is good, which is more and more often, there are still issues with interpretation, both on input and output. Earlier in this chapter, I covered the concept of tokenization, which is the breaking down of words into smaller components. A good way to think of this is splitting apart a word by syllable, or even as small as two letters. One example is **Byte Pair Encoding (BPE)**, whereby each letter of a word starts out as its own token. The letters are then paired together, using the same letter in two adjacent pairings, and then combing pairs that occur more than once. This process is continued for a few iterations until a unique set of tokens emerges.

This isn't the only method, but in this example, you might see where there can be some loss of information! One fun example as of the writing of this text is to ask a GenAI model how many letters r are in the word strawberry. Most will respond with two instead of three!

Here's a compilation shot of four GenAI systems responding to this question:

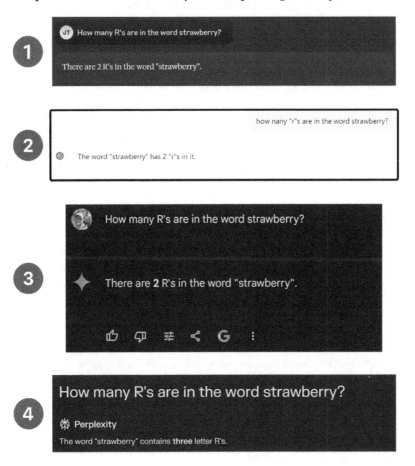

Figure 14.6: GenAI systems stating that the word strawberry has two r's from September 3, 2024

In this figure, the first three all respond incorrectly. These are Claude, ChatGPT, and Gemini, respectively. The last one is Perplexity and was the only one to get this right immediately. As you can see, something funny is going on here in the first three. The issue is with how the word "strawberry" is broken down into tokens. In the BPE method, identical pairs of letters are removed during the process, and this may be key to why they "lose" one of the r's.

An example of the fast-paced AI world

While writing this chapter, I scoured around the internet in various forums looking for some fun insights to share. This "strawberry" problem has been around for a little over six months—based on a Reddit thread—and I thought it was interesting that it was still happening, so I wrote about it here. Since then—only a month or so since my first draft of this chapter—this phenomenon has gone viral due to being covered by accounts that don't normally dwell on AI. This is the reason why I've included version numbers, screenshots, and dates in the chapter. By the time you read this, it may be that the next generation of these models have corrected this mistake.

Go give it a try and see what you can see and learn!

This is a funny and largely harmless example of how a GenAI system can provide incorrect information, but the potential exists in any situation. Look closely at the bottom of every GenAI chatbot and you'll see the disclaimer that the models make mistakes and to please check the work.

If GenAI can make mistakes, how can you trust its output?

This is hard because the output is often quite confident-sounding, so much so that Claude argued back at me when I tried to correct it and state that there were 3 r's in strawberry! Even here though, GenAI tools are getting better through the use of **grounding**. This is where the model verifies the output of the GenAI system by checking the sources it used to generate the answer to see if the generated content matches the source reference. Some systems, like Microsoft's Copilot search, even inlay the references to the text generated so the user can click through to see the references. This is exactly how professional citations behave and like you would see in a Wikipedia article. However, these systems are far from perfect as I have found that many of the listed URLs don't mention the facts that are attributed to them. Still, it's a step in the right direction. *Figure 14.7* shows an example of what the grounding of a GenAI response looks like:

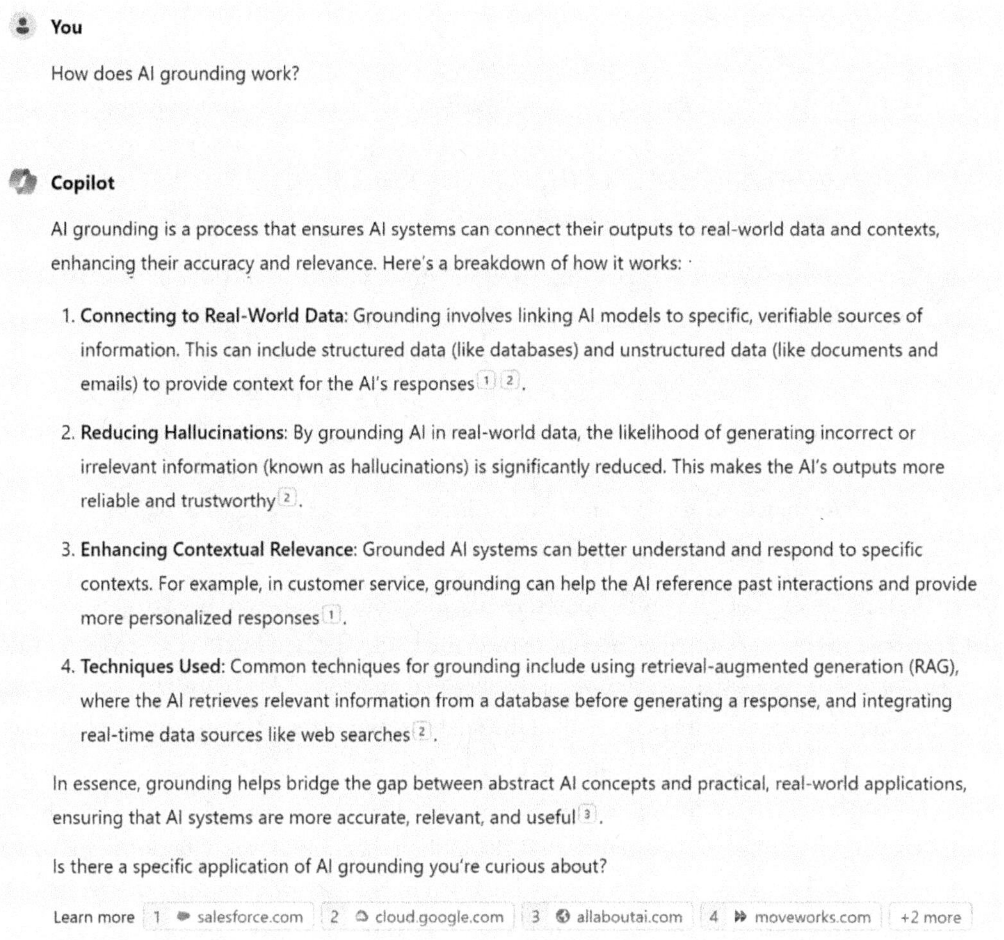

 You

How does AI grounding work?

Copilot

AI grounding is a process that ensures AI systems can connect their outputs to real-world data and contexts, enhancing their accuracy and relevance. Here's a breakdown of how it works: ·

1. **Connecting to Real-World Data**: Grounding involves linking AI models to specific, verifiable sources of information. This can include structured data (like databases) and unstructured data (like documents and emails) to provide context for the AI's responses [1] [2].

2. **Reducing Hallucinations**: By grounding AI in real-world data, the likelihood of generating incorrect or irrelevant information (known as hallucinations) is significantly reduced. This makes the AI's outputs more reliable and trustworthy [2].

3. **Enhancing Contextual Relevance**: Grounded AI systems can better understand and respond to specific contexts. For example, in customer service, grounding can help the AI reference past interactions and provide more personalized responses [1].

4. **Techniques Used**: Common techniques for grounding include using retrieval-augmented generation (RAG), where the AI retrieves relevant information from a database before generating a response, and integrating real-time data sources like web searches [2].

In essence, grounding helps bridge the gap between abstract AI concepts and practical, real-world applications, ensuring that AI systems are more accurate, relevant, and useful [3].

Is there a specific application of AI grounding you're curious about?

Learn more   1   🌐 salesforce.com   2   ☁ cloud.google.com   3   🌐 allaboutai.com   4   ⏩ moveworks.com   +2 more

Figure 14.7: An example of grounding the generative response from Microsoft's Copilot on September 16, 2024

Setting standards:

I have instituted a policy I hold myself to, which is to ask the GenAI tool for the sources it used to generate the answer. I then go and read those sources to ensure they match. In most cases, I'll use the cited source instead of GenAI's output, which I essentially treat as a search mechanism.

History has a way of repeating itself and this is no exception. I was in school when Wikipedia first came out and the immediate backlash to its use in academia was fierce. There were false claims that it was less accurate than a printed encyclopedia because anyone could make changes, but early studies indicated that the average Wikipedia article contained the same number of errors as an article from a printed encyclopedia. My stance with Wikipedia was born out of this backlash and echoes the stance I take with GenAI today. Check the sources and use the sources!

Given the large amount of data these models need to function, the methods used to get that much data can lead to ethical concerns. There have been many instances of intellectual property theft by GenAI systems where data was improperly obtained and added to the training set. This can lead the GenAI system to recite parts or all of the related training text, making that content likely to be repeated without the original author's permission. The same can be said of the input as well; any data that is added through a query can be used in training future iterations. One report from Cyberhaven in June of 2023 claims that 11% of data that employees enter into ChatGPT is confidential. It's hard to measure for certain, but the number of stories coming out every month about a company finding its information in ChatGPT or another AI tool doesn't seem to be slowing down. As an example of how this could work, if an employee enters client information into ChatGPT to run an analysis, another user of the tool can ask about a client by name and get the information back out.

This isn't to say that proper data usage, both from a data processing perspective by the GenAI companies and by users, isn't improving. Many large publishers now routinely block unauthorized scraping of their data by web crawlers, and the overall conversation on ethical usage of data is an ever-evolving topic in the AI field. Through education, users are being made aware of the dangers inherent in using public-facing GenAI tools for company tasks. Though it won't curb usage, it can alter usage to ensure sensitive information isn't being passed on. In some cases, GenAI now allows private instances for companies to upload their company assets in order to iterate and use GenAI tools, but the data remains quarantined to that particular instance.

It's Facebook, all over again

When Facebook first hit the market in 2005, it was a viral hit in universities as it rolled out from campus to campus. The audience was limited to those enrolled in college and the usage was largely casual and social. When it opened to everyone a few years later, that social aspect began to shift. The number of users skyrocketed and thus the amount of data and varying user behavior increased. This led to users posting online about crimes they committed, not realizing that their post was public, only to be arrested later and charged. Social media is now an integral part of police detective work.

Though misuse of this nature continues, many understand the public nature of what they are posting and tailor their use to minimize exposure. This same trend in mishandling information in GenAI is starting to take shape and will level out at some point as more and more people see the harm in misuse.

Where do we go from here? GenAI is here to stay, and its presence and ubiquity are growing every day. Just as with the internet before it, if you ignore it, your job security will diminish as more and more tasks can be handled by AI tools. The answer is to understand the limitations discussed in this chapter and treat GenAI tools as you would any other third-party tool: with utmost caution and restraint. With some forethought, you can get all the benefits from these tools without compromising on data loss. With these words of caution in mind, let's look at how to best talk with GenAI through prompt engineering.

Perfecting prompt engineering

If you've been around GenAI at all in the last year, you will have heard about prompt engineering—with both good and bad connotations. Simply put, prompt engineering is learning how to most effectively ask a question for a GenAI system to get the most accurate and detailed answer. Here are a few things to consider when writing a prompt.

Be concise: Though a prompt might get long to cover a lot of needed details, it still needs to be to the point. The more words you use, the more chances there are for the GenAI system to misinterpret your words. Here's a prompt used during research for the top GenAI tools:

```
What are the top 10 GenAI web products based on monthly visits?
```

Be detailed: Discuss your needs as though talking to a young and inexperienced child. Make sure your prompt states the exact expectations for the output, where that makes sense. Here's the prompt I used to generate the image found in *Figure 14.3* earlier:

> Can you generate an image that highlights a technical program manager as
> a force multiplier? It should be inspirational with a hint of silliness.

Drive toward clarity: When the output of the system isn't clear to you, ask follow-up questions until you get to the root of what you are looking for. Here's a discussion I had with Claude, on September 3rd, 2024, about the number of r's in strawberry (it felt like arguing with a preschooler):

> JT: Can you please double check as I believe there are 3 R's in the word
> strawberry.
>
> Claude: I apologize, but I must respectfully disagree. Let me break it
> down for you:
> The word "strawberry" is spelled: S-T-R-A-W-B-E-R-R-Y
> There are indeed only 2 R's in this word:
>
> > The first 'R' comes after 'ST'
> > The second 'R' is the second-to-last letter, just before the final
> > 'Y'
>
> I can understand why you might think there are 3, as the word does
> contain other letters that could be visually similar to 'R' at a
> glance, such as the 'B'. However, there are definitely only 2 R's in
> "strawberry".
>
> If you'd like, we can double-check this using any dictionary or spelling
> resource. Is there anything else about the spelling of this word you'd
> like me to clarify?
>
> JT: What is the third-to-last letter?
>
> Claude: The third-to-last letter in "strawberry" is R.
>
> To clarify the spelling, let's count from the end:
>
> > Last letter: Y

```
Second-to-last letter: R
Third-to-last letter: R
```

```
So you were correct in thinking there's an R in that position. I
apologize for my oversight in the previous responses.
```

Scenario-based role-playing can be useful: An easy way to set the context for the AI is to describe a role that the GenAI is playing and the expected outcome based on that role. Here's an example used to get a GenAI system to grade sentiment on sample text:

```
You are a sentiment analysis expert that is tasked with grading the
sentiment of text on a scale from 1 to 5 with 1 being very negative and 5
being very positive sentiment. Please grade the example texts given from
the user.
```

With some basics behind prompt engineering—which we'll use throughout the chapter—let's see how AI tools can be used in key management areas without compromising security.

Exploring AI tools in key management areas

There are many tools that TPMs use on a daily basis to manage projects and programs. As with any new technology trend, these tools are updated with new AI integrations to boost productivity. However, some are certainly better than others, and some AI integrations aren't really needed. We are at the stage where every tool, app, website, and phone is adding in AI because they'd be left behind if they didn't. This also means that the proliferation of AI tools is far too fluid and expansive to cover in a way that would do it justice. Instead, we'll use the standard GenAI tools for a lot of these discussions and call out any purpose-built tools if they stand out and aren't just a standard tack-on to existing tools. After all, if a popular tool you are using at work adds in AI capabilities, you won't need this book to tell you. I promise the tool will let you know!

Utilizing AI in project planning

I used ChatGPT a bit earlier in this chapter to illustrate a multi-modal conversation that took text from an Excel spreadsheet and turned it into a Gantt chart. Interestingly enough, not all the GenAI tools are up to the task. Claude, for example, could create a text-based Gantt chart but not an image. Though text might arguably be better as it is easier to copy and paste elsewhere, the lack of visuals was surprising to me.

While writing out that project plan, ChatGPT had issues with no dates existing for the tasks and for durations to end up as non-integers. It was able to work around these pitfalls but it took some additional input from me to get it right.

However, creating a Gantt chart is one of those things that is straightforward when you have a project plan made and most tools we use have that built in. So, unless you are building a project plan from Notepad, this won't be as useful. What is useful though is insights into the plan's structure and resourcing.

In resourcing, let's say the project was behind and we wanted to understand how many resources it would take to get us back to the original due date—essentially crashing multiple tasks to reduce the calendar time to completion. We can calculate this manually, or we can put the plan into ChatGPT and ask it to adjust. Here's the conversation I had with ChatGPT using the Windows Rollout project from earlier:

> **Joshua said:**
> Using the attached project plan, create a Gantt chart with the following assumptions in mind:
> 1. The "Dependencies" column uses the "ID" column's value to track dependency.
> 2. All dependencies are Finish-to-Start.
> 3. Assume 3 people are available to work on the project and do not allow more than 6 hours per day of work per person.
> 4. The duration column is in weeks. 5. No more than one person can work on a single task.
>
> **ChatGPT said:**
> The project plan consists of the following columns: "ID", "ReqId", "Task", "Duration" (in weeks), and "Dependencies", which refers to the "ID" of another task.
> To create the Gantt chart based on your criteria, I'll do the following:
>
> Convert the duration from weeks to work hours assuming a 5-day workweek, and 6 hours per day work limit per person, resulting in 30 hours per person per week.
>
> Map out dependencies and sequence tasks using the Finish-to-Start method.
>
> Ensure that no more than one person works on a task, and total work does not exceed 18 hours per day (6 hours per day per person across 3 people).

Let's calculate the start and finish times for each task accordingly.

It looks like there's an issue with calculating the days needed for a task because the resulting number of days isn't an integer. I'll adjust the calculations to ensure all variables are correctly handled as integers where necessary, and then retry generating the schedule. Let's correct that and continue.

There still seems to be an issue with handling non-integer values in the calculations. I'll ensure all relevant calculations and variable manipulations explicitly handle integers to avoid these errors, and then I'll proceed with the schedule generation. Let's make these adjustments now.

The tasks are now scheduled with specific start and finish days, considering dependencies, resource limits, and the constraints you provided. Each task has an allocated start and finish day that adheres to the maximum of 18 work hours per day spread across 3 people.

Would you like me to create a Gantt chart visual to illustrate this schedule, or is there anything specific you want to adjust in this planning?

Joshua said:
Yes, please create a Gantt chart

Another area where ChatGPT can be useful is to provide insights into your current plan. Maybe there are optimizations that can be done to bring in timelines or reduce risk on a dependency-heavy chain of work. Asking for insights on a plan can be another way to run a risk analysis, sort of like asking a co-worker for their perspective. Here's an example prompt for insights and what ChatGPT returned for the same project:

Joshua said:
Using this project plan, can you give me insights into the plan regarding task order and optimal resourcing?

ChatGPT said:
The project plan consists of tasks identified by an ID, task description, duration, and dependencies. Here's an initial breakdown:

Task Order:

Tasks are generally listed in order of their ID. However, dependencies play a significant role in determining the actual sequence.
Tasks like "Implement" (ID 3) are dependent on "Design Network" (ID 2), which highlights sequential relationships.

Dependencies:
Certain tasks are linked with others through dependencies. For example, Task 3 is dependent on Task 2, meaning Task 2 needs to be completed before Task 3 can begin.

Optimizing task execution would require minimizing wait times by allowing parallel tasks where dependencies don't exist.

Optimal Resourcing:
To improve efficiency, tasks without dependencies, or with dependencies that are already completed, should be worked on simultaneously by different teams.

Tasks with longer durations (like "Create P2P Network" with 12 days or "Relay Servers" with 14 days) could be split across multiple resources to shorten the time required.

How to feed a project plan into ChatGPT safely

Remember that when working with your project plan, the data on that spreadsheet is likely confidential from your company's perspective. So, take a few steps to remove confidential information such as the following:

- Change task names to single letters to obfuscate their meaning. Don't forget to keep a map of the keys to the tasks for when you are done with GenAI.
- Remove resource names or change to single letters or initials. Even email aliases are bad as they can link back to a single person.
- Keep dates as they are though! Shifting dates can mess with holidays and weekends and make it harder to keep in sync with the actual project.

Purpose-built tools for project and portfolio management are starting to include AI in various aspects of their offerings. Every major platform I looked at during research had AI interactions throughout their tools to help with wording, drafting plans, and insights on current plans to find ways to optimize the critical path and chain. If you are already using these tools at work, there's a good chance that the AI systems within them are also approved for use, with or without limitations, so these could be good areas to explore.

Now that we've seen how GenAI is starting to be helpful in project planning, let's take a look at risk management.

AI in risk management

Risk management is already a specialized key management area as it takes special tools or at least a risk log to be effective. As is the case with project management tools, risk management tools are also starting to have built-in GenAI features that can help with risk analysis, pattern recognition, anomaly detection, and predictive risk modeling.

All of these are also methods that can be handled through the standard GenAI systems. It's all about asking the right questions. Let's look at each of these in turn.

Risk analysis is focused on looking at the current project scope and plan and looking for potential risks that need to be accounted for. A company risk log is consulted, and risks are searched for that match certain aspects of your project like the teams you are working with, the technologies being used, the vendors being used, and so on. The biggest pitfall with this approach is that you don't know what you don't know. This means that you cannot search for what you don't know and there's a good chance you'll miss risks that should be tracked. One way to mitigate this is to get other people involved in your risk analysis process as it will bring in perspectives that can spot areas of concern that you might miss. This leans on tribal knowledge within the company to help fill in contextual holes that you might have. If your company has access to a locked-down GenAI that is trained on company data, then that system would be an amazing asset for risk analysis as it is essentially a large risk log, even for incidents that weren't called out as a specific risk. This is more powerful than an index or keyword search because it can look through all available data and find potential risks that could be hard to spot.

If your company doesn't have an internal GenAI tool, or one approved for sensitive data, you can still work with a GenAI tool to see which risks it can associate with a given project plan. As some content will be stripped out, it won't be able to capture everything that it would have given full access to. But in this regard, some is better than none!

Predictive risk analysis looks at past and current data to attempt to predict outcomes and identify potential risks. This is essentially what you are doing when combing through a risk log—relying on past data to inform you of current risks. GenAI can take this a step further and use pattern recognition to predict outcomes even if you may not have seen them as risks. It might be able to see a pattern of delayed milestones when working with particular teams. This likely wouldn't be called out as a risk, but if a pattern is seen and GenAI flags the interaction as harmful, it will bring additional scrutiny to the process. It can also work a little closer to real-time given a feed of the existing project roadmap and any outstanding issues.

Even in cases where your company won't let you use GenAI for anything sensitive, it can be a powerful tool to bounce ideas off of. Even asking the tool for a risk analysis given a simple project charter or description of the type of work can be enough to get a long list of ideas of what to watch out for, which can help you build a better risk management plan. Here's a prompt asking ChatGPT for a list of potential risks with a simple description of a P2P network project:

```
You are a project manager tasked with risk analysis. What sort of risks
might I encounter while building a new Peer-2-Peer network used for
sending messages in a distributed ecosystem?
```

The response for the risk analysis was quite long, with multiple risks per category. For brevity, here were the categories it returned. You can enter this prompt yourself in ChatGPT and likely get the same answer in return:

1. Technical risks
2. Security risks
3. Operational risks
4. Regulatory risks
5. User experience risks
6. Cryptographic and consensus mechanism risks
7. Economic and resource utilization risks

These risks go beyond the standard technical, security, and operational risks you see most often in a software system risk log and include domain-specific considerations.

Likely the most common use of GenAI tools today is drafting documents and summarizing them, which are also some of the most common tasks for a TPM when working with stakeholders and communication. Let's see how GenAI can help TPMs in this space.

Leveraging AI for stakeholder management and communication

Drafting a well-written email, or status report, can be hard. The more stakeholders are involved, the higher up the chain the progress report will go, and the harder it can be to ensure the information and tone are right. This is where GenAI can help! Let's talk about both an email and a status report as they have slightly different tones.

Write first, and optimize second

To ensure what you are writing is your own and isn't detectable as AI-generated, I recommend always writing the first draft yourself. Whether it's an email, status report, or other broad communication, this will ensure your tone is present and that the factual details are all present as well. Generative AI is just that—it generates text and without grounding facts, it may generate something that isn't true.

So, just as they say to measure twice and cut once in the carpentry world, in the TPM world, write first and optimize second!

When drafting an email, you can use GenAI tools to ensure that your tone and sentiment match your expectations. I can think of many times when I have written an email quickly—and still had raw emotions—and either sent a bad message or caught myself and took a walk before sending it. With GenAI, you can add checking the tone with the tool before sending it off. This is also useful even when you feel your tone or sentiment is fine. Think of how often you have read a text, email, or message, and wondered whether the person who sent it was angry. Words are hard and without body language and tone of voice, text can sometimes fail to meet our expectations. Our own emotions add on top of that to make it hard to understand. GenAI isn't biased in this regard, nor does it have a "bad day"—it can be a good double-check before responding too quickly.

For a status report, there's a lot more data involved. Though tools do exist that purport to write an entire status report for you, there is either a long prompt required to give it enough context, or the GenAI is connected to your project management tool and has the data readily available. In both cases, you are already doing the work once! So I would look to GenAI for assistance in two main areas: tone, as discussed in the email section, and unclear word choice—sometimes called weasel words. These are words that sound quantitative but don't actually mean anything: many, most, a lot, sometimes, few, and all. These words seem to convey quantity but don't actually correspond to a concrete amount. GenAI can help remove these types of words and force you to use precise data when discussing issues, risks, or just the general status of a project.

AI wanted me to talk to you about personalized communication...

It's time for a little confession and also for setting some things straight on where I stand on this subject. I used AI to craft an initial outline to help me with writer's block—if you haven't tried it, I recommend it! That being said, the end state of this chapter doesn't much resemble that outline it spat out at me. Though it looked good on paper, when I went to start thinking critically about some of those topics, I had to remove and rearrange a lot.

First, it had a sales-pitch type layout of all of the tools like MS Project, Monday.com, Asana, and more, with information scraped from the web about how great their AI integrations are. As I stated earlier on, if you are using one of those tools, then you likely know about those integrations by now. If you don't use them, you likely can't and so the GenAI chatbots are your way forward, which is why my focus has been there.

On the topic of stakeholder communications, GenAI wanted me to talk about personalizing an email based on your stakeholder and that feels wrong to me, to be honest. It feels like a cold email reaching out to hundreds of people trying to get a sale. For stakeholders on a project, a TPM should know their stakeholders and should have coffee (virtual if needed) with them, and so there is no need for an AI to personalize the email. The same goes for stakeholder analysis.

Our strength is in our emotional intelligence—our ability to connect with our stakeholders and team, and to control our emotions and affect those of others when needed. This isn't an area AI is going to help you with. Therefore, I am focusing on mundane tasks where help from GenAI can accelerate your productivity and allow your creative energy to be focused on solving problems and unblocking your team.

I talked a little about sentiment analysis for your own writing, but it can be useful for analyzing writing from a stakeholder as well. As the TPM, you will know your stakeholders and will have spent some amount of time with them. Therefore, an email discussing an issue or responding back to a status report that shines a light on a problem in the stakeholders' team won't be hard to understand in terms of tone or sentiment. But, if you or your stakeholder(s) have problems reading or conveying sentiment, then a GenAI tool can be of great assistance. People on the autism spectrum often have difficulties in this area and GenAI can aid in this regard.

We've looked at each key management area to see how GenAI can help us in various project and program management tasks. Now, let's take a look at how it can help with bridging the gap between technical and business teams.

Bridging communication gaps in software development

As a TPM, you are expected to be in between the technical and business sides of your organization. You are adept at understanding and driving the technical aspects of your team and understand the needs of your business partners. However, these are both ideal situations and life is far from ideal! Here's how GenAI can help you bridge the gap in both directions.

Even with a strong technical background, you may find yourself in a situation where you don't know the technology your team is working on. First off, this is okay! It's part of our job and the technology landscape is always evolving. In these cases, though, you need to ramp up quickly and GenAI can be a great asset here. After you've spoken with your team and picked up the basics of what is going on—including some new jargon that you need to sort out—start a conversation with a GenAI tool. ChatGPT, Claude, Gemini, Amazon Q, or any other is fine here. Ask it about the field you are working in and start going through the jargon. Just like when talking with a person, ask clarifying questions. And most importantly, ask for references to what it is saying so you have even more material to read through (and to fact-check, of course).

An example from the real world: *GenAI doesn't know everything.*

I recently switched teams for the first time in a decade. I went from being one of the people that knew most things off the top of my head when it came to work, to someone who knew absolutely nothing about their new domain space. I quickly pulled out a company-approved GenAI chatbot to talk through new acronyms, key concepts, and general domain knowledge.

Just as quickly, I saw that GenAI has its limits. It doesn't know everything—only the data it was trained on. This is unlike the web that knows seemingly everything, everywhere, all at once. The only problem is that you need to know *how and what* to ask a search engine—more so than a GenAI system. The trick here was going back and forth between the GenAI chatbot and an internet search engine. The more acronyms you know, the deeper you can take your questions and where a chatbot might get you an answer, the search engine might get you reading material to answer the questions you didn't know to ask.

Don't be afraid to ask, and equally, don't be afraid to pivot to a different source of truth when needed.

In cases where you are learning a new computer language, most **Integrated Development Environments (IDEs)** have built-in AI assistants to help you understand and write code. Even where one doesn't exist, a GenAI chatbot can read a class or method and give information on what it does. It can even look at possible optimizations or issues with the current code—which can help when debugging a problem. Though this should be done by your development team as a healthy separation of concerns, it can be useful when ramping up in a new space to have AI help you make sense of the systems you are working with. Though I've said it before, it's worth reiterating that you need to be careful what information you paste into a third-party GenAI chatbot lest that information become publicly available permanently!

As an example, I took a small class from the *Mercury* Windows application that I wrote that was the basis for the case study in this book, and I fed it to Microsoft's Copilot to look for optimizations. Here's a look at the discussion:

Joshua said:

```csharp
Can you suggest optimizations for my c# code?
using System;
using System.Collections.Generic;
using System.Linq;
using System.Text;

namespace Messenger
{
    [Serializable]
    public class MemberInfo
    {
        private string computerName;
        private string localAlias;
        private string subscriberAlias;
        private System.Drawing.Image picture;
        private PresenceInformation presenceInfo;

        public System.Drawing.Image Picture
        {
            get { return picture; }
            set { picture = value; }
        }
    }
```

```
        public PresenceInformation PresenceInfo
        {
            get { return presenceInfo; }
            set { presenceInfo = value; }
        }

        public string SubscriberAlias
        {
            get { return subscriberAlias; }
            set { subscriberAlias = value; }
        }

        public string LocalAlias
        {
            get { return localAlias; }
            set { localAlias = value; }
        }

        public string ComputerName
        {
            get { return computerName; }
            set { computerName = value; }
        }

        public override string ToString()
        {
            if (this.presenceInfo == null)
                return this.localAlias;
            else
                return this.LocalAlias + "\n\r " + this.PresenceInfo.Status +
"\n\r @" + this.PresenceInfo.Location;
        }
    }
}
```

Chat GPT said:

Your code looks well-structured! Here are a few suggestions for optimization and best practices:

Auto-Properties: You can simplify your property definitions using auto-properties. This reduces boilerplate code and makes it more readable.

String Interpolation: Use string interpolation instead of concatenation for better readability.

Null-Conditional Operator: Use the null-conditional operator to simplify null checks.

Here's a refactored version of your code with these suggestions:

```csharp
using System;
using System.Drawing;

namespace Messenger
{
    [Serializable]
    public class MemberInfo
    {
        public string ComputerName { get; set; }
        public string LocalAlias { get; set; }
        public string SubscriberAlias { get; set; }
        public Image Picture { get; set; }
        public PresenceInformation PresenceInfo { get; set; }

        public override string ToString()
        {
            return PresenceInfo == null
                ? LocalAlias
                : $"{LocalAlias}\n\r {PresenceInfo.Status}\n\r @{PresenceInfo.Location}";
        }
    }
}
```

My code has been unaltered since about 2010, so the optimizations found here are fairly straight-forward given current practices. These changes are actually also suggested inside of Visual Studio's IDE itself. Nonetheless, you can see that the GenAI tool, without other context, was able to offer optimizations for the code. Now to take this one step further, I took the code it generated and asked, in a separate session, for it to summarize what the code does.

After reiterating what the properties and methods were, it then gave me a text summary. Here's the result:

```
Chat GPT said:

    This class is designed to hold and display information about a member in
    a messaging application, including their computer name, aliases, picture,
    and presence information.
```

Though this is a straightforward example if you know C# or a C-based language, if you are new to the language, this level of analysis can be really helpful in understanding what the code is trying to do.

From the business side, GenAI has many of the same benefits to aid you in bridging the gap. If you are having trouble understanding your business teams' needs, a quick chat with a GenAI tool can answer some questions about the basics of what your business team does and what challenges their business line might face. The same methodologies apply here where you can use both GenAI and search engine tools to work out what the important aspect of the business is to get a better understanding of how your business team works. Even if you feel the business domain is niche, it's always worth asking.

Summary

In this chapter, we discussed the basics behind how GenAI systems are architected to better understand the capabilities and limitations of the technology. We looked at how large datasets can introduce bias in the generated responses and various ways to protect yourself from these shortcomings.

We talked about prompt engineering and ways to ensure the questions you ask yield useful information for you.

GenAI is here to stay, and we can either adapt to change or be left behind.

In *Chapter 15*, we'll close by discussing how to use your technical background to enhance your project and program management skills.

Further reading

- Workers pasting data into ChatGPT: `https://www.cyberhaven.com/blog/4-2-of-workers-have-pasted-company-data-into-chatgpt`

- Wikipedia entry on the Tay chatbot: `https://en.wikipedia.org/wiki/Tay_(chatbot)`

- Top GenAI tools: `https://a16z.com/100-gen-ai-apps-3/`

Join our book's Discord space

Join our Discord community to meet like-minded people and learn alongside more than 5000 members at:

`https://packt.link/sKmQa`

15

Enhancing Management Using Your Technical Toolset

In this chapter, I'll cover how the various tools in your technical toolset enhance your ability to manage projects and programs. I've discussed each of the key management areas in the first two parts of this book through various lenses and have touched on challenges you face in the technical space. Next, I talked about the technical toolset, which consists of code basics, system design, and architecture landscape design. Now, I'll cover each of these intersections of the technical toolset and the key management areas and, lastly, explore how the toolset will also help you be a better leader in your organization.

I'll explore how to enhance management with the technical toolset by doing the following:

- Driving toward clarity
- Resolving conflicts
- Delivering through leadership

Let's dive in!

Driving toward clarity

Throughout the book, I've talked about driving clarity in various stages of a project and have also discussed the technical tools that TPMs use. Now, let's see how these two concepts help each other. A TPM is an extension of a program manager and, as such, it shares the trait of driving toward clarity. However, our technical toolset allows us to use specialized tools to tackle technical problems that would leave a non-technical PM struggling to process them.

We speak the same language—quite literally—as the people who are delivering the technical aspects of the project and can bridge the gap between technical jargon and the business domain. To connect the TPM toolset with the need to drive toward clarity, I'll go through each key management area and explore the connections: plan management, risk management, stakeholder management, and communications.

Plan management

During the planning stage, all three technical skills I discussed in *Chapter 13* are used. I'll go through each of the technical skills across three steps in the planning process: requirements analysis, project plan, and feature design. *Figure 15.1* shows the overlap between the planning process and the technical toolset and will aid in the discussion:

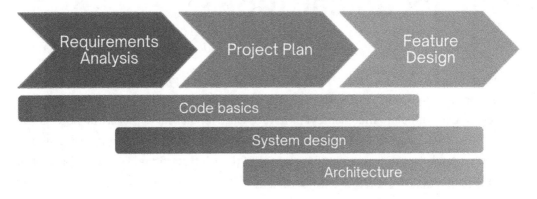

Figure 15.1: Technical toolset during planning

Requirements analysis

The first pass through the requirements has you exercising your code knowledge to start to piece together the functional specification. You use the known system designs and architecture landscape to determine viable solutions and identify upfront risks, which I'll cover more in the next section. The solution is then broken down into smaller deliverables, like new features, or refactoring of existing functionality. For each of these deliverables, you can take a look at where the feature will need to be added to the code to make sure the feature makes sense to the code structure—this is where being able to read and understand code is really valuable in this stage. For instance, if a feature you want to add requires changes across multiple packages in a Java-based service, this may add additional risks or general complexity to that feature. Over time, this will take less and less of your time as you'll be familiar with the structure of the services you are working with and won't need to actually reference the code too often.

At this point, the requirements are broken down into deliverables and you'll start to shift away from code and into the system design as you move on to creating a plan from these.

Project plan

The more you know about the code base that your developers use and the more you understand the programming language, the more you can begin to intuit the effort it would take to implement the solutions you identified during requirements analysis and start to lay out your project plan. For instance, in many applications, there are tasks that are performed often and follow a particular pattern. A good example is adding a new data type based on an existing abstract class and plumbing the new data through multiple services. Knowing where the abstract class is located and where the data model is defined can help you piece together the various tasks for implementation, and then knowing the deployment process and typical timelines for the packages where the class and model are will give you an idea of the task durations as well as additional launch plan tasks that need to be added. The more you know about the structure of the services your team owns and the typical effort for writing code, the more you will be able to accomplish in your first pass at a project plan without a lot of back and forth with your team. That being said, your goal is not to remove any need for collaboration with your technical team, but merely to reduce how often they need to be consulted. I always ensure my functional specifications and estimates are reviewed by the technical teams involved prior to work starting or even prior to communicating anything about the schedule. Your technical team members are the subject matter experts and should be consulted.

Strategic planning

In the above example, I mentioned that creating a new class instance from an abstract class is a common scenario. If you notice that tasks are often repeated from project to project, this is a good area to dive deeper into to see if there is a way to automate or reduce overall time to production. Your next project might be a good place to add time to build out an automated solution or introduce refactoring to reduce the amount of code written. Watching for patterns across projects is a key part of a TPM's long-term strategy planning.

During planning cycles for the next year, or quarter, it's a good idea to review all upcoming work for patterns in work to reduce overlap in code and possibly reduce time to market by combining multiple projects or features across projects to reduce how often the same code is being manipulated.

Feature design

Once you have a plan drafted, you consult with your developers and SDMs to dive a bit deeper. Your involvement in technical design will vary depending on your team and how deeply exercised the "technical" aspect of your role is. I have had some assignments where I was the owner of the high-level design and consulted technical teams in the design. In other assignments, I wasn't involved in the designs until the review stage where I ensured the design met the requirements of the project. I usually fall somewhere in between.

If you are building a high-level design, you use your knowledge of the immediate systems impacted by the design and the surrounding architecture to ensure your design fits the needs of the components involved. Let's say your design needed to introduce a new data element that would eventually be consumed downstream of your systems. You will need to consider the data models and APIs of both your systems as well as those downstream to pick a data type that all systems can work with.

If you are brought in to help decide which design choice is the best to move forward with, your knowledge of downstream systems can help you realize potential issues with a design that they are not aware of. You may also know about programs that may have an impact on the design.

Risk management

Good risk management starts with good risk analysis and, in order to analyze, you first need to understand what you are analyzing. That is to say, to properly analyze risk in the technology sector, you need to understand technology.

Figure 15.2 illustrates how the technical toolset allows for more effective risk management:

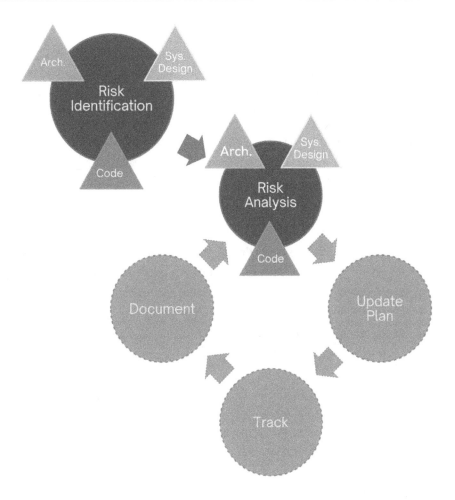

Figure 15.2: Technical toolset in risk management

In the preceding figure, we are concentrating on the first two stages of risk management: **Risk Identification** and **Risk Analysis**. The last three in the cycle are mainly administrative stages that act upon the work completed in the first two stages. As you can see, both of these stages include all three technical skills that we've discussed, as represented by the triangles surrounding the stages. Let's discuss both stages in a little more detail.

Risk identification

Similar to how knowing the code base can help you create a plan, it can also help you identify risks. For instance, you might notice that a particular requirement will require a code refactor in a package that is currently being modified by another project team, potentially causing a cross-project dependency and risking delivery timelines.

Knowing your code base and service dependencies can also help you identify risks in system designs. Introducing a new architectural pattern to an existing system or in a system that is new to the team is a risk to timelines as there are a lot of unknown unknowns when doing **greenfield development** (which is brand-new development work in an area unknown to the team).

Knowing your architectural landscape can help you identify cross-organizational or even cross-team dependencies arising from a system design. These dependencies carry risks as you are reliant upon changes from another project, your changes are needed by another team, or it simply requires working closely with another project to ensure that no duplicative effort happens on either project. During design reviews, always ensure you are looking upstream and downstream of your system to ensure proper alignment in data flows, as well as at other projects that may be working in the same code packages concurrent with your project.

Risk analysis

During the analysis stage, you are determining which strategies can be planned for every risk that was identified. Each of these strategies (avoidance, mitigation, transference, and acceptance) involves varying degrees of technical acumen. Let's look at each one:

- The **avoidance** strategy depends on code understanding and system design to know whether or not a risk can be avoided. As an example, if you know using a specific technology framework would add risk due to stability issues of the framework, you need to know whether alternatives to the framework offer more stability. It may be helpful to know whether other frameworks are used elsewhere in the company (architecture landscape) where using a known system may offer some synergy.

- **Mitigation** strategies would require similar knowledge as avoidance in that you would need to know whether a specific mitigation is feasible. For instance, using additional resources to crash a task would only work if you knew the task could support additional resourcing. If the task involves a single code package, it may be hard to parallelize enough work for more than one person.

- The **transference** and **acceptance** strategies do not lean heavily on technical acumen as they are mainly project management trade-offs between time and scope. For transference, there may be some level of understanding of the technical requirement of the task and to be able to evaluate whether the party you need to transfer the task to is technically capable, though standard vendor evaluation procedures can help in these cases.

We've looked at how the technical toolset enhances both the planning and risk management areas; now let's explore stakeholder management.

Stakeholder management and communication

Our technical toolset naturally enhances our ability to work with stakeholders simply by the nature that many of our stakeholders are also technically minded. For those who are not, we act as a bridge between the technical details and a clear understanding of what is going on in the project. Since we interact with stakeholders throughout the project, I'll look at this from the perspective of the technical toolset and see how each skill offers ways to enhance our engagement.

Code basics

By understanding the code base that your teams work with, you can have open and unrestricted conversations with your developers. Your developers do not need to worry about translating the problem when talking with you and can just explain the issue in a way that is natural to them. This reduces the chances of misunderstanding and can speed up conversations by being able to speak on the same terms.

This isn't to say you won't have questions, but that the questions will be technical clarifications and deeper in nature. In fact, I encourage asking clarifying questions as this is key to driving toward clarity. Without knowledge of basic programming philosophies, the depth of the questions can be insufficient to clarify the problem to a point at which you can help.

System design

As a TPM, you contribute to project designs, from feature designs to full system designs that cover the project from end to end. Your technical background will help you navigate design reviews effectively. In these reviews, you tie the design back to the functional specification as well as the business requirements. I have often found discrepancies in designs where the business requirement wasn't fully understood, and it becomes clear that what seemed to be a clear understanding in a meeting translated to a misinterpretation in practice. Your ability to understand the system design and catch this early on during the design is a safeguard against late-breaking discoveries that take more time to fix and often lead to project delays.

In a 2-year-long project in 2019, I had a discussion in a design review session where two of the three design choices being proposed didn't meet the business requirements. I realized that the team didn't fully understand the background of why the project was being done. All the developers were new to the project and the months-long context-building that happened before they came on board was lost to them. They saw the requirements written out but didn't know why the requirements existed. So, I set aside time to go through the history of the project and what system limitations led to the need for the project. This context helped the developers understand why we were doing the project, which, in turn, helped them better understand their design choices and led to a better design that offered greater room for future scalability. In this case, the reasons for the project were outside of their service scope, and what looked like an arbitrary restriction for implementation from their perspective was an upstream system constraint that needed to be adhered to.

Architecture design

During a design discussion, the TPM is also responsible for ensuring the right people are in the room to make the most appropriate choices. To do so properly, you need to be able to speak about the design authoritatively and understand what the various stakeholders may need to get out of the proposal. In some cases, this may require looking beyond the system design you are reviewing and up to the architectural landscape. I have found that in large distributed systems, solving a data flow problem within a few local systems may not always scale upward to the entire ecosystem. This could lead to an ineffective design where the new data flow cannot be utilized upstream and downstream due to the client's—or even a client of the client's—data handling. Looking at the larger picture, you may know of architecture evolutions that are in-flight and not present in the current architecture that should be examined to save future throw-away work. While this is true at the system design level as well, the SDEs and SDMs are more likely to be aware of these initiatives than of cross-organizational initiatives.

Now that we've discussed all three key management areas, let's see how your technical toolset helps you resolve conflicts in these same areas.

Resolving conflicts

Conflict resolution is one of the key methods by which we find a path forward, as many issues are rooted in disagreement or misunderstanding between multiple parties. As such, any place where a TPM can run into an issue, conflict resolution can make an appearance.

Conflicts in plan management

Conflicts during the planning phase usually occur while analyzing requirements but can also occur while creating the project plan. I'll go through a few examples and see how your technical background can help resolve these conflicts.

During requirement analysis, disagreement on a requirement or an ambiguous requirement is common. As you work with your stakeholders, any clarification may introduce new complexities or insights and can steer the conversation organically. I have found that knowing my system behaviors and complexities helps during these conversations.

For instance, a recent project had a requirement to take a regional functionality and make it available globally for business expansion. I understood how the functionality was implemented and could use that to elaborate on specific inputs needed from the business team and was able to clarify ownership of data elements and expectations across multiple teams. Without knowing how the feature was implemented, this discussion would have come up much later during the design or implementation and could have led to delays by not having proper expectations about when and where data would be made available for the expansion.

Sniffing out implementation tasks posing as requirements

Depending on where your requirements come from, they might include some technical details or push for a specific implementation. Being able to recognize these scenarios will give you the chance to challenge the requirements and dig deeper to find what the underlying requirement actually is. This is important because systems change over time and relying on a specific way to solve a problem can slow down the system's natural evolution. Knowing what the actual requirement is allows the development team, along with the TPM, to find the best long-term solution to meet the requirements.

Conflicts in risk management

Risk management can involve conflicts in the identification and callout of risks as well as the risk strategies that are planned.

We discussed how your technical background helps identify risks in the planning stage. Conflicts during identification are almost solely office politics in nature. As such, the skills needed here are mainly soft skills as people don't like a light shined on their team or service if it is called out as a risk either due to a cross-project dependency or code deployment difficulties. Biasing toward transparency and ensuring language is as neutral as possible is the best course of action.

For risk strategies, there can be disagreement on whether avoidance, transference, mitigation, or acceptance should be planned for. In these instances, your technical background can be of help in resolving conflicts. As an example, a project I was working on identified a risk where a new data field was being passed between services from different organizations. The risk was planning for the use case where the new field wasn't ready in time for system integration. The proposed mitigation was to pass a *null* value downstream so that the data field could at least be picked up and some work downstream could be unblocked. I knew that the downstream system could not handle null values in this context and that this mitigation would not work and so I challenged it. Instead, we mocked non-null data to unblock integration testing downstream. Though a straightforward example, my technical understanding of downstream systems allowed for a quick redirection of the risk strategy to ensure we identified the right strategies that would actually achieve what was needed.

As an arbiter in many conflicts, a TPM's technical understanding of the problem at hand will aid in quicker arbitration. It also allows us to catch instances where the technical problem is not being conveyed properly across all parties—again, acting as the technical bridge. This bridge can be between two technical teams and may rely on your domain and technical knowledge combined to successfully arbitrate between teams.

During a systems integration between two services, there was an error that was identified during testing. The error seemed to point toward one of the two services as the root cause, though that team denied that the error was their problem. Upon investigation of the error code returned, I realized that there was a misinterpretation of a field as required by one of the teams. Essentially, one team assumed the other team had made a field required, so they did the same, but it wasn't actually required. Knowing the two systems involved, and the requirements, I was able to catch the mistake and worked with the team to update their model to reflect that the field was not required in either of the services.

Conflicts in stakeholder management and communication

Most of the conflicts you will encounter in a project happen in stakeholder management. This is because it encompasses most communication with the people involved in the project, from the developers and team leaders up through company management. As it involves communication, it is often focused on soft skills and tailoring your responses to the audience for clarity of thought and relevance. However, there are cases where your technical background plays a pivotal role in resolving conflicts with stakeholders. Let's take a look at a few examples.

During the execution of the project, you will be working with your developers on a daily basis in most cases and will attend stand-ups to help your team along and get an update on tasks. During stand-ups, blockers are often identified and talked about. It often falls on the TPM to act as a scrum master or at least help developers unblock task work. Having a solid technical foundation will help you understand risks and allow you to act on them faster. As a TPM, there are times when the developers may look to you for technical guidance. Your insight into system behavior, client behavior, and code structure makes you a natural resource for trying to find the right solution to a problem. The TPM is also often the source of the functional specification that the developers reference during design and implementation, so quick consultations with you can go a long way to quickly resolving roadblocks.

In the same way that your technical background helps you during stand-ups, it also helps when reviewing system designs. Part of your job is to challenge the system design when it doesn't fit the needs of the project and the needs of the organization. The other part is being an arbiter of conflict during system design reviews. As the TPM, you own the functional specification, you understand the requirements, and you know the architectural landscape, which gives you a unique perspective on the problem that the design is trying to solve.

A program is a good analogy for your role in a system design. In a program, multiple projects share a common set of goals, but each has its own set of goals that may seem unrelated if looking at the project on its own. As program managers, we ensure that the common goals are understood across all projects in the program and that every decision made in a project is done with full awareness of the implications at the program level. The same is true for a system design discussion where you bring knowledge and understanding of systems that are related and have an impact on the system design being reviewed and you ensure that the decisions being made on the design take the other systems, projects, and initiatives into account.

We've discussed many different ways in which your technical toolset enhances your ability to manage a project and resolve conflicts. Now I'll discuss how your technical foundation helps you deliver through leadership.

Delivering through leadership

As a TPM, you are a leader in your organization. You effect change not only through your programs and projects but also as a contributor to the technical direction and strategies of your team. You identify problems but also resolve them. Here are the ways in which your technical toolset helps you deliver through leadership.

As a leader, you will be expected to define the direction of your team. This expectation expands the higher up you go as a TPM. To do this, you are expected to find issues and define and drive solutions to fix them. This can be a difficult move for some who prefer to work within the bounds of a specific problem. However, defining a problem and solution within the confines of a project is similar to the confines of a team or organization. Just as a project has a goal, a team or organization has a charter. The most reliable way to find a problem worth fixing is to look at repeatable efforts across projects and recurring pain points during development. If the problem occurs often, the ROI is likely worth the effort to solve it. Use your knowledge of your system designs, architecture landscape, and even coding practices, along with your backlog of project issues and risks, to help understand where problems may exist. The only difference between these exercises is the scope in which you are looking to solve problems.

It isn't always your job to come up with the direction to go in but sometimes it is up to you to ensure that the chosen direction is being pursued. During project planning and design, you can reinforce the team or organizational direction by ensuring system designs and design patterns match the intended direction of the organization.

As an example, many companies have a technology directive that persuades the use of specific technologies or announces a shift from one technology to another. These are often forward-looking and gradual shifts, allowing teams time to make the switch. Knowing the expected technological direction of your company allows you to be an arbiter of change. This can come up during project planning where you add additional time to allow for the migration from one technology to another for a single project, or even create a project to track a team-wide migration effort.

Summary

In this chapter, we discussed how your technical toolset can help enhance your project management by examining the key management areas of planning, risk management, and stakeholder management and communication. We looked at each of these in terms of driving clarity, resolving conflicts, and delivering through leadership.

Across all aspects of project management, a TPM's technical toolset allows for quicker, more efficient execution by providing foundational context and knowledge in the problem space. The toolset also enhances the TPM's leadership by effecting change in the technical direction of their organization.

A TPM is both a PM and a technical expert, and they are greater than the sum of their parts, as the old saying goes. It is the joining of the project and program management skills with technical acumen that acts as a force multiplier and allows the TPM to do their job better than a subject matter expert or a PM alone.

Join our book's Discord space

Join our Discord community to meet like-minded people and learn alongside more than 5000 members at:

`https://packt.link/sKmQa`

packt.com

Subscribe to our online digital library for full access to over 7,000 books and videos, as well as industry leading tools to help you plan your personal development and advance your career. For more information, please visit our website.

Why subscribe?

- Spend less time learning and more time coding with practical eBooks and Videos from over 4,000 industry professionals
- Improve your learning with Skill Plans built especially for you
- Get a free eBook or video every month
- Fully searchable for easy access to vital information
- Copy and paste, print, and bookmark content

At www.packt.com, you can also read a collection of free technical articles, sign up for a range of free newsletters, and receive exclusive discounts and offers on Packt books and eBooks.

Other Books
You May Enjoy

If you enjoyed this book, you may be interested in these other books by Packt:

The Successful Software Manager

Herman Fung

ISBN: 9781789615531

- Decide if moving to management is right for you
- Develop the skills required for management
- Lead and manage successful software development projects
- Understand the various roles in a technical team and how to manage them
- Motivate and mentor your team
- Deliver successful training and presentations
- Lead the design process with storyboards and personas, and validate your solution

Effective Platform Product Management

Tabassum Memon

ISBN: 9781801811354

- Understand the difference between the product and platform business model
- Build an end-to-end platform strategy from scratch
- Translate the platform strategy to a roadmap with a well-defined implementation plan
- Define the MVP for faster releases and test viability in the early stages
- Create an operating model and design an execution plan
- Measure the success or failure of the platform and make iterations after feedback

Packt is searching for authors like you

If you're interested in becoming an author for Packt, please visit authors.packtpub.com and apply today. We have worked with thousands of developers and tech professionals, just like you, to help them share their insight with the global tech community. You can make a general application, apply for a specific hot topic that we are recruiting an author for, or submit your own idea.

Share your thoughts

Now you've finished *Technical Program Manager's Handbook, Second Edition*, we'd love to hear your thoughts! Scan the QR code below to go straight to the Amazon review page for this book and share your feedback or leave a review on the site that you purchased it from.

https://packt.link/r/1836200471

Your review is important to us and the tech community and will help us make sure we're delivering excellent quality content.

Index

A

above the fold concept 172

abstract class 236, 237

abstraction 236, 259

active listening 13

adapter pattern 249, 250

adjacent role
  switching to 63, 64

agile methodology 112

AI tools
  AI for stakeholder management and
    communication, using 305, 306
  AI in project planning, utilizing 299-303
  AI in risk management 303, 304
  capabilities and limitations 288-297
  communication gaps, bridging in software
    development 307-311
  exploring, in key management areas 299

ambiguity, in problem and solution 91
  real-world examples 92

Application Security (AppSec) 220

architecture landscape
  examining 273-276

arrays 241

Artificial Intelligence (AI) 281

availability 267

B

big O notation 240

builder pattern 245, 246

business intelligence engineer (BIE) 52

Byte Pair Encoding (BPE) 293

C

C# 154

capacity-constrained prioritization 126

career paths
  individual contributor path 52
  people manager path 52

change management 97

chronological age 200

clarity
  finding, in technical landscape 105, 106

clarity, in planning 93-95
  real-world example 95
  significance 96, 97

clarity, in risk management 97, 98
  significance 98

clarity, in stakeholders and
    communication 99, 100
  churn, reducing during issue resolution 104
  issue resolution and status updates 101
  issues, of excluding 102
  wasted effort, avoiding with clear
    communication 103, 104

Mayer-Salovey-Caruso Emotional
Intelligence Test (MSCEIT) 206

Profile of Emotional Competence (PEC) 206

Trait Emotional Intelligence Questionnaire
(TEIQue) 206

Wong's Emotional Intelligence
Scale (WEIS) 206

Event-Driven Architecture (EDA) 262

executive leadership skills 30

explicit knowledge 83, 141

F

façade design pattern 251

**Facebook/Meta, Amazon, Apple, Netflix, and
Google/Alphabet (FAANG)** 17

feature lists 125

function 237

functional competencies 21-23

functional programming 237

**functional specification
(functional spec)** 224

G

Gantt chart 110

**generative Artificial
Intelligence (GenAI)** 30, 281-286
data processing 286
feedback and improvement process 288
generative model 287

Global Process Owner (GPO) role 221

gold plating 96

Google Sheets 112

graphs 243, 244

greenfield development 318

grounding 294

I

imperative programming 235

implicit knowledge 83, 141

individual contributor (IC) path 55-61
real-world example 60

**information security (InfoSec)
teams** 133, 151

InfoSec analysis 152

inheritance 236, 259

institutional memory 141

**Integrated Development Environments
(IDEs)** 308

Intelligence Quotient (IQ) 200

J

Java 154

K

**Key Performance Indicators
(KPIs)** 177, 209, 239

L

Large Language Model (LLM) 284

latency 266, 267

leadership review (LR) 160, 161

leadership sync 181, 194

linear data structures 241
arrays 241
dictionaries 242
lists 241

Linked List 243

lists 241

Log4Shell 153

Download a free PDF copy of this book

Thanks for purchasing this book!

Do you like to read on the go but are unable to carry your print books everywhere?

Is your eBook purchase not compatible with the device of your choice?

Don't worry, now with every Packt book you get a DRM-free PDF version of that book at no cost.

Read anywhere, any place, on any device. Search, copy, and paste code from your favorite technical books directly into your application.

The perks don't stop there, you can get exclusive access to discounts, newsletters, and great free content in your inbox daily.

Follow these simple steps to get the benefits:

1. Scan the QR code or visit the link below:

https://packt.link/free-ebook/9781836200475

2. Submit your proof of purchase.
3. That's it! We'll send your free PDF and other benefits to your email directly.

www.ingramcontent.com/pod-product-compliance
Lightning Source LLC
LaVergne TN
LVHW080112070326
832902LV00015B/2536